THE
CREATION
OF THE
FUTURE

THE CREATION OF THE FUTURE

THE ROLE OF THE AMERICAN UNIVERSITY

FRANK H. T. RHODES

Cornell University Press   Ithaca & London

The author's royalties are being donated to the
Cornell University Scholarship Fund.

First published 2001 by Cornell University Press

Printed in the United States of America

Library of Congress Cataloging-in-Publication Data

Rhodes, Frank Harold Trevor.

   The creation of the future : the role of the American university /
Frank H.T. Rhodes.

      p. cm.

   Includes bibliographical references and index.

   ISBN 0-8014-3937-X (cloth : alk. paper)

   1. Education, Higher—Aims and objectives—United States.   2.
Universities and colleges—United States.   I. Title.

   LA227.4 .R49 2001

   378.73—dc21   2001002214

CONTENTS

ACKNOWLEDGMENTS

To write a book about an institution in which one has spent a lifetime is to acknowledge a profound indebtedness to many individuals, not least to those who have, over the centuries, created and sustained the universities to which our past and present owe so much and on which our future will heavily depend. It is also to recognize the influence, understanding, and help that so many of my own teachers, students, colleagues, mentors, and friends have provided — and continue to provide — day in and day out, over the long years.

Left to my own devices, it is most unlikely that I should ever have had any serious contact with universities. I grew up in wartime England, graduating from high school in the summer that saw World War II come to an end. My own plans — well-defined, but influenced, no doubt, by the mood of the times, as well as by a strong family tradition — were to enter the British Army and pursue a career as a regular officer. My parents (far wiser than I) thought otherwise, and, after conversations with two of my schoolmasters — Colin Hey and A. L. McKenzie, who knew me well — urged me to go to university first, before beginning a military career. Doubtfully, and against all my own instincts and judgment, I followed their advice. They were right; I was wrong. I shall never cease to be grateful to them for their wisdom, their love, and their support. Their advice opened up a world of learning and discovery that has been one of the joys of my life.

So I do not pretend to be an uninvolved observer of the university. I have had the immense good fortune of seeing the university from many perspectives: as undergraduate, graduate student, postdoctoral fellow, lecturer, professor, department head, dean, provost, president, trustee, external examiner, accreditor, consultant, visiting scientist, senior Fulbright fellow, honorary fellow, and more. And I have had the added benefit of being a member of universities on two continents and of becoming familiar with those of other lands. To these institutions, their trustees, students, faculties, and staff, and particularly to those who have been my closest colleagues in them, my gratitude is great.

I had the immense good fortune to work under a series of "bosses" from whom I learned much, and each became a close friend. The late Frederick Shotton was the head of the department in which I had my first academic job:

a student demonstrator. King Dunham (Sir Kingsley Dunham) was the department head in the university (Durham) where I had my first full-time teaching appointment, and the late George W. White was the department head at the university (Illinois) where I had my second. The late John Fulton (Lord Fulton) was the principal of the university in which I had my first junior administrative appointment (University of Wales-Swansea), and Bob Fleming (Robben W. Fleming) was president of the university (Michigan) where I had my first senior administrative position. The late Eric Ashby (Lord Ashby), former master of Clare College and vice chancellor of Cambridge, was someone from whose life, writings, and friendship over the years I have learned much. And successive chairmen of the Cornell board of trustees, the late Robert W. Purcell, Jansen Noyes Jr., Austin H. Kiplinger, Stephen H. Weiss, and Harold Tanner — my "bosses" at Cornell over eighteen years — have been, and are, an unfailing source of encouragement, support, and friendship.

In writing this book I have had outstanding help from four people, to whom my indebtedness is substantial, and to whom I am especially grateful. Connie Bart Kintner helped me at every turn, writing a first draft of part of two chapters and reading and editing the whole manuscript with meticulous care; Lisa Bennett wrote the faculty profiles, conducted the public interviews that are the source of some of the quotations, and read and edited an early version of the manuscript; Sam Siegel wrote material that became an early draft of part of Chapter 8; and Joy Wagner, my executive assistant for more than two decades, typed and retyped the text with forbearance and constructive comment, constantly pushing me to finish it. I am immensely grateful to all four of these good friends. I also acknowledge with particular gratitude the financial support from a foundation that made this assistance possible. I am grateful to William G. Bowen, president of the Andrew W. Mellon Foundation, Ronald G. Ehrenberg, professor of labor economics at Cornell, and Grey Osterud who read the manuscript and gave me valuable advice. Professor David Lipsky, also of Cornell, has been especially helpful in discussing distance learning. I am grateful, too, to the Rockefeller Foundation, for the benefit of a month's stay at Bellagio, where I wrote a first draft of this manuscript.

I am grateful to certain publishers for their permission to reprint sections of this book that have appeared in, or formed the theme of, a few articles in various publications. These include: "The University and Its Critics," in *Universities and Their Leadership*, ed. William G. Bowen and Harold T. Shapiro (Princeton: Princeton University Press, 1998), 3–14; "The Advancement of Learning: Prospects in a Cynical Age," *Proceedings of the American Philosoph-*

ical Society 142, no. 2 (June 1998): 218–43; "The Art of the Presidency," *The Presidency* 1, no. 1 (1998): 12–18; and "Speedbumps in the Road Ahead," *Trusteeship* (May/June 1999): 8–12, copyright 1999, Association of Governing Boards of Universities and Colleges; all rights reserved.

There is one other person I must acknowledge, from whom after forty-nine years I still learn every day, and who has been my fellow student, adviser, companion, and friend on the long academic journey. My gratitude to her is profound. That's why this book is for my wife, Rosa.

FRANK H. T. RHODES

INTRODUCTION

The university is the most significant creation of the second millennium. From modest beginnings over nine hundred years ago, it has become the quiet but decisive catalyst in modern society, the factor essential to its effective functioning and well-being. The university promotes neither political action nor government policy, but it provides the knowledge and data on which both are developed. It manufactures no products, but it creates the science and technology on which those products depend. It produces no mass circulation newspapers, magazines, or television programs, but it trains their publishers, writers, and producers. It informs public understanding, cultivates public taste, and contributes to the nation's well-being as it nurtures and trains each new generation of architects, artists, authors, business leaders, engineers, farmers, lawyers, physicians, poets, scientists, social workers, and teachers — as well as a steady succession of advocates, dreamers, doers, dropouts, parents, politicians, preachers, prophets, social reformers, visionaries, and volunteers — who leaven, nudge, and shape the course of public life.

No longer an ivory tower, the university runs demonstrations of agricultural projects in the desert, grapples with the social problems of the inner city, develops alternative energy sources, provides the most sophisticated health care, monitors natural hazards, shelters and informs the debate on every vexing issue of public life, provides most of the basic scientific and biomedical research, and, in the United States, educates half of the population directly and all the rest of us indirectly. Cherishing the independence and autonomy society has granted it, the university has, for nine long centuries, been a place of "full and fair enquiry, bringing wisdom to bear in human affairs."[1]

In fact, American universities are enjoying a period of unprecedented success. Talented students the world over clamor for admission to their programs. American universities are, as Stanley Ikenberry, president of the American Council on Education, recently summed it up, "at the top of their game."[2]

Because knowledge has become the dominant economic force, the importance of the university can only grow and its influence increase in the new millennium. But this growth will occur in a rapidly changing environment.

American higher education is about to become deregulated. The centuries-old monopoly on education enjoyed by the universities is over, a casualty to new means of learning (information technology [IT] and the Internet) and new providers (especially corporate America and for-profit vendors). The universities once controlled access to knowledge, represented by both their vast research libraries and the professional skills and expertise of their faculties. They controlled accreditation, graduation, and certification, and they controlled the place, time, style, and substance of learning. No more. The traditional pattern of learning — by college-age students enrolled on a full-time basis in a residential, rigidly sequential program — is already being replaced by on-demand, anytime, and often on-line learning from an increasingly competitive "knowledge business." Skills are acquired as needed for changing careers and changing job demands by cost-conscious knowledge shoppers of every age.

In a millennium in which knowledge has become the new economic capital, the universities — the traditional providers of knowledge — face both extraordinary challenges to which they must adapt, and extraordinary opportunities that they must seize. Natural selection operates in society more subtly than in the biological realm, but just as surely. Survival requires adaptation; it is those better fitted to their environment that leave descendants. The inadaptive perish.

Some thoughtful critics see the university as a dinosaur — huge, lumbering, splendid in its own quaint way, even endearing; prodigious in the variety of forms it has developed; ancient in its lineage; once long ago unrivaled in its preeminence; exquisitely adapted to conditions that are now vanishing, and therefore doomed by the rapidity of the changes that have overtaken it; waiting in these end-Cretaceous times for the asteroid to strike. They see the university as ill suited to the changing world and ill adapted to new technology, just-in-time knowledge, skills on demand, and cost-effective learning. The need the university once filled has not vanished — far from it. Rather, time has passed the university by, with nimble, low-cost, low-overhead, mammalian competitors — corporate knowledge-dispensers and for-profit information vendors — filling its niche, eating its lunch, nudging it out.

These critics, though they have their differences, generally reflect the view represented by Peter Drucker: "Thirty years from now the big university campuses will be relics. Universities won't survive. It's as large a change as when we first got the printed book. . . . Already, we are beginning to deliver more lectures and classes off-campus via satellite or two-way video at a fraction of the cost. The college won't survive as a residential institution. Today's buildings are hopelessly unsuited and totally unneeded. . . . I consider the American research university of the last 40 years to be a failure. The great educational needs of tomorrow are not on the research side, but on the learning side."[3]

In discussing what life is like today at the leading public and private universities, I confine myself to the 125 or so institutions that are often called "major research universities," places where professors and their graduate students — the professionals and professors of tomorrow — are actively engaged in original scholarship and research and professional service, as well as teaching the accumulated knowledge of the present and past. For it is research universities that have shown the most striking changes, particularly since World War II; it is they that provide a unique range of educated leaders, knowledge, and services to society; it is they that are least likely to be replaced by developments in information technology (although they will likely be major players in its development and application); and it is they whose future is most dependent on the public's understanding and goodwill.

Throughout the book, I draw heavily on my experiences at Cornell University, an independent, Ivy League university where I served as president for eighteen years, and also at the University of Michigan, a distinguished public research university, where I previously had held professorial and administrative posts. These are the universities I know best, but they are also institutions that, between them, reflect many of the major trends impacting American higher education in the twenty-first century.

In explaining research universities, some of whose activities scarcely existed when the grandparents of today's students were young, I shall make the case that they are an irreplaceable resource, quite literally a national and international treasure, whose value must be preserved through judicious renewal and reform, beginning with a rededication to teaching as a moral vocation. And if they renew themselves — applying old virtues to new realities — they are likely to strengthen public confidence in their work. The public understands intuitively — without, in most cases, the benefit of reading Plato or Jefferson — that education is the most fundamental of all social responsibilities. Without it, there can be no democratic state, no personal freedom worthy of the name. With it, a society may achieve greatness.

Universities are, to a unique degree, the conservators of human experience; the custodians and transmitters of the best that has been thought and written, said and done; the embodiment of openness, rational discourse, and experiment. They are also critics of the very knowledge they conserve, and of the society that supports them. Not least, they are the creators of new knowledge, fresh insight, novel techniques, and creative approaches.

There is tension between the creation of new knowledge and the conservation of existing knowledge, but the university must accept both roles. The growing flood of data will be of limited value to those who lack the discernment to differentiate between conflicting trends and judge between contrasting views. Information remains just that — information — to the person who lacks a grounding in critical thought and understanding of the basis of knowledge. Those who wrestle with social issues without any knowledge of the past lack a critical dimension. New discoveries in one field often provide a wholly new approach to problems in another field. It is here that the community we call the university is so important: testing, sifting, contesting, refining, and applying all manner of knowledge; analyzing and addressing all kinds of issues; and doing all of this in a spirit of rationality, integrity, openness, and civility.

Universities are communities of debate and discovery. But they do not exist in isolation. They embody all the tensions and advocacy of our larger society and the noisy and rancorous debate that that tension sometimes generates. But they also are committed to fairness, reason, and civility, and hospitable to disputes, different viewpoints, competing explanations, and alternative approaches, persuaded that, in the end, understanding emerges from dialogue in community. To the extent that they have fallen from their own high standards and lofty calling, they must be reclaimed, not by an enforced return to a vanished nineteenth-century homogeneity and orthodoxy, but by the restoration of a community of learning, based on engagement with the issues of our day within the context of the enduring values that have shaped both our universities and our civilization.

The future of our universities is a matter of far more than academic interest. The degree of public understanding and support that they enjoy will determine whether we either neglect a treasure that has taken more than 350 years to build or affirm the faith in the importance of knowledge and the value of full and fair enquiry that has enabled our universities to serve society well. It is our universities that will also shape the kind of society we are, the kind of nation we hope to become. The university's unique function is not only to provide technical skills of the highest order, but also to bring each new generation together with a community of more senior scholars to reflect on the great issues of life and to confront the overarching challenges of society. The university equips young scholars to play an informed, energetic, and responsible role in addressing such issues and challenges. That experience leavens the life and promotes the well-being of the nation. Alfred North Whitehead once wrote, "The task of the university is the creation of the future, so far as rational thought, and civilized modes of appreciation, can affect the issue."[4] That is a task as daunting as it is inspiring. We should settle for nothing less.

THE
CREATION
OF THE
FUTURE

{ 1 }
THE RISE OF
THE AMERICAN
UNIVERSITY

The quality of life enjoyed by the people of the United States in the opening years of the new millennium rests in substantial part on the broad foundation provided by the American university during the twentieth century. Higher education has been the doorway to advancement and participation for countless citizens and dozens of immigrant groups. It has been the path to social attainment for millions from impoverished backgrounds, the generator of the nation's leaders in every area of life, the key to vastly improved professional services from health care to technology. It has been the foundation of growing national economic prosperity and manufacturing success, vast improvements in the products of agriculture and industry, and undreamed-of access to new means of communication. And beyond all those benefits, it has provided to successive generations the opportunity for meaningful careers, for service in a free society, and for access to the riches of human experience, aspiration, and achievement. For all its shortcomings, the American university has been an unambiguous influence for good. To a degree unknown elsewhere, it has educated a steadily growing proportion of the population and thus nurtured the democratic spirit and enlivened the nation. It has trained the workforce, enriched the individual experience, and enlightened public life. It has quickened the social conscience and empowered and inspired each rising generation.

What accounts for the distinctive strength and singular contribution of the American university? How did it come into existence? What forces have shaped its development? How well is it situated to contribute to the future?

Distant ancestors of institutions are as notoriously difficult to identify as those of organisms, and the precise origins of our own and other species involve substantial speculation. Phylogenies become matters of strenuous contention, and the precise age of any ancient lineage is often a matter of lively debate. As with human origins, so it is with the American university. What is possible, with institutions as with humans, is to pick some conspicuous milestones on the path of development, turning points on the long, unfolding journey to the present. Perhaps we might choose five universities to mark the path by which the modern American university came into being: Bologna, Harvard, Virginia, Cornell, and Johns Hopkins.

Lying at the base of the Apennine foothills on the fertile plain between the Reno and Savena Rivers is an unassuming city, carrying its ancient history lightly under a facade of mellow brick. Its splendid pedestrian arcades, its turrets and its towers (two of them leaning at perilous angles), its wealth of Renaissance and Baroque churches, its aristocratic palazzos, and its spacious piazzas all offer a gentle contrast to the bustle of a modern industrial city, producing everything from pasta to chemicals, sausages to shoes. It was here in the eleventh century that the Western university, represented by the University of Bologna, came into existence. Students from all over Europe came to Bologna, and by the middle of the twelfth century students are said to have numbered nearly ten thousand. The names and arms of those elected as representatives of their nations are still preserved in the ceiling of one of the city's oldest buildings.

The ancient university had no campus; it owned no buildings. It was a loose community of professors and students (a *universitas magistorum et scholarium*) with the professors often teaching in their own apartments, paid by the students lecture by lecture for their services. It was five hundred years before the University of Bologna had its own buildings. So Bologna, like other older universities, was — to use modern jargon — a virtual learning community, long before it was formally recognized as an educational institution. Formal recognition came first from the chancellor of the local cathedral, who licensed instruction outside the cloister, but in time the reigning pope or emperor recognized the older and more distinguished institutions as *studia generale,* whose graduates had the right to teach at any institution, without further examination.

A flowering of legal studies in Bologna about the year 1000, spurred in part by legal disputes between the pope and the emperor, led to the rise of the university. So studies in both canon and civil law flourished side by side with student guilds — the Ultramontani and the Citramontani — protecting the interests of their members, many from foreign lands and many of established position and mature years. By about 1200, faculties of medicine and philosophy (the liberal arts) came into being, while theology followed later.

Bologna is not the oldest university-like institution. Salerno, for example, had a famed school of medicine at least as early as the ninth century. Centers of higher learning were associated with some of the larger mosques of the Islamic world. But Bologna was the first to develop a comprehensive range of studies, balanced faculties, both professional and liberal arts, and perhaps the first to create student colleges and a deliberative assembly, presided over by a rector.

The founding of Bologna was followed by a remarkable growth of universities in other Italian cities — among them Reggio nell'Emilia, Modena, Vicenza, Padua, and Naples. Elsewhere, in such places as Paris, Oxford, Cambridge, Valladolid, Salamanca, Seville, Coimbra, Prague, Cracow, Vienna, Heidelberg, Cologne, Louvain, Leipzig, and St. Andrews, others followed. In a span of two centuries, the university came into being across the length and breadth of Europe.

In 1636, the new institution reached North America, when the first American college was established in New Towne, Massachusetts, lying on the Charles River across from the city of Boston. It was in this same place, on July 3, 1775, that Washington was to take command of the Continental army. The general court of the Massachusetts Colony voted £400 to create a "schoale or colledge." Two years later, the site of its founding was renamed "Cambridge," in honor of the university where many leaders of the colony had been educated. John Harvard, a Cambridge graduate and Puritan minister, left half of his estate (almost twice the sum of the colony's funding) and his library of 260 books to the fledgling college. The purpose of Harvard's founders is touchingly summarized in their statement: "After God had carried us safe to *New England*, and we had builded our houses, provided necessaries for our liveli-hood, rear'd convenient places for Gods worship and settled the Civill Government; One of the next things we longed for, and looked after was to advance *Learning* and perpetuate it to Posterity; dreading to leave an illiterate Ministry to the Churches, when our present Ministers shall lie in the Dust."[1] In 1642, Harvard awarded its first degrees — the degree of bachelor of arts — to nine young men. The charter of 1650 established the college for "the advancement of all good literature, arts and the sciences" and "the education of the English and Indian youth . . . in knowledge and godlynes." It also provided for an independent, self-perpetuating corporation consisting of the president, treasurer, and five fellows to govern the college subject to confirmation by a board of overseers. This board, though at first jointly representative of the state and the church, later became a lay board, elected by the alumni body.

The foundation of Harvard was followed by the creation of other colonial colleges. The student experience at these various colleges was remarkably similar, including compulsory attendance at the college chapel, pursuit of the classical curriculum, participation in the extracurricular literary societies (which encouraged debates, readings, lectures, and other activities), and the senior capstone course in moral philosophy — the "great glory" of the curriculum — taught generally by the president.

As the young nation grew in numbers and expanded its frontiers, it faced a steadily growing need for both educated citizens and trained professionals, and public funding was contributed by a number of states — Virginia, North Carolina, and Michigan among them — to meet this need.

This led to the creation of public universities, funded largely by the states. The best known of these — though not the most typical — is the University of Virginia, founded by Thomas Jefferson at Charlottesville, in the shadow of the Blue Ridge Mountains. The campus echoes the Jeffersonian dream. Jefferson planned every aspect of its development, choosing the site, planning the layout of the "academical village," designing the buildings, creating the curriculum, selecting books for the library, appointing the founding faculty, and serving as the first rector. "Mr. Jefferson's University" was chartered in 1819, and opened in 1825 with eight members of the faculty. Forty years later, it was second only to Harvard in size.

The University of Virginia had two distinctive features. Unlike other universities of its time, it had no religious affiliation and required no religious assent of its students.

It also broke from the classical curriculum, which was then dominant, by creating eight schools, each headed by a professor: ancient languages, modern languages, anatomy and medicine, law, natural history, mathematics, natural philosophy, and moral philosophy. These schools, designed to grow as funds permitted, were later to be joined by commerce, diplomacy, and manufacture. This rich assortment of offerings was to allow an elective program of study, in contrast to the rigid requirements of other colleges. The architecture matched the curriculum, with each school housed in its own pavilion, with students living on the campus, "in watchful proximity" to their professors' residences.

For all its creativity, the University of Virginia provided no model for other institutions. Its style was distinctive to the point of eccentricity. Jefferson had opposed the granting of degrees, for example, as "artificial embellishments," and the baccalaureate degree was not offered until 1868, although the university awarded the M.D. degree in 1828 and the master of arts — its primary degree — in 1831.

But the massive growth of public funding of higher education began with the Morrill Act of 1862, signed into law by Abraham Lincoln, which provided grants of federal lands to the states for the establishment of public universities and colleges. These "land-grant colleges and universities" were to provide for "the liberal and practical education of the industrial classes in the several pursuits and professions of life."[2] This act led to the creation in every state of a new kind of college that was distinctively American. Perhaps no university is more typical of the fusion of scholarly inspiration and worldly practicality, on the one hand, and of the joint power of private philanthropy and public expenditure, on the other, than Cornell University.

Frederick Rudolph, in his magisterial book on the university curriculum, describes the impact of the founding of Cornell as follows:

> Cornell brought together in creative combination a number of dynamic ideas under circumstances that turned out to be incredibly productive. . . . Andrew D. White, its first president, and Ezra Cornell, who gave it his name, turned out to be the developers of the *first American university* and therefore the agents of revolutionary curricular reform. . . .
>
> Ezra Cornell, whose wealth and imagination allowed him to be Western Union's largest stockholder, turned these same assets into a few words that transformed the American college curriculum: "I would found an institution where any person can find instruction in any study." Andrew D. White, the university's first president, translated a classical education at Yale, scholarly training in European universities, and experience on Henry Tappan's faculty at the University of Michigan into a resolution to create a great American university.[3]

So, with the founding of Cornell, a new kind of university came into existence. When Ezra Cornell spoke of "any person" he meant poor as well as rich, as he provided work and scholarships; women as well as men, as he built a women's college as an integral part of the university; "the whole colored race and the whole female sex," in White's words.[4] Ezra Cornell was equally serious when he spoke of "any study," leaping over the weary debate on the traditional classical curriculum in relation to more modern studies. Law and languages, agriculture and architecture, engineering and English jostled together, with the student encouraged to make informed choices within a range of nine "departments" broadly aimed at professional careers, while the division of literature, science, and the arts allowed nonprofessional students five routes toward a general course of study. "Discipline comes," White declared, "by studies which are loved, not by studies that are loathed."[5]

"In walking away from choice and embracing all alternatives, White made an American decision consistent with Ezra Cornell's democratic intentions and the imprecise, but clear obligations of the Act of 1862," Rudolph wrote. "Practical vocationalism, scientific research, applied technology, classical learning, and university scholarship all found a welcome."[6] "The Cornell curriculum brought into imaginative balance the openness of American society, the temporary nature of its directions and opportunities; it multiplied truth into truths, a limited few professions into an endless number of new self-respecting ways of moving into the middle class."[7]

Ezra Cornell and Andrew Dickson White insisted on one other concept; their university was to be nonsectarian, with a board of trustees in which members of no one denomination should have a majority. So Cornell was to become hospitable to all religious persuasions, but committed to no one denomination.

To the Morrill Act of 1862, two other pieces of federal legislation were later added: the Hatch Act of 1887 provided federal funds for research and experiment stations, while the Smith-Lever Act of 1914 provided additional funds for extension programs, designed to bring to their communities the benefits of new campus-based research.

But when Cornell was founded, there was precious little research to extend. The universities of the mid-nineteenth century were teaching institutions, in which scholarship, though prized, was generally understood to mean high competence in one's field, whether in theory or in practice. In contrast, the German universities of this period became centers of research and graduate study, spurred on, to some extent, by industry's need for technical and scientific research. Many of the professors of America's new universities had themselves been students in these German graduate schools, and, almost imperceptibly, the Germanic scholarly influence, and the new knowledge it created, seeped into the American curriculum.

"The consequences," Rudolph observed wryly, "have generally been appropriately described as both profoundly inventive and overwhelmingly destructive."[8] They were inventive because they led to an explosion of knowledge in every field. They were destructive because they undermined the reigning assumptions of the unity of the traditional liberal arts and sciences and weakened the centrality of humane learning. Specialization, professionalization, and narrow inquiry were all very well for the European undergraduate, product of the demanding *gymnasium,* but they "left the college, the society's repository of liberal values and humane learning, crippled and confused."[9]

Just how far this was a problem is shown by our fifth landmark, Johns

Hopkins in Baltimore, Maryland. It was Baltimore's importance as a port and center of communication that led indirectly to its distinctive contribution to the growth of the American university. Its excellent harbor had long made Baltimore a leading shipping center, while its position on the National Road contributed to its early eighteenth-century growth. But the completion of the Erie Canal threatened its prosperity, and a group of wealthy local investors chartered the Baltimore & Ohio Railroad — the first public U.S. railroad — to strengthen its access to the west. Among these investors was Johns Hopkins (1795–1873), who gave his fortune of $7 million and his name to a new university. Johns Hopkins's first president, Daniel Coit Gilman, made advanced scholarship, scientific research, and graduate study the university's main purpose, though it also included an undergraduate college. The Hopkins model — serious scholarship, graduate study, the Ph.D. degree, the specialized academic major and expansive minor, a pervasive spirit of inquiry and an earnestness of purpose that went with it — soon influenced the new universities and aspiring colleges, both private and public.

"The presidents of state universities . . . knew that they could not be universities in reality until the spirit of Johns Hopkins had become as pervasive as that of Cornell," concluded Rudolph.[10] Opened to great acclaim in 1876, Hopkins in its preoccupation with research served as the model for a number of other embryonic universities — Clark University, Catholic University of America, and the University of Chicago among them. But though total immersion in research to the exclusion of substantial concern for the well-being of undergraduate students and professional studies proved an unsuccessful recipe, Hopkins's great contribution to the development of the American university was to inject a spirit of advanced study, serious inquiry, and scholarly emphasis into the Cornell model of wide access, expansive scholarly and professional programs, and institutional autonomy. Its influence remains strong today.

By the final quarter of the nineteenth century the general form of the American university had taken shape. It had become a learning community with a largely residential campus, embracing both a college of liberal arts and sciences and graduate and professional schools, devoted to both teaching and research, committed to widening access and expanding public service. That structure continues into the twenty-first century.

The contemporary American university, however, is a distinctive product of the twentieth century and especially of the last fifty years. There are several particular trends that have altered the shape, though not the structure, of the university.

The university has seen a deliberate growth in social inclusiveness, with a major expansion in the proportion of the traditional college-age population attending college and a more recent but rapid increase in lifelong learning, including both continuing professional education and distance learning.

There has been a growth in number and size of institutions to accommodate this growing student enrollment and the differentiation of institutional style to respond to differing educational needs and opportunities.

The university has seen increasing intellectual inclusiveness, with growing professionalism both in the "established professions" such as law, medicine, and engineering and in new ones such as architecture, city planning, and business, as well as the specialization and growing professionalization of the traditional disciplines.

Finally, universities have experienced the disproportionate expansion of science and the science-based professions, supported by infusion of federal funding for research, and their growing influence in shaping the culture of the campus.

I discuss professionalism and science in Chapters 2 and 3. In this chapter, I want to explore the impact of increased student access and institutional growth.

The colonial college, large in aspiration but small in size and modest in the range of its curriculum, was unambiguous in its educational purpose, selective in its admissions, and homogeneous in its student body. Its aim was typified by that of Yale: that "Youth may be instructed in the Arts and Sciences who thorough the blessing of Almighty God may be fitted for Publick employment both in Church and Civil State." Its membership was predominantly white, male, and Protestant.

The subsequent history of higher education is one of larger purpose, steadily expanding access, and growing inclusiveness. The Morrill Act established new land-grant universities to educate "the industrial classes." Institutions like Cornell welcomed the rich and poor of both sexes and all races and religions. In comparison with contemporary European universities, this was an extraordinary degree of inclusiveness. Yet women and nonwhites remained a rarity and small minority on the university campus. It would take another half century before dramatic increases in inclusiveness would take place.

In 1900, only 237,592 men and women attended college, about 4 percent of the college-age population. By 1940, total enrollment had reached 1.5 million, about 12 percent of the college-age population. The passage of the G.I. Bill at the end of World War II represented a national decision to extend the benefits of a college education to a greater proportion of the population, offering support to returning veterans, and thus giving a major boost to college attendance. By 1998, a record 67 percent of the graduating high school seniors were enrolled in college, most of them as full-time students at four-year institutions.

But inclusiveness involved more than attendance ratios. Thirty years ago, universities set out to make their campuses look more like America. It was a mission supported, monitored, and overseen by federal and state governments on the basis of widespread agreement on this threefold premise: education provides a foundation for personal growth, professional training, and social mobility; women and minority groups have been historically underrepresented on college campuses and in professional and leadership roles in society; and universities should pursue affirmative policies to recruit these groups and so remedy past underrepresentation.

Although the concept of affirmative action is now the topic of litigation and lively public debate, the striking growth in numbers of women and previously underrepresented minorities in both higher education and public life is evidence of the success of this venture. Also notable are the growing presence of students from families of lower income levels and the growth in numbers of female and minority faculty. Until recently, university admissions were guided by the *Bakke* case, a 5–4 decision of the Supreme Court that prohibited discrimination by race, but allowed race to be used as one positive criterion, among others, in college admissions.

The future of affirmative action is unclear. The rejection by California voters of racial preferences (Proposition 209), the prohibition by the University of California Board of Regents of their use in admissions, and the recent *Hopwood* court decision concerning admissions to the University of Texas have had a profound effect on universities in those states. In the first year following the Texas and California decisions, there was a precipitous decline in minority student applications and enrollment. In the law school of the University of Texas at Austin, for example, once a significant source of black graduates, the number of new black students enrolling in 1997–98 plunged to zero. At California's flagship public universities — Berkeley and the University of California at Los Angeles — admission levels of underrepresented minorities are down substantially from pre–Proposition 209 levels. As of 1999, they were down 44 percent at Berkeley and 36 percent at UCLA.[11]

Several alternatives to traditional affirmative action programs are now being suggested. Some argue for the use of nonracial "class-based" criteria in admissions, assuming that this could still produce enrollments that resemble current college levels of racial diversity, since black and Hispanic students are three times as likely to come from low-income families. What such arguments overlook, however, is that these minority students represent only a small minority of the low-income population and that many minority students achieve relatively low SAT scores. This would mean that to retain anything approaching present minority enrollment levels, a very large intake of low-income students would be required, thus further limiting access for middle- and upper-income students. Others have urged the use of geographic origin — zip code — as an admissions criterion, but this may involve similar problems.

The impasse here is real, and the implications are serious. California voters' rejection of affirmative action and the judicial rejection of racially based admissions criteria in other states are both clear. But equally clear is the need for access to the ranks of the professional workforce for all Americans as a foundation both for a comprehensive and effective educational setting and for a harmonious and just society. As yet, no simple numerical criteria seem capable of providing this.

Fortunately, an alternative admissions model exists. If each student applicant is treated as an individual — rather than as a racial representative or a disembodied numerical test score — and admission is based on consideration of essays, class ranking, teacher and counselor reports, civic and community service, leadership, extracurricular activities, socioeconomic background, and other factors, race may still be taken into account, as one factor among others. Where this is done, numbers of black and Hispanic students continue to increase or hold steady.

Consider one example. For the Cornell University Medical College class of 2000, there were 7,602 applications for 100 places. The faculty conducted 1,339 interviews, and the class finally selected contained 24 black and Hispanic students. That number was achieved without quotas or set-asides, without admitting the unqualified or the uncommitted. It was achieved by considering each individual as an individual, representing a range of abilities, skills, experience, backgrounds, and characteristics — of which race can legitimately be considered to be one among others.

In large public universities, where student numbers make such personal interviews difficult, new programs that offer blanket admission to the top 10 or 20 percent of all graduating seniors of all high schools, whatever their test scores, seem at first glance to offer encouraging results. These programs have liabilities, as well as benefits. They leave untouched, for example, the important issue of admissions to graduate and professional programs. They typically guarantee admission to only one of the various state colleges and universities, with a consequent concentration of the best minority students in a few and a "cascading" of the rest. In an age when over 60 percent of all high school graduates enroll in college, these programs leave out the many able minority students who do not make the 20 percent cut. What has been interpreted by some as an easy solution to the problem of maintaining both race-blind admissions and campus diversity turns out to be far from a panacea.[12]

With growing inclusiveness has come growth in campus size. The early American college was a small, compact, homogeneous community. Two hundred years ago, Harvard enrolled some 57 students, a hundred years ago 3,373, and today 18,700, of whom about 6,800 are undergraduates. A century ago the University of Michigan had 3,303 students on its campus in Ann Arbor; today it has about 50,000 on three campuses, located in Flint and Dearborn as well as in Ann Arbor. For virtually every college and university in America, the same story of growth could be told, though the details would differ.

It is easy to forget how this growth in size has changed the culture of the campus. In 1891, for example, James Angell, the president of the University of Michigan, had no secretary, answered all letters himself in longhand, personally enrolled all students in the Literary College, taught courses in international law and the history of treaties, conducted all the chapel services, and knew each of the 103 members of the faculty, as well as hundreds of the 2,420 students. "No part of the curriculum was mysterious to him," commented Howard Peckham.[13]

Few of the charms of that small campus remain in the university of today. Although nationally the average enrollment on a single campus is 4,034, the research universities tend to be substantially larger: fifty-three universities, for example, have enrollments greater than 25,000 students.

But if the American university has lost the intimacy of a small campus, the growth of higher education has brought immense benefits. Along with the new inclusiveness have come new programs, most of them professional or technical, which have brought benefits to the nation.

The extraordinary medical successes of the last century, for example, are the direct result of the Flexner Report of 1911. In 1900, medical training involved a system of apprenticeship, with little formal education beyond the sharing of treatments and remedies, many of quite limited effectiveness. Flexner recommended not only the transfer of all medical education to the universities, but also its linkage to research in the basic sciences, which have since provided the groundwork for pathbreaking medical advances.

The pattern of incorporating professional training into the universities has been repeated in other professions. Within universities, preprofessional education has been linked to systematic professional training; research has been linked to professional practice; ethical standards have been created along with the expectation that personal practice will be linked to public service. All these developments have brought positive benefits to the public at large.

Professional education and sophisticated training are no longer limited to the "college years" or the period of on-campus enrollment. Growing numbers of professional continuing education programs are provided, often at remote sites, as well as short residential postgraduate refresher courses, workshop introductions to new developments and procedures, reference resources, and on-line consulting and advisory services.

The rise of the American research university reflects a pattern not seen elsewhere on anything approaching the same scale. In Europe, for example, at the close of the nineteenth century, a handful of universities — Berlin, Cambridge, the Ecole Polytechnique, Göttingen, Heidelberg, Oxford, and the Sorbonne among them — represented the standard toward which all other universities aspired. A listing of the world's top ten universities would have included, at most, only one or two American institutions. A century later, such a list might have included two-thirds or more universities from the United States.[14]

What were the distinctive factors that produced this transformation? Institutional mission has played a significant role. Whether developed out of older colonial colleges (Columbia, Harvard, Princeton, Yale), created by nineteenth-century benefactors (Chicago, Cornell, Duke, Hopkins, Stanford, Vanderbilt), or established by states in response to public needs (California, Illinois, Michigan, North Carolina, Virginia, Wisconsin), all American research universities embraced a mission of research; undergraduate, graduate, and professional education; and, especially in the state universities, a wider role of public outreach and extension. This mixture of functions produces tensions — research versus teaching being a frequent complaint — but it also produces benefits of cross-fertilization and professional cooperation. The performing arts exist alongside law and medicine. Philosophy and public health share a common home with economics and environmental engineering. All disciplines, together with their students and faculties, are swept up in the atmosphere of inquiry and discovery that pervades the campus. All this has been developed around the core of a college of arts and sciences, a legacy of both the colonial college and the need to educate large numbers of undergraduates coming from a variety of precollege backgrounds. This large undergraduate student body, representing a rapidly growing proportion of the traditional college-age group, distinguished the American university from its more selective and elite European counterpart until the last few decades.

The sponsorship of American research universities is distinctive. There is no one sponsor, no overseeing ministry, no national plan or government regulation. Decentralized, feistily independent, uncoordinated, pluralistic, American universities have been opportunistic, adaptive, creative, and responsive to new opportunities. The pattern of state control and centralized funding, so typical of most European universities, is in the United States replaced by a decentralized system consisting of fifty states, each with distinctive goals and needs, and scores of independent institutions, each with its own goals and traditions. While internally American universities — whether public or private — tend to assume a broadly similar functional organization, their independence from central government planning and control gives them a vigor that has proved more elusive in the regulated European institutions, where faculty members are often civil servants and where central government control extends not only to management of institutional enrollment and programs, but also to regulation, budgeting, and evaluation of individual academic departments. It is ironic that, whereas the older universities in Europe — including the great civic universities of the nineteenth and early twentieth centuries — were privately founded by religious orders, individuals, cities, and other communities, they were later effectively nationalized into a system of higher education rigidly planned, budgeted, and controlled by a central ministry. Even in those countries, such as Germany and Switzerland, where local states *(landes)* supported universities, they did so within the context of a well-defined national plan.

In contrast, the great state universities of the United States have tended to become more diversified over time, with each state supporting a distinctive range and style of institution, many of which have gained a substantial degree of autonomy. Unlike the planned "command" educational systems of Europe and elsewhere, the unplanned, opportunistic, pluralistic "system" of the United States has proved adaptable, flexible, and remarkably successful.

The governance of American universities has been distinctive. The typical board of the colonial college, made up of independent "gentry," developed into the lay board of trustees of the private university, whose independence became a model for the generally less independent, politically appointed or elected board of regents of the public universities. These boards, though of variable quality, have tended to have far more authority and autonomy than the typical boards of universities in other lands. Because the boards of American institutions had a major role in justifying and providing funding for their individual universities — as opposed to dispensing what was provided from a remote central government ministry — their identification with the aspirations and success of their universities was immediate and strong. This has led to a degree of interinstitutional competition unknown elsewhere, which, though it has its liabilities, has been a force for good. In this respect, the great private universities — the Ivy League, Stanford, Chicago, CalTech, MIT, and others — have been pacesetters not only for the independents, but also for most of the publics. It is not that private universities are unknown in other nations, but rather that their limited number and particular role (specialized professional in France, the United Kingdom, Germany, and Sweden, serving particular religious or ethnic communities in Canada, devoted to expanded undergraduate education in Japan, Brazil, and Venezuela) have made them much less influential.[15]

The leadership of American higher education has had a strong influence on its development. Though many would argue that there has been a decline in the influence of presidential leadership since the giants of the late nineteenth and early twentieth centuries, still the power of the American university president has typically been substantially greater than that of his or her counterpart elsewhere. Supported by a strong faculty and a committed board, presidents have shaped and nurtured their institutions to a remarkable degree. Andrew Dickson White at Cornell, Charles Eliot at Harvard, Daniel Coit Gilman at Johns Hopkins, David Starr Jordan at Stanford, and many others seized the responsibility entrusted to them and led their universities to greatness.

The American university remains an organizational enigma, whose loosely coupled structure and collegially based organization defy the established canons of management. But the very flexibility of the internal organization of the American university has nurtured its entrepreneurial spirit. The basic unit of organization — the department — is not, as in some other countries, the domain of a single professor, presiding over it, sometimes with a heavy hand, for an indefinite and often prolonged period, but an alliance of more or less equal colleagues, democratic in spirit if not always in fact. The elected chair, the first among equals, serves for a specified term — often three or five years — renewable by agreement. This system, while it has imperfections — lack of continuity and lack of strong leadership — has major benefits in its lack of rigidity and in the entrepreneurial opportunities it provides for all its members.

So, too, does the academic career ladder, where a full professorship can be the career aspiration of not one, but most faculty members of a department. The incentive to continued striving provided by this structure contrasts sharply with the more restricted career opportunities of the traditional academic hierarchy in other countries.

While the department chair in the American university has been relatively weaker than his or her opposite number in other countries, the office of dean has typically been relatively stronger, representing a substantial level of administrative and financial independence and academic responsibility. This, too, has fostered a sense of entrepreneurial initiative and scholarly creativity. Behind much of the success of the American university lies the steady leadership and vision of generations of deans who have nudged the aspirations and nurtured the creativity of their colleagues.

The size of most American research universities has been a positive factor in allowing a critical mass of faculty in those areas, especially the sciences and science-based professions, where scale and teamwork are critical to success in research. While size is less important in the arts or humanities, the larger size of the science-based faculty allows a degree of specialization and cooperation that has major benefits in research. This does not mean, of course, that a physics department of sixty faculty members is necessarily superior to one of thirty, but there are few eminent small departments.

The pattern of federal support for research has been critical to the success of the American research university. A variety of federal agencies — the National Institutes of Health, the National Science Foundation, the Department of Defense, the Department of Agriculture, the Department of Commerce among them — have offered financial support at growing levels, aimed at varying national needs, from national defense to health care, from environmental conservation and agricultural productivity to regional economic development. Almost all this support has been based on proposals designed by the professor-investigator, rather than being contract work designed by the sponsoring agency, and it has been awarded on the basis of the merit of the proposals submitted, with awards screened and largely determined by independent panels of expert peers. This pattern, first established by Vannevar Bush more than half a century ago (see Chapter 9), has returned an incalculable dividend on the nation's investment in research.

In other nations, much of this type of research is performed in national institutes or academies, having little linkage to universities.

None of this would have been possible without an unabashed competitive spirit and entrepreneurial attitude within the university. The long traditions of strong alumni financial support in the great private universities, the openness to industrial and state partnerships pioneered by the leading land-grant universities, and the existence of charitable foundations willing to share in the educational and research enterprise by supporting everything from mul-timillion-dollar telescope systems to inner-city poverty– and drug abuse–prevention programs have represented an extraordinary opportunity for the American university.

These factors, taken collectively, have shaped the history of the American university over the last century. It would be rash, of course, to suppose that any one factor has been decisive. Quite different patterns of organization and oversight, for example, have been used by the various states in their support of the great flagship public universities. But collectively these features have defined the characteristics of the most successful universities. Unplanned, opportunistic, well governed, well led, as conservative in some respects as it has been entrepreneurial in others, the research university is one of the great success stories of America's twentieth-century history.

Colleges and universities are a traditional part of the American landscape. For every family taking its aspiring high school junior on the round of campus tours, there are countless others for whom fall football weekends, New Year's Day bowl games, spring NCAA championships, and early summer commencements are established benchmarks in the subconscious annual calendar. The college campus, with its stately colonial architecture, its carillon resounding through leafy quadrangles, splendid in perpetual autumnal dappled sunshine, is part of our collective consciousness.

This familiarity is not surprising. There are 4,096 colleges and universities in the United States today, double the number that existed fifty years ago. Private colleges and universities, although they make up more than half (58 percent) of all these institutions, enroll fewer than a quarter (22 percent) of all students, a proportion that has fallen by more than half in the last half century.[1]

During the same period, there has been a major increase in the proportion of the traditional college-age population enrolled in college, from 30.2 percent in 1950 to 43.5 percent in 1998. The growth in enrollment of "nontraditional" college-age students has been even greater.[2]

This enrollment gives the United States one of the highest participation rates in higher education of any country in the world; 32.1 percent of American twenty-four year olds have a first university degree. Only the United Kingdom, with 35.1 percent, has a higher rate. Japan's rate is 28.0 percent, Norway's is 25.8 percent, Germany's is 24.3 percent, and China's is 1.4 percent.[3]

The average size of the American campus has also grown in the last fifty or so years, from an average student enrollment of 879 in 1940 to 4,034 in 1998. Most of the smaller institutions are private. For example, there are 525 private colleges with fewer than 500 students, but only 85 public. Women and minority students have accounted for a steadily growing proportion of the total enrollment since 1940.[4]

Today's 4,096 colleges and universities represent a bewildering variety of institutions, and that huge number does not include another 6,737 vocational institutions. All of them, however, have deliberately improved access for students and have sought to increase the enrollment from groups previously underrepresented. Flexible attendance schedules, financial aid, and a wealth of institutional programs and types have facilitated this access. Of the 14.6 million students enrolled in universities and colleges, more than 5 million are enrolled in community colleges,[5] which offer open access, remedial education, and a vast range of programs to those from nontraditional backgrounds or those who have not pursued or qualified in the typical precollege curriculum, and they also provide well-established transfer opportunities to four-year colleges and universities. The number of students enrolled in these and other two-year colleges has grown disproportionately in the last fifty years, from 200,000 in 1950 to 5.5 million in the late 1990s, accounting for 9 percent of the total enrollment in higher education in 1950, and 38 percent in 1996. In contrast, enrollment in research universities, liberal arts colleges, doctorate-granting universities, and master's degree colleges and universities has grown relatively slowly.

Some topics I want to discuss — the nature of effective teaching, for example — are relevant to all of these institutions. Others apply chiefly to the small group of institutions — the research universities — with which this book is chiefly concerned.

In an ideal world, of course, it would be tautological to speak of a "research university," a little like talking of a "musical rock group" or an "artistic painter." But in the real world, not all rock groups are notably musical and not all self-styled painters are particularly artistic. And not all universities are unambiguously devoted to research, so rather arbitrary financial and enrollment definitions are used to indicate a substantial preoccupation with research. That preoccupation reflects a conviction that research and teaching, the "advancement and diffusion of knowledge," are mutually reinforcing and are best conducted by the same people in the same community, governed and guided by that conviction, living together in the same place.

How do we define research universities? What distinguishes these institutions from all the rest? Research universities are distinguished chiefly by having a substantial number of doctoral students and a significant commitment to organized research. Perhaps 125 or so institutions might be grouped as research universities.

Even this number includes a variety of universities. Some are public — 86 of them — and others private. Some, such as Catholic University of America, have strong religious affiliations. Some, such as MIT and CalTech, are devoted chiefly to scientific and technological studies. Some are household names: Harvard, Stanford, Michigan, and Berkeley. Others are little known outside their immediate area. Some are huge: Minnesota's and Ohio State's main campuses each have more than fifty thousand students enrolled. Others are of modest size: Rice has about four thousand, for example.

This group exercises a major influence, both as a pacesetter for other colleges and universities and as the major source of most of the research conducted by the nation's universities and colleges. For example, the "top 100" universities in research and development expenditures accounted for 72 percent of all university science and engineering research space in 1996 and some 77 percent of all research and development expenditures in 1997, the most recent year for which data are available.[6] Research universities also accounted for the large majority of doctoral and professional degrees: about three-quarters of all Ph.D.s (the future faculty members of all colleges and universities) and about 35 percent of all professional degrees.

To an overwhelming degree, it is the graduates of this small handful of universities on whom the nation depends for the success of its continuing everyday functions. Manufacturing, business, health services, agriculture, the legal system, research, conservation, the arts, design and planning, and more — all rely on these universities and their graduates, not only for a large proportion of the nation's professional baccalaureate degrees, but for virtually all the nation's professional and other doctoral degrees.

Even within this restricted group, there is, of course, nothing that can be identified as "The American University." Nevertheless, most people think of the American university as a substantial institution, with an established campus, a large enrollment, a significant residential component, a comprehensive scope, graduate programs, professional schools, and a commitment both to undergraduate education and significant research. Others have described it in less-flattering terms. "Featuring the size of a small city," Charles Clotfelter has written, "the complexity of a major conglomerate, the technical sophistication of the space program, the quaintness of a medieval monastery, and the political intrigue of a Trollope novel, the modern research university in this country is a peculiar institution indeed."[7]

Size, Style, and Uniformity

The research universities, for all the importance of their contribution, occupy only a small niche within the larger framework of higher education. Before we turn to the research university, I want to say a word about their sister institutions, the other 3,900-plus colleges and universities. As colleges and universities have increased in number and size, one might suppose there would also have been an increase in variety and richness of offerings. In some colleges, there has. The rapid increase in community and junior colleges, for example, reflects a recognition of the value of providing technical skills linked to local employment opportunities, as well as more general educational offerings. In these colleges there is a rich variety and creative experiment. They are one of the nation's unwritten success stories.

But one of the unintended — and paradoxical — consequences of growth in student numbers has been a trend toward uniformity of educational styles. And in the universities and many former colleges that have declared themselves "universities," that trend has been especially notable. The established research universities, virtually all of them a century or more old, have been supplemented by a host of newer universities. And the model of the older research universities has been widely adopted by many of these newer institutions.

The development of many former public teachers' colleges into full-fledged universities reflects the general recognition by state legislatures of the need for expanded local opportunities for undergraduate and professional education. But growth of these "new universities" has brought surprisingly little variety of subject matter and teaching style. The blinkered goal of each new institution seems to be to become another Harvard, offering as full a range as possible of traditional undergraduate, graduate, and professional programs. Although here and there we find an enterprising exception to the monotony of the educational landscape, by and large the most striking thing about the newer universities is the similarity of their style and the unimaginative uniformity of their substance. Even the prewar denominational colleges and universities, which added variety and conviction to the educational enterprise, seem to have lost their intellectual moorings. Perhaps, in one sense, Kingsley Amis was right when he predicted that "more would turn out to mean worse," at least in terms of educational variety.

It may be argued that this aspiration to "climb the academic ladder" is praiseworthy; that it does no harm; that research will be sifted and judged, ideas criticized in time, and valuable knowledge assimilated. In science and related areas, that is the case. Every new discovery and hypothesis is quickly exposed to rigorous review and searching analysis. But in other areas, as Alan Wolfe and others have argued, "the system often produces perverse results" as the scholarship produced becomes increasingly "self-referential," the discourse more and more restricted and the audience more and more limited.[8] It is then the public as well as the students — both undergraduate and graduate — who are the losers.

The casual assumption that research — of whatever quality — is somehow superior to teaching leads, in many cases, to a reduction in concern for the essential responsibility of teaching, in which the institution may have a long and distinguished record, and a devotion to graduate study and research, for which it may be ill equipped. This leads to an unreasonable emphasis on research by institutions and individuals whose real forte is — and should often continue to be — teaching. We can never, in principle, have too much knowledge, of course, but frequently the gain in knowledge that is produced by this change in collegiate status is not worth the loss of time and attention devoted to first-rate teaching and to student interests. Graduate education, as Pelikan has remarked, is not an extension of a professor's undergraduate teaching, but an extension of a professor's research.[9] If there is no significant research, there can be no significant graduate program.

Yet, for all this Harvardization of aspiring universities, America's colleges and universities still display a remarkable diversity and pluralism: public and private, large and small, urban and rural, general and technical, religious and secular, coeducational and single sex. That variety, so unlike the regulated systems of other industrial nations, deserves emphasis; it is healthy. In every category, two-year colleges, women's colleges, land-grant universities, liberal arts colleges, four-year universities, multicampus state university systems, there are examples of flourishing institutions that are performing superbly in their chosen roles. That is why the earlier thoughtless drift of so many institutions toward the development of new graduate professional courses and the addition of specialized Ph.D. programs has been a trend of questionable value. The nation needs a variety of postsecondary educational offerings, each strong and effective in its own role. The richness of this educational variety, with the wealth of opportunities it provides for students, is likely to be increased by greater specialization of institutional function and differentiation of role in the years ahead.

That there is competition among these institutions, both within their various sectors and between them, is not, it seems to me, without benefit to the student in particular and the public in general, any more than industrial competition is without public benefit. Competition in both provides a healthy antidote to complacency and inefficiency. Of course, for public colleges and universities, funded from the public purse, duplication disguised as competition can be both costly and wasteful. The solution here should surely be, not to eliminate competition by some heavy-handed regulation but, to encourage competition and require both partnership and accountability.

So let me make it clear that, in focusing on the research universities, I am not advocating them as a model or a standard for all the rest. We should, rather, expect and encourage a thoughtful and healthy variety of institutions.

The Research-Intensive University

The arbitrary definition of the research university in terms of the level of Ph.D. production and federal research support captures part, but only part, of its essence. The research university is a substantial institution seriously engaged not only in research, but also in the pattern of formal scholarly apprenticeship and partnership that leads to a Ph.D., and sufficiently competitive in the quality of its work to attract both graduate students and research support in the fiercely competitive system of merit review and peer evaluation on which federal funding is based. It is tempting to gloss over these characteristics — substantial size, prominence of research, significant graduate student enrollment, and success in attracting external, especially federal, funding — as matters of only taxonomic convenience in identifying the research university. But they also define its character and give rise to some of the tensions that so concern several of its critics.

Size, while essential to provide the critical mass of faculty, staff, students, and facilities, brings with it problems of intellectual isolation, disciplinary fragmentation, and multiplicity of aims. The intimacy and easy collegiality that are one of the great strengths of the typical liberal arts college, for example, are less easily achieved in a large university. There they have to be nurtured and encouraged by incentives, sometimes rather artificial, if they are to provide the benefits of contrasting viewpoints and interdisciplinary approach so useful in both teaching and research. The success of much research depends on a precise and narrow focus, but comprehension of the larger issues of life requires a wider perspective.

The prominence of research and the significant presence of graduate students on the campus have been seen by some as diminishing the centrality of undergraduate education. Certainly, they create a community in which the education of undergraduates is no longer the sole common concern. But it is replaced by a larger sense of common purpose — inquiry and discovery — that permeates everything, and gives to the undergraduate experience a rich and distinctive flavor. In this community of inquiry, where there is no longer a division between teachers and learners, but where everyone is a scholar, the undergraduate is caught up in an atmosphere of personal exploration and discovery that forms the basis of an attitude of lifelong learning. And, while graduate students do compete for faculty attention, they also play a useful role as teachers and mentors to undergraduates. To be sure, their teaching role has been criticized by some, and it requires both training and careful oversight by faculty members to assure its effectiveness.[10] But, on balance, the spirit of inquiry fostered by research on the campus is an enormous asset, not only to the undergraduate experience, but to society at large.

Competition for research funding is part of a larger pattern of interinstitutional competition in everything from the quality of dorm rooms to intercollegiate athletics. Apart from occasional excesses in these two areas, most of this competition is probably healthy. In research funding, for example, success depends on the quality of proposals by faculty members, which are evaluated by panels of expert peers. The entrepreneurial nature of these research proposals and the care given by these panels to their scrutiny and evaluation are one of the great strengths of the research enterprise in this country. No other nation approaches the United States in the level of basic research performed in its universities. Elsewhere, much of this government-funded research is conducted in government laboratories, where direction and an inevitable degree of bureaucracy inhibit the vigor and entrepreneurism of the American partnership between the federal government and the universities. Though that system has recently experienced some strains, it remains a model of effectiveness and productivity, as reflected, for example, by the overwhelming dominance of the United States in producing winners of the Nobel Prize, or its strength in such university-developed industries as biotechnology. About 10 percent of all university research funding now comes from industry, and while this is not without some tensions, that figure is likely to grow in the future.

No system, of course, however successful, is without its downside. The federal funding of research brings with it a substantial burden of regulation and accountability. The system can be abused, both by government (administration and the Congress) and by the universities, and it may distort both university priorities and those of the individual investigator. Some federal research support has tended of late to drift toward a pattern of procurement of results, or purchase of services, rather than funding investigator-initiated proposals, while the level of support for the indirect costs of research (building operations, library resources, and so on) has been such that many universities complain that they are compelled to subsidize these costs from other sources. Each of these concerns is real, but for all its imperfections, the model of federal support of university-initiated research proposals is one of the greatest and most distinctive strengths of the American university.

Other tensions inherent in the research-intensive university are less tangible, but no less important. The growing influence of research, together with the concentration and reductionism it typically involves, has reduced the influence once enjoyed by the liberal arts in the university as a whole, while the growth of professionalism and science has lessened the role of the liberal arts in undergraduate education. That diminution, while perhaps predictable, should not be accepted as inevitable, for the wider moral concerns and intellectual cohesion long represented by the liberal arts have never been of more importance in both professional practice and society. The research-intensive university has a unique opportunity to harness those concerns and viewpoints to the most pressing issues of our time. But this will not happen without leadership, structures, and incentives that encourage this vital interaction. Professional schools must be viewed, not as the opponents of the vision and breadth of the liberal arts, but as laboratories where the virtues of the liberal arts can be applied to professional practice and where their concepts can be tested and refined in the demanding context of daily life.

The research university places heavy demands upon the individual faculty member: he or she must be a successful investigator, a scholar of originality, a successful entrepreneur and fund-raiser, a substantial author, an effective mentor of graduate and professional students, a challenging and inspiring undergraduate teacher and adviser, an effective participant in the life of the department, an informed citizen in the affairs of the college and university, and a responsible public servant contributing the benefits of professional insight to the continuing needs of the local community, the larger society, and the professional guild. Given this lengthy list of expectations, it is not surprising that the faculty member is challenged to cover all the bases, devoting the most attention to those areas that provide the most direct support. High on this list come research, grant seeking, and the professional guild. Research is the basis of public recognition, grants support that research, and the various professional guilds provide rewards and recognition. In contrast, great teaching and effective mentoring are more private, less easy to evaluate; they receive less recognition, less acclaim. And effective citizenship, whether on or off the campus, is celebrated least of all. Small wonder, then, that many lament the loss of institutional loyalty by the faculty. But perhaps the greatest surprise is that, given these competing distractions, so many faculty members continue to exhibit such devotion to their students and such commitment to their universities. Let us look in on a few professors in action.

Consider Jody Maxmin, an art history professor at Stanford who is known to spend more time making comments on term papers than some students spend writing them and who has won six teaching awards. On a sunny May day, Maxmin walks into the drab green room in the basement of the Stanford arts building where she teaches Greek and Roman art history. A slight woman with long brown hair, she wears a purple skirt, white blouse, and not a trace of makeup. In front of thirty-five undergraduates, many of whom are football players, she appears dwarfed by a gang of giants.

Her strategy for winning them over is disclosed one small move at a time. First she returns student papers to which she has added her own essays as commentaries on theirs (it is a level of attention, she notes, that inspires them to spend far more time working on them). She then pauses a few seconds by their desks. "How are you doing?" she asks one student. "You look tired." She asks another about a game he was in, another about a friend, another about work. Can any student in this class feel like a lost and lonely undergraduate among the competitive crowd? Not likely.

Turning then to the day's lecture topic, the building of the Coliseum as a tactic for unifying the Romans, Maxmin turns off the lights, flips on the projector, and slides into a lecture that seems both spontaneous and planned down to the smallest detail and joke. Emperor Nero is described in passing as having spindly legs and a pot belly, Otto as having a double chin and hound-like eyes, Vespasian as having a face so rough that if you kissed him on the cheek, you would need lip balm afterward.

It is, to be sure, a somewhat quirky way of teaching, far from staid and remote. By peppering her lecture with details, both objective and personal, Maxmin never allows the students to mistake history for a dry account from books but motivates them to see it as stories about the follies and successes of people. In this way, she teaches them that history follows the same dynamics we continue to engage in, in one way or another, today. The details may vary, but "the history of everything" boils down to two facets of experience, which, Maxmin notes, the Romans wisely named Venus and Mars, or love and war. We build things up, she says, then we burn them down. The cycle is forever repeated.

As she continues to speak — of the art, the politics, the people, the myths — Maxmin's students listen closely to her stories, laugh at her jokes, ask their questions, and answer hers. They spot the connections between classical history and our times, and they seem to absorb the wisdom of myths as easily as if they were stories from the newspaper. If learning about Roman history in sunny California seemed foreign to them on the first day of class, it seems very much a part of life on this, one of the last days.

And in this fact, as in the evidence of the excellent marks more than 90 percent of the class earns on very detailed and challenging exams, Maxmin shows she has prevailed — indeed, shows herself to be the perfect metaphor for the Greeks, who were small *and* capable of conquering the far larger and more numerous Persians.

Their secret, she explains, was in their approach to education: they believed one had to develop one's body and, as she puts it, the great muscle between the ears. As their myths taught them, she says, "You've got to be clever. You've got to be wily. You've got to do it your own way."

But there is another element she would add in explanation of her teaching strategy, one borrowed from Odysseus and rare in these Freudian-swept times: "You've got to lose self-consciousness."

In other words, to do something, anything truly well, one must know it so completely that one feels free to forget oneself, to forget the impression one is making, and to play — to play at the work. This, of course, requires more than the usual amount of work; Maxmin works from 8 A.M. to midnight every day. But this, she says, is what it takes to teach in both an informed and spontaneous fashion, and it is this combination that gives birth to creativity and the possibility for true connections with students: for the transformation that is the aim of deep education.

Or consider John Hsu, the Old Dominion Foundation Professor of Music at Cornell. John Hsu has heard music in his head at least since he began piano lessons at age three in his native Swatow, China. On planes, he prefers reading music to listening with earphones. Once, when he left a concert that his companion enjoyed but he found lacking, he was heard to say, "I hear a better concert reading the music."

Whether he is conducting, lecturing, or teaching the nuances of bowing a baroque instrument, Hsu speaks quietly, evenly, patiently. When he leads the Cornell Chamber Orchestra, he rises on his toes and his thin body bends with the music toward the instruments he is addressing; but his gestures are graceful, not flamboyant. In rehearsal, his directions may be as simple as a gentle "ssh" to the first violins or, to the horns, "Measure three: da-da-bup, da-da-bup; okay, let's move on."

He is personally modest and loath to sound highbrow about baroque music. He won't say a bad word about rock. It is in music itself that he expresses his passion for music; and, indeed, he says the reason music matters is that it fulfills people's need to express their feelings: "If there were no music or painting, every human being would write poetry."

Shelves in his office and home are lined with family photographs from former students bound to Hsu by his personal generosity and the love of music that shines through his unassuming manner. Some of the students now teach; some perform; some are bankers or lawyers. They were all enriched by the music in Hsu's head.

Yet some critics might complain that John Hsu doesn't pull his load. If they looked for him in his office or in the classrooms of Lincoln Hall, they would find no sign of him most mornings and might conclude that, after about forty-five years of hard labor, he was enjoying some well-earned leisure. How wrong a conclusion that would be, though it is the kind often drawn by those who say a professor's nonclassroom time can't possibly be the same as, well, real work.

Hsu usually begins his fourteen-hour workdays around 7 A.M., in two converted bedrooms of his modest home two miles from campus. One room, the house's only one that is air-conditioned, contains a small wooden chair, a music stand, a floor-to-ceiling rack stuffed with sheet music, and — the reason for the air conditioning — Hsu's cello. That was the instrument he studied at the New England Conservatory, that he played at the New England Opera Company in Boston, and that he taught before coming to Cornell in 1955.

After an hour with Mozart, Haydn, or Bach, Hsu walks across the upstairs hall to the other converted bedroom to work on a research project that will produce seven volumes and will consume something like fifteen years' effort. Volume 4 came out in 1998. Piled on a small desk, which sits beside a vertical Chinese scroll painting, are up to thirteen versions of the same sheet music, collected from publishers and libraries in France, Switzerland, Germany, and the United States. Hsu is editing the first complete modern edition of the 598 works of the French baroque viola da gambist Marin Marais (1656–1728). Meticulously comparing thousands upon thousands of bars of music, he looks particularly for little xs that Marais added late in life because he thought beauty would be served by extending some notes beyond their usual length.

Hsu is one of the world's leading viola da gamba players, having traveled widely in America and Europe to perform and record baroque works. His life is animated with teaching, conducting, lecturing, and listening. Why would he also make the commitment to the arduous and tedious detective work of cross-checking editions of Marais? Wouldn't he rather, being over sixty years old now, spend more time with his wife at the Caribbean time-share condominium that he gets himself to for only one week a year?

This research project is like that of the classicist who keeps working to produce a more perfect English and Latin edition of Cicero's letters or Caesar's *Gallic Wars*. It can be argued that old editions tell us all we need to know of republican Rome — or that it really doesn't matter much if future musicians have a slightly more accurate rendering of Marais's intended sound. Remember, John Hsu has had tenure and an endowed chair for years. He is not doing the research for gain or vanity. He is doing it because truth, beauty, and perfection matter to him, because if he does not work for Marais's perfection, perhaps no one will. A certain kind of mind could call this work a waste of time and money. It is quite true that while he is bent over his thirteen editions, he cannot be in a classroom earning his salary directly from tuition-paying students. And no one contends that this research will reach many or that it will, as biochemistry might, have a significant ultimate effect on mankind. Yet I believe it is good for posterity and good for Cornell students today that John Hsu should be paid for that time in his upstairs bedrooms.

The main reason is that it enriches the work he does on campus and enriches the lives of others far beyond it. The way it does so explains a lot about the difference between a research university and a more traditional college. Back in 1960, Hsu was a young assistant professor teaching chamber music, cello classes, and a daily 9 A.M. class in music theory. He was also lead violinist in the Cornell orchestra and cellist in a trio that performed every Sunday on local radio, and in the afternoons he coached student ensemble groups and individual cellists. In the midst of all that, some senior colleagues asked Hsu if he'd be willing to learn to play the viola da gamba, a baroque-era six-stringed instrument that is held between the knees, played with a curved bow, and similar in range to the cello. He said yes, Cornell bought three of the instruments from Germany, and, with Hsu's maiden recital on campus in the spring of 1961, the practice of playing eighteenth-century music on historically correct instruments began in America.

But before he could play, John had to do months of detective work, at the Bibliotheque Nationale in Paris; he had to reconstruct the playing technique of masters like Marais and Forqueray, and he had to divine from their notations their musical and aesthetic intentions.

That research has borne fruit far beyond the broadening of Hsu's own knowledge. First came his *Handbook of French Baroque Viol Technique*, then his initial editing of Marais. Hsu formed the Haydn Baryton Trio, a much-acclaimed ensemble devoted to playing and recording 126 divertimenti on restored instruments; the seventeen-member Cornell Chamber Orchestra (made up mostly of undergraduates who are not music majors); and the Cornell Summer Viol Program, to which a small group of advanced gamba players come each year to improve their art with Hsu's gentle help. Thanks to John Hsu, Cornell has become a center for the study of historic instruments, granting a Ph.D. degree in performance of eighteenth-century instruments.

Hsu's research makes him a better performer and teacher; his teaching makes him better understand what research should yield. And Hsu himself makes Cornell a better place. A senior chemistry major who had played the violin since the age of six and who was, only for relaxation, in a quartet led by Hsu, put it this way: "His great insight has given me an enriched and a deepened understanding of music. I'll have it for life."

The research university provides an atmosphere of instruction and a context of learning that are distinctive, intensive, demanding, practical, professionalized, personal, and unending. Learning becomes a lifelong quest, meticulous attention to detail becomes the benchmark. The results, for individuals and for society, can be transforming.

{ 3 }
TRANSFORMING
PROFESSIONALISM

"A college becomes a university," it has been said, "when the faculty ceases to care about the students." That observation is as cynical as it is false, but it highlights one matter of lively debate: the rise in professionalism on campus and its impact on students. To understand this shift, let us consider again the roots of the American university.

As the undergraduate colleges were assimilated into the new university, they became a transformed central component for a larger enterprise. Undergraduate education continued to be a vital function of the newly emerging institutions of the late nineteenth century, so the values and goals of a liberal education were not lost. But alongside liberal undergraduate education, two other functions emerged — graduate education to supply the increasing demand for a professoriate, and research in the basic disciplines to fill the nation's research needs. The training of new professional classes needed to serve the growing country.

Indeed, in little more than a decade or two, in the late nineteenth century, the university became comprehensive, offering instruction in all the practical affairs of life, including architecture, veterinary medicine, mining, and home economics. Later, in the twentieth century, a sweeping range of professional skills was added, from business management, public policy, pharmacy, dentistry, nursing, health administration, operations research, industrial engineering, regional planning, education, social work, library science, and gerontology, to industrial and labor relations, hotel management, nanofabrication, international diplomacy, journalism, landscape architecture, and forestry.

From a national perspective, the evolution of the American university was piecemeal, uneven, and rarely fully planned in form or fully comprehended in impact. In vain, some within the academy, such as Robert Hutchins of the

University of Chicago, argued that not all subjects were equal. Chiropractic and homeopathic medicine, cosmetology, criminal justice, and fashion design were soon to follow in some institutions, though rarely in universities. And why not? many people asked. If universities were to serve the public good, why set any bounds?

The association of professional schools with colleges of arts and sciences reflects the conviction that each has something to contribute to the other. The association of the humanities, the social sciences, and the natural sciences within a single college — a grouping virtually nonexistent in other countries — represents the same conviction. Beyond the more obvious links between, say, the basic sciences and medicine, or between economics and business, other linkages continue to prove fruitful: the social sciences and law and engineering, engineering and architecture, psychology and medicine, environmental science and city and regional planning, agriculture and nutrition. And of course we must not forget the value of history, philosophy, religion, literature, drama, music, and art to all the others. This is true at every level, from undergraduate programs to faculty research. The challenges of life and the needs of society defy traditional disciplinary boundaries, and the collective expertise of the campus is an asset of growing value that is widely acknowledged, though not yet fully utilized.

The other striking feature of the American university is that it is not only the same institutions but also the same people who are involved in these complementary functions. Only rarely will universities appoint "research professors" or "graduate professors." The general assumption is that research and undergraduate and graduate teaching are everyone's responsibility, not to be differentiated and meted out to a small select group. That some faculty members will be more versatile than others is acknowledged, but the assumption is that all will gain by the shared responsibility. John Slaughter, former president of Occidental College, put it this way: "Research is to teaching as sin is to confession. Unless you participate in the former, you have very little to say in the latter!"[1]

Behind this diversity of America's universities there lies a multiplicity of particular aims and a bewildering variety of support and function. Even among the leading research universities, the differences are immense. CalTech is unlike Chicago in many respects. Princeton bears little close resemblance to Purdue. American universities do not constitute a system, and that is, on balance, one of their great strengths. Their dependence on no single source of support and authority gives them a vigor, independence, and pragmatism unknown in some other places.

There is, however, behind this variety, not only the shared conviction that collegiality is a unique source of strength, but also the further conviction that this is particularly important in relation to the professional schools. The very name *universitas* refers to a group of people organized for a purpose. The Latin *collegium* has the same implication.[2] It was the group, the college, the whole association, that was distinctive, not only, as is sometimes stated, a curriculum of universal studies. Students educated in a research environment develop a lifelong curiosity and outlook from which they continue to benefit, whatever their chosen fields. Professional education gains from interplay with the arts and sciences and vice versa. Research is often most fruitful at the boundaries between existing disciplines. New studies in neuroscience, for example, draw on the expertise of four or five traditional disciplines. Modern medicine is becoming heavily dependent on biochemistry, structural chemistry, genomics, and X-ray crystallography. It is the university, acting in this collegial fashion, that has, over its long history, proved to be the most effective environment for both learning and discovery.

Yet, today, a century of explosive growth and a mixture of institutional opportunism, legislative concern, personal entrepreneurship, and collegiate absentmindedness have turned the American university into an indigestible hodgepodge. A great university, it was once said, is known by what it chooses not to do, as well as what it chooses to do. These are wise words. Indeed, there are some who lament the growing presence of professional studies within the university, claiming they dilute "purer" scholarship. But it is too late now. We are what we are, and there is no realistic possibility of going back, even if we wished to do so. *E unum pluribus.*

But we should not wish to go back to simpler days. It would be churlish to deny the real gains in the quality of professional service that growth has produced. They are immense. The remarkable level of scores of professional services, from surgery to retailing, the quality and value of hundreds of products, from fruit to computers to freeway design and automobile safety, reflect the benefits of this growth in university professionalism. So we should be thankful for this new professionalism. It has served our nation well.

I was particularly conscious of this some time ago when I broke my hand. I had supposed my hand would require an orthopedist to pin it back together, and so it did, but my orthopedist — for whose superb skill and personal care I am deeply grateful — was one of six at the Hospital for Special Surgery whose practice was limited to surgery of the hand. And my physical therapist — equally superb — was one of a half dozen at the hospital who deal exclusively with treatment for the hand. From this specialization, and the superior services it provides in hundreds of fields, the public derives daily benefits.

So the university today "reeks of professional dominance," to use Burton Clark's words. That is a fact of life that we should neither bemoan nor regret. The nature of the professions requires it. The sweeping range of services the university provides for its members (including athletic teams, sports facilities, orchestras and repertory companies, theaters and studios, museums and libraries, health services and police protection, dining halls and dormitories, counseling services and career advice, transportation services and military training, university presses and national laboratories) requires it.

There are, of course, major differences among the various professions as represented on the campus. Let me add a word of explanation about the term "professionalization," for the concept of professionalism has, as Walter Metzger and others have shown, undergone a remarkable transformation in the last half century.[3] The earlier concept of a profession was of an occupation requiring a high level of technical competence and serving a commendable public purpose. Typically, it involved admission into membership of a corporate guild and/or state licensing, which both established and required high standards of performance.

Under this arrangement, the public granted professional autonomy in exchange for a fiduciary commitment to high ethical and professional standards and a personal obligation to responsible public service. The more recent decline in public esteem for some professions reflects, perhaps, not only allegations of individual malpractice and incompetence, but a more serious drift toward what is seen as antisocial behavior and self-serving activities on the part of some members of the professions at large, particularly law. Public esteem has also been diluted by the explosive growth in occupations now described as professional, from baseball to law enforcement, from catering to pest control. In many of them, there is no public licensing, no formal personal commitment to responsible service.

There is, however, another tendency that is chiefly responsible for the growing professionalization of the university. It is claimed there are now over 8,500 definable fields and subfields of knowledge.[4] The explosive growth in knowledge has reduced the possibility of any serious claim to general knowledge at anything except at the most superficial level. For as knowledge increases, so, too, must individual ignorance of fields other than one's own, and even within one's own selected field, personal competence tends to become increasingly specialized and refined.

This specialization and professionalization affect not only the "service" professions but all knowledge. They are as characteristic of philosophy and physics as they are of pediatrics, as characteristic of literature as of law. And while their growth is inevitable and their benefits are substantial, they have a less benevolent impact upon undergraduate education, weakening the possibility of common learning. Professional writing, for example, has always involved writing for one's peers, but such writing has become less and less accessible to those outside the fields. Writing for a more general public is, at best, little valued by many fellow academics, and, at worst, is described slightingly by some as cheap popularization and dismissed by others as an act of intellectual vulgarity.

The inclusion of professional studies within the university provides the benefits, not only of intellectual cross-fertilization between, say, medicine or engineering and the basic sciences, but also of reflection on the ethical obligations and social consequences of each profession. This is not a substitute for either professional self-regulation or public oversight, but it provides an intellectual framework within which responsibilities can be analyzed and assumptions challenged. If professions are to play an optimal role in public life, such scrutiny becomes ever more important.

The Price of Professionalism

But no benefits come without costs. The enormous growth of professional education and the professionalization of what were once the liberal arts have had several major effects on the university.

Professionalism has tended to shift student interest from pursuing an education to getting a job. "Developing a coherent philosophy of life" topped the list of student goals a quarter century ago. Now "getting a job" and "succeeding in a career" are the goals of most of the present student generation. Between 1966 and 1993, for example, the number of B.A. degrees awarded to students majoring in one of the fields of the arts and sciences (humanities, social sciences, mathematics, and sciences) fell from 48 percent to about 35 percent.[5] Indeed, "liberal arts" colleges now compete for students by offering management programs, allied health majors, and a remarkable array of vocational programs. The same trend is reflected by the steadily rising proportion of college graduates who go on to graduate or professional school.

More and more, the undergraduate degree is practically based, as the postbaccalaureate professional degree casts a long shadow of requirements on what should be the carefree intellectual exploration of the undergraduate years. ("Of course, we encourage you to take a history degree. . . . You'd be a better doctor for that, no doubt . . . but we know you're going to need organic chemistry and physiology, and calculus would help.") In this trend there is a real loss. Focused professionalism and blinkered careerism, applied early and rigidly, impoverish the variety and vigor of the undergraduate experience.

Professionalism has caused knowledge itself to be seen as a commodity, a product to be purchased and applied. Education has increasingly become vocational training and learning a skill, rather than personal illumination. Understanding is seen as operational rather than comprehensional, as instrumental rather than insightful. Ethical standards, once at the heart of the university's existence, are now imposed by professional bodies and external boards, rather than being personally derived.

No one has diagnosed this danger of unfettered professionalism to professional practice better than Lewis Mumford, when he indicated the dangers of a life "governed by specialists, who know too little of what lies outside their province to be able to know enough about what takes place within it: unbalanced men who have made a madness out of their method. Our life, like medicine itself, has suffered from the denouement of the general practitioner, capable of vigilant selection, evaluation, and action with reference to the health of the organism or the community as a whole. Is it not high time that we asked ourselves what constitutes a full human being?"[6]

Professionalism has diminished the influence of the liberal arts themselves, and, in turn, reduced public discourse and diminished professional practice. The nagging questions of our common humanity once confronted by the liberal arts are now hushed or ignored, even though we have never needed them more. A young man or woman will become a more humane physician after some exposure to Shakespeare and Dostoyevsky. The time to reflect on our mortality is not in the operating room, but in the classroom. The time to debate the appropriate level of a patient's bill is not in the hospital examination room; it is in the economics seminar room. What is true of medicine is true of every other professional field: we need specialist professionals with a generalist view, whether in estimating the costs of environmental conservation or the ethics of genetic engineering.

One particular danger of narrow professionalism is that it insulates the professional from extraprofessional dialogue and may even, in extreme cases, deflect attention from the basic goals of the discipline that gave rise to the profession itself. This is a danger in any professional field; in the humanities it is a catastrophe, for these, of all disciplines, once spoke to us across our boundaries of birth and divisions of belief.

Frank Kermode has described the breakdown of what had been a steady dialogue between the experts, on the one hand, and the educated public at large on the other, as a consequence of professors' increasing tendency to speak and write only for one another, "inventing arcane dialects to keep out the uninitiated." In response, the lay public no longer looks to professors for wisdom or assumes that the humanities offer "a defense against the increasing horrors of modern life, as it was believed that they did in the time of the great nineteenth-century periodicals. And there are few inducements of the gentler sort, that simply make the reading of literature a task in which the pleasure might conceivably outweigh the labor."[7]

Centripetal professionalism, with its growing isolation and its threat to the benevolent influence of literature, is also a threat to the other professions and the wider benefits they provide. The antidote is intelligent dialogue, informed debate, not only within the professional groups, but among the professional groups, embraced by that larger community of discourse that is the university.

Professionalism has shifted the allegiance of the faculty away from the university. Consultancy arrangements, company directorships, royalty and patent rights, clients who are wealthy and influential, benefactors bearing gifts, coveys of assistants, generous fees from professional practice, enviable research support, favorable salaries, popular books, successful videotapes, the international lecture circuit, superior working facilities — these are all typical involvements and enjoyments of the most successful members of the professional faculty. Successful professors view themselves as favoring the university by their presence. It is their base, but scarcely their employer. Rather, they are entrepreneurs, paid a substantial retainer for their services, but free to exercise their judgment on what to teach and study, how to do it, and even when to do it. Their allegiance is not to their institution, not to their college, not primarily to their students, but to their profession, their guild, their colleagues, most of them beyond the campus, and to their clients.

So the collegial lines are weakened. Common discourse and informed communal debate decline. The department becomes the whole world of the faculty member and also, often, of the student. This is both tragic and ironic: tragic because we lose so much, both as individuals and as a nation, by limiting our contacts and isolating our activities, and ironic because it was precisely to avoid this isolation and fragmentation that universities were established. A meaningful life consists of linkages, and without those larger connections we wither. Learning was intended to be richer in community than it ever could be within the monastic cell. But in our academic structures the subdivisions of department and center become the new monastic cells. Clark Kerr was not being entirely facetious when he quoted Robert Hutchins's description of the modern university as a series of buildings, loosely held together by a central heating system.[8]

Professionalism has diminished what was once a common concern for the well-being of the individual student, reflected in the earlier "pastoral" role of the faculty — embodied in the phrase in loco parentis. The faculty member is now the student's "instructor" and at a more personal level his "academic adviser." (When I first began teaching at the University of Durham in the 1950s, each student had a "moral tutor," who was a member of the faculty. If the name was quaintly archaic, the intention was not; it was to assure that the educational experience was optimally useful in the development of the student as a whole person.) The personal relationship between student and faculty member has been qualified and restricted. A legion of others — professional specialists all — deal with every other segment of the student's life: financial aid counselors, study-skills experts, chaplains, coaches, career advisers, health care specialists of every variety, residence hall advisers, judicial advocates, ombudspersons, deans of this, directors of that. All offer advice on every aspect of student life, from contraception to community service, from social life to study abroad. Nothing is forgotten, except, perhaps, the need to deal sensitively with the student as a whole person.

Professionalism has caused the loss of an implicit set of moral assumptions that once provided an educational framework for the curriculum. The earliest American universities reflected the Christian roots of the ancient European universities and the Protestant heritage of the New England colleges. Even the nineteenth-century private universities, while anxious to assert their sectarian independence, were also quick to declare their ethical moorings. "We will labor to make this a Christian institution," declared Andrew D. White of Cornell, "A sectarian institution may it never be."[9] The leaders of the public universities were no less emphatic. In their report of 1841 to the superintendent, the University of Michigan Regents stated, "Whatever varieties of sect exist in these United States, the great mass of the population profess an attachment to Christianity and, as a people, avow themselves to be Christians."[10] These statements were not, I think, doctrinal declarations, but rather a shorthand statement of the moral aspirations that were regarded as the foundation of a successful education.

But the twentieth century saw a de-Christianizing of the nineteenth-century university, and with this secularization, the once-common set of moral assumptions that lent an ethical context and educational framework for the curriculum has collapsed. Moreover, this framework has been re-placed, not by an alternative viewpoint or another coherent educational structure, but rather by a collective moral and intellectual ambiguity. The very lack of shared conviction has become the hallmark of the new academy, whose only collective assertion is likely to be the validity of all viewpoints and convictions and whose only prohibition is the critical judgment of competing values or the open evaluation of alternative worldviews. The ultimate goal thus becomes the avoidance of offense rather than the attainment of truth, and the supreme virtue an open-mindedness that leads to perpetual suspen-sion of critical judgment rather than the discernment of the true and merito-rious. And, given no agreement on the nature of the good life or even the ra-tional basis of understanding, agreement on educational goals becomes impossible, and their very discussion an embarrassment. A person can spend a lifetime in the professorial ranks and never participate in a collegial discus-sion of such matters. It is not that academic rigor is abandoned. It is pursued, with professional pride, in exquisite refinement and extraordinary detail. But the broader picture, the larger issues of life about which the student yearns for some understanding — these are the casualties of the new enlightenment.

No one, of course, would wish to turn back the clock to the preprofes-sional days of the educated generalist or the informed amateur. The victories of professional knowledge have been hard-won, and we are all the beneficia-ries of those whose professional devotion and skill have achieved them. But they come at a price. Alfred North Whitehead once remarked that profession-alism "produces minds in a groove. Each profession makes progress but it is progress in its own groove." And minds in a groove lead easily to lives in a groove — "the celibacy of the intellect," as Whitehead called it — and the loss of wholeness and richness that that involves.

Redeeming Professionalism

Having said all of this, let me be clear that I am not arguing against profes-sional education itself; I am arguing against its reduction to narrow job train-ing. The first is large, expansive, having the spirit of the liberal arts, setting skills as means within larger ends, concerned not with "the job" but with life and with the social goals the profession promotes and the ethical standards it demands. The second is narrow, restrictive, developing specific skills in preparation for routine tasks, sometimes very technical or scientific; it in-volves knowledge for specific ends, raising no questions of larger significance;

it is impervious to social context, oblivious to moral choice. A liberal outlook may be nurtured within the context of professional education. It soon withers in the presence of narrow training for a particular job. Indeed, today we have law devoid of ethical context, health care systems unconstrained by economic reality, engineering and architecture uninformed by aesthetics, public administration uninvolved with sociology, and management isolated from both psychology and ethics.

In the few cases where a particular skill is regarded as vital to a profession, the disciplines themselves have been captured, harnessed, and tamed. Consumer economics, rural sociology, agricultural entomology, business English, marketing psychology, food chemistry, and more — all these areas now serve the growing professional needs and appetites of the New American University. Useful? Yes, I think so. Educationally desirable? No, I think not. We need to reconsider how to meet these needs. We must not allow the basic disciplines to lose their edge or their influence.

But we cannot go back. Much as we may lament the loss of shared educational goals and common ethical assumptions, we must live with what we have: the secular university, vast in its scope, professional in its orientation. The question is not whether we can restore a vanished prototype: who would wish to? Extinction, after all, is forever. The question is whether we can recapture the sense of common educational purpose, personal concern, and individual scale that marked the best qualities of the university but that have become the casualties of the new professionalism.

So what shall we do? I wish I had a simple answer. I have only some thoughts. And I hesitate to offer them, because they seem so inadequate against the entrenched strength of the professions. Perhaps narrow careerism is a requirement for success in twenty-first-century life, after all. Perhaps the view that we can and must learn from one another is only quaintly nostalgic, an impossible dream in the hard realities of our age. I hope not, but I may be wrong.

But suppose for a moment that I am right. Suppose that by exploring alternative viewpoints, by sharing common experiences, by developing additional models — suppose that by doing these things, personal experience can be enriched, professional practice can be improved, and community life can be enlarged. Would it not be worth the effort?

Edward O. Wilson, who has done more to bring the biodiversity crisis to the attention of the American public than most scientists in or out of academia, thinks so. He would like nothing better, he once said, than to leave his position at Harvard University, trek to Brazil, and never come back. In the in-

troduction to his book *The Diversity of Life*, the two-time Pulitzer Prize winner lovingly describes what he sees, hears, and smells in the rain forest. Then,
as if still there, he observes, "It struck me how little is known about these creatures of the rain forest, and how deeply satisfying it would be to spend
months, years, the rest of my life in this place until I knew all the species by
name and every detail of their lives."

Back at Harvard, where he holds the Pellegrino University Professorship,
Wilson explains why he doesn't fulfill his desires. "I have a feeling of mission.
If I thought the world was in good order, the rain forests were saved and the
world was full of conservationists, I would go off somewhere, definitely. I
would go off and enjoy nature."

But with his firsthand knowledge of the damage being done in the rain
forests, and his understanding of the implications of the stripping of nature's
diversity, Wilson does not have the conscience to skip town — conscience, in
his case, being a fair term. "My religious background is another reason why I
am what I am," says Wilson, who is a Southern Baptist.

Wilson's roots as a naturalist came from his experience of growing up in
rural Alabama, the only child of divorced parents. Because his father's position as a government accountant required them to move often, he attended
sixteen schools in eleven years. No surprise, he had little opportunity to develop friendships.

But he did find companionship in nature. He put on rubber boots and
walked the fields and swamps wherever he went. And wherever he went, there
were some familiar things, of which he never let go. "Like most children," the
New York Times wrote of him in a 1990 magazine cover story, "Wilson went
through a bug phase, but he never grew out of his, never on to the larger creatures most naturalists drift toward. To use his own lingo, Wilson was pre-
adapted for ant work."

Now the world's leading authority on ants, Wilson, along with Bert Holl-
dobler, the Alexander Agassiz Professor of Zoology at Harvard, is the author
of the most complete book ever written on the subject: *The Ants*. It won the
1991 Pulitzer Prize for General Non-Fiction and put Wilson on the morning
television and radio programs *Good Morning America*, *The Today Show*, and
National Public Radio's *Morning Edition*.

Why ants? "They are," he writes, "the little creatures who run the world."
Without them, he says simply, the earth would rot. Ants make and keep soil
fertile. If they didn't, vegetation would pile up and close channels of nutrient
cycles, and vertebrates would die off.

But, of course, there are endless topics, both serious and consequential, that vie for the public's attention. The quality that attracted television audiences to Wilson and his ants was his unusual style of telling a story. This quality can be seen in Wilson's *On Human Nature,* which won the Pulitzer Prize in 1979, a book that argues that genetically determined patterns of human behavior, such as altruism and aggression, still guide our behavior today. It can be seen in *The Ants* and in more recent books as well.

"A scientist is much more of a storyteller and a myth-maker than I think most scientists realize or at least care to admit," he explained in "E. O. Wilson: Reflections on a Life in Science," a videotape distributed by Harvard. "The scientist is in fact a storyteller looking for a story to tell, not of fiction, but certainly a product of imagination passed through the crucible of testing in the real world."

In *The Biodiversity of Life,* for example, Wilson wrote as a novelist might the story of the evolution of and threat to biodiversity. He developed protagonists. He described a crisis (the imminence of mass extinction), he relaxed tensions (with suggestions of how to avoid the crisis), and he struck mythic themes (the apocalypse).

In this approach, Wilson is unlike many university professors who are concerned that such experimentation will risk their reputations as serious and objective scholars. He is able to take the risk, he explains, because he has proven his credibility as a scientist. But he also feels compelled to do it to fulfill his sense of obligation that he use his expertise to communicate to students and a wider general audience. "If we speak out too forcefully on what we see as a problem — global warming, toxic pollution, extinction — then our colleagues are likely to regard us as representing a political or ideological constituency. But if we don't speak out at all or speak out too weakly, then we have abandoned the responsibility to say something," Wilson says. "This, I think, is an important role that university research personnel can and should play."

Recommendations

There are several steps that the university and professions can take to capture the broader potential of professional education.

Universities and the professions should pause to examine the assumptions, requirements, and outcomes of professional education. There is nothing sacred, or even uniquely effective, in the present practices. Other countries have very different approaches and produce skilled physicians, lawyers, engineers, and managers. Russia and China both have universities solely devoted to particular careers: railroad engineering, agriculture, or telecommunications, for example. Of course, direct comparisons aren't easy. European schools, Japanese legal systems, and the British health care system all differ from ours. But why should journalism, business management, and architecture be offered as undergraduate degrees in some reputable institutions but limited to graduate degrees in others that are equally reputable? What are the differences in recruitment, context, employment, and outcome? What are the costs, and what are the benefits? Or consider engineering. Is a four-year undergraduate degree appropriate for what, in an earlier period, was always a five-year program? Or medicine: Does the present pattern of education provide the optimum experience for the surgical profession? It is time for each profession to reexamine its present educational practices. I would make a requirement, if I could, that the body that reexamines the education of each profession have a significant number of members from outside that particular profession.

Universities should bring the liberal arts, with the broad human concerns they represent, inside the tent of professional courses and programs. We need not a new curriculum, but a new spirit of learning — some simple, meaningful, achievable educational goal. Save for the most basic information, it is no longer necessary, at the college level, to commit vast amounts of knowledge to memory. Data can be retrieved and utilized through a host of information sources and technologies. Of more lasting value are the broadly applicable skills and wide-ranging interests and perspectives that the traditional liberal arts curriculum once sought to provide (see Chapter 6).

Universities should require that all committees for faculty recruitment and promotion have one or two members from outside the particular discipline or profession represented. Joint appointments, team teaching, and cooperative research will all contribute to a restoration of community.

Universities should provide incentives for such cooperation. At present, all the pressure is centripetal, directed inward to serving the interests of the department. Worse yet, contacts outside the department or profession are sometimes regarded with suspicion and hostility as disloyal and distracting. This is a mistake for which society at large pays the price. The university must foster linkages, not undermine them.

One simple and inexpensive place to start might be the introductory courses. Gerald Graff and others have described the success of learning communities, formed around broad themes — human nature and law in nature, society, and language, for example.[11] In these communities, existing courses in science, the humanities, and social sciences would be brought together, thus exploring common issues between them that remain unaddressed in the existing cafeteria-like curriculum.

Such a move, encouraged from the top but developed from bottom-up debate by the faculty, would have a refreshing effect on everyday campus life for all members of the community. Unlike other schemes of so-called reform, it would require neither the renunciation of scholarship nor the denial of difference, ambiguities, and tensions among both the disciplines themselves and their practitioners. It would promote face-to-face discussion as a powerful antidote to electronic estrangement, and interdisciplinary debate as an alternative to intellectual isolation.

These changes will strengthen rather than weaken professional performance: they will enlarge it, not reduce it. Until now, professional education has prospered by its zealous concentration, and we should cherish that. These strategies would enrich its role in society by enlarging the intellectual foundation on which it is based.

But does that matter? Does it make any *practical* difference? Professionals are busy people. Is there time to pursue what some busy practitioners would regard as peripheral, or even distracting, questions? I believe it does matter, that it will make a difference, and that time must be found. It is not only the effectiveness of professional practice that is at stake here. It is the well-being of our society. The complexities of life and the comprehension of experience often elude the exquisite concentration and rigorous abstraction that professionalism increasingly requires.

Rebuilding Discourse

To John Henry Cardinal Newman, writing in 1873, the idea of the university was powerful, precise, and simple. In Newman's university there was no place, no provision, and scant respect for the professions.[12] Science existed on sufferance, present but peripheral on the campus. The arts — liberal, traditional, scholarly — were not only at the heart of the university, they *were* the university. It was the arts that formed and shaped the gentleman, and it was the gentleman — informed, humane, reflective, enlightened — who defined and embodied the professions. It was not the profession that molded the man; it was the man that made the profession. The role of the British professor was, in Mark Pattison's words, to produce "not a book, but a man." Newman's idea persists, but it persists only in a small and dwindling number of colleges. It is the idea of a college; it is not the idea of a university. Perhaps it was never more than what Newman called it: an idea. Even Newman's beloved Oxford, with its cloistered halls and dreaming spires, was never quite so pure, so free of professional entanglement, as he remembered it.

Today's university has no acknowledged center. It is all periphery, a circle of disciplinary and professional strongholds, jostling for position, and surrounding a vacant center. Among the members of the neighboring fiefdoms, there is little meaningful contact. The humanities, which once inspired and anchored all the rest, are rich in learned clamor and dispute, but provide no coherent vision and address few significant questions. Yet the great themes for which they stand — the overarching issues of experience and meaning, of significance and purpose, of freedom and responsibility, of fidelity and truth — have never been more significant or more relevant. Meanwhile, the learned professions each ply their craft — efficient and effective, but unengaged with, and sometimes unresponsive to, the wider issues and concerns of the clients they serve. Exhaustively trained, exquisitely skilled, they perform their various functions and exercise their various skills, each constrained and isolated within the enveloping cell of their own professional education.

Yet how much more effective their ministries would be if these professional practitioners, as they developed their skills, were seriously engaged in a discussion of the contextual issues within which they perform their several roles. The challenge for the American university is to recreate that comprehensive community, to restore that vanished dialogue. That will not be easy. It will demand dogged perseverance and patient advocacy, with liberal doses of "carrot" and occasional touches of "stick." But what is at stake here is the health and future of our fragmented society. A society may be endangered, not only by too little professional expertise, but also by too much, if that expertise is unguided by serious reflection on the goals and priorities of the society it seeks to serve.

{ 4 }
RESTORING COMMUNITY

If I were allowed only one word to describe the distinctive method by which the university pursues its multiple tasks of learning, discovery, and service, it would be the word "community." Without community, knowledge becomes idiosyncratic: the lone learner, studying in isolation, is vulnerable to narrowness, dogmatism, and untested assumption, and learning misses out on being expansive and informed, contested by opposing interpretations, leavened by differing experience, and refined by alternative viewpoints. Without community, personal discovery is limited, not because the individual inquirer is any less creative or original than the group, but because his or her conclusions remain unchallenged and untested; private knowledge is knowledge lost.

It is not only the testing of conclusions that requires community. Increasingly, identifying issues of importance, specifying the problem to be addressed, framing the experiment, designing the study, and developing the competence and skill to pursue it also require the teamwork and joint effort of a community. And effective service — the humane application of knowledge — cannot be pursued in isolation; its very nature involves the recognition of *need* in others, and the deliberate application of knowledge and dedication of skills to meet that need. The effective university depends on community, because the interacting community multiplies the power and extends the reach of its members.

Universities came into existence as communities designed to counteract the isolation of the solitary scholar. They reflected the conviction that growth of knowledge was only in part the result of individual insight and of personal discovery. Its testing, its refinement, its implications, and its applicability were largely the result of communal challenge, debate, and disputation. Until the eighteenth century, formal disputation was a daily event within the university. The university lived by disputation, believing that conclusions must be challenged by others in order to be tested and thus established or rejected. To-day, the public defense of the Ph.D. thesis is the only reminder of the ancient custom of formal disputation.

In the early American college, the predecessor of some of today's research universities, the community was designed and established by Christian de-nominations — Harvard by Congregationalists, Princeton by Presbyterians, Yale by Puritans, Columbia by Anglicans — although the latter community was committed to being interdenominational from the beginning. The earli-est faculty members of these colleges shared both a common faith and a com-mon sense of mission. These were communities of conformity. Their stu-dents, sharing at least nominally these same convictions, pursued a common curriculum, which gained a unity and coherence from those convictions. That they did so by rote learning did not necessarily reduce the closeness of the small communities in which they lived.

By the late nineteenth century, the long-established pattern of Christian influence in higher education was declining, diluted by the creation of large secular state universities. And the coherence that the curriculum once had was weakened by the intellectual fragmentation accompanying the growth in specialized knowledge — especially in the sciences — and by the emergence of the various disciplines in the sciences and the humanities as distinct and autonomous fields of endeavor. The void that was left by the eclipse of Chris-tian influence was only partly intellectual: it was also partly moral and partly social. It was intellectual because it was no longer clear that there was any ul-timate unity, or even harmony of knowledge to which one could aspire. It was moral in that the earlier tradition had sought to encourage and promote right conduct — to produce a well-rounded "Christian gentleman" — and had provided a broad cohesion of integrating purpose for the larger educational enterprise, and, indeed — the social part — for a life of meaningful purpose and fulfillment within a just and benevolent society.

In its absence, our forebears looked to the humanities to provide both a new intellectual framework and a pseudospiritual dimension concerned with culture, character, and values. Perhaps through the aesthetics of great litera-ture, art, drama, and music, one could still grapple with the overarching is-sues of existence. So the liberal arts, variously defined, represented the hope of a new civic virtue.

At first, that hope seemed well-founded. All that was needed, it was sup-posed, was to bring people together — faculty and students, scholars of different interests — and a meaningful community would emerge. Thus, An-drew Dickson White at Cornell created a fund in 1866 to supplement professorial salaries so that students might be invited to tea to satisfy "the want of free intercourse, and even of acceptance, between professors and students."[1]

In other universities, both those founded by states under the Morrill Act and those established by private individuals, community was encouraged at the outset. Asked what had made Johns Hopkins a great university in so short a time, its first president, Daniel Coit Gilman, is said to have replied, "We went to each other's lectures."

In the contemporary university, with increasing size and growing specialization, a sense of community is now much less common. But does that matter? Is the loss of community not a reasonable price for the spectacular success we have enjoyed? Is it not a reality of modern life — regrettable, perhaps, but inevitable — that many once-supportive communities have declined over time?

In the case of universities, loss of community is not a mere misfortune; it is a catastrophe, for it undermines the very foundation on which the universities were established: the conviction that the pursuit of knowledge is best undertaken by scholars, living and working, not in isolation, but in the yeasty and challenging atmosphere of community. Knowledge is constrained if disciplines and narrow subspecialties lack the challenge of open discourse and debate to test their assumptions and amplify their conclusions. Student understanding is impoverished without exposure to contrasting and contesting viewpoints. The openness of the university to the public that supports it is diminished, and its influence and usefulness are thereby reduced, because the problems of society come, not in neat disciplinary or professional packages, but sprawling across their jealous boundaries.

It would be both naive and unproductive to pine for a vanished, homogeneous community that can never return. But a new community, based on engagement, openness, and candor, can emerge without sacrificing any of the strengths the university now enjoys and without encouraging a superficial uniformity that has been outgrown.

Such a community does not imply agreement or even harmony, but it does imply interaction. That is how a community is defined. It is a group of individuals interacting in a common space. Our present loss of community reflects not a lack of agreement, not even a lack of cohesiveness, but rather a lack of discourse, an absence of meaningful dialogue, an indifference to significant communication. For we are not only a group of individuals sharing a common space; we also share some quite basic common concerns and goals.

Enclaves of any kind that shelter their members from lively interaction with the wider community reduce the value of the campus experience for all.

Under such conditions, separation soon gives rise to isolation. Our task is to educate citizens of a new society, embracing diversity with confidence rather than escaping from it in cloistered isolation, facing the challenges of disagreement rather than sheltering from them in a capsule of silent indifference.

There is one other aspect of the campus community that is worth remembering: it can be led and encouraged, but not managed. Wholesale adoption of ready-made solutions based on popular management models from the world of manufacturing is unlikely to solve the most pressing problems facing the academy. These models, designed to create standardized, efficient, simplified production processes, with tight control and central planning, and a narrow focus on instrumental learning and bottom-line results, are more likely to corrode the foundation of the university than to improve its performance.

Restoring a meaningful campus community is one of the most difficult and urgent tasks for the university, but before we can discuss its restoration, we need to analyze further the reasons for its decline.

It is ironic that the twenty-first-century university — for all its undisputed success — has diminished in community. Stronger in countless ways than its forebears, it is today perhaps more fragmented and more intellectually divided than at any time in its past. Part of this is the inevitable consequence of growth in size. How can you speak of a meaningful community of 45,000 students? Part is the result of proliferation of purpose and multiplicity of goals. Part is the result of the growing intellectual inclusiveness of the curriculum, as schools of real estate management, forestry, industrial and labor relations, public administration, hospitality, and more are embraced within the context of the campus. "How," President Charles de Gaulle is said to have complained, "can you govern a nation that produces 650 varieties of cheese?" How, we might ask, can you have a community with such a proliferation of interests? And part, as we have seen, is the result of growing professionalism, not only in the traditional professions, but within all those areas that were once thought of as the core of liberal learning.

The Success of Science

Perhaps the most significant factor in the decline of community has been the growth of science with its attendant technologies, not only because of the impenetrability of its jargon and the inaccessibility of some of its premises and conclusions, but also because its methods have been widely, and sometimes unwisely, emulated by other disciplines, whose stature and scope have thus diminished.

In the early American college, science scarcely existed. In the mid-nineteenth-century American university, it had a respected, though limited, place. Today, together with the professional schools, it exerts a major influence on the campus. It sets the pace for institutional growth. It provides the curricular basis for much technical professional education. It enjoys vast research support. And it has changed our attitude toward knowledge — indeed, toward life itself.

It is in science, both pure and applied, that the university now makes its major investment, building costly facilities, licensing its products, constructing research parks and incubator facilities for its exploitation, and often investing resources in its corporate ventures. The center of gravity of the New American University has shifted toward a science-based culture that permeates much of the life of the institution.

This has produced over the last fifty years a golden age in science, a period of heroic enterprise and extraordinary discovery. Three developments of the last fifty years led to the rapid growth of academic science.

The growth of professions based in science has required it. From medicine to manufacturing, from agriculture to engineering, professions that require a scientific foundation have required a substantial expansion of the teaching of science in the nation's universities.

National policies have demanded it. Military technology, environmental conservation, nuclear testing, nutrition, atmospheric pollution, earthquake prediction, highway safety, space exploration, alternative energy sources, food production, and more — all have imposed substantial requirements on science to provide both well-trained graduates and new knowledge. Every part of our contemporary existence has become more science dependent.

National and professional demands have substantially increased both public and private funding for science, and this, in turn, has brought new facilities, improved instrumentation, higher levels of graduate enrollment, and expanded technical support. Science is now a major enterprise, and its pursuit requires increasingly elaborate and costly university facilities, from radio-astronomy observatories to particle accelerators, from experimental farms to elaborate hospital facilities. And new partnerships and associations have developed. Large research teams of twenty or more members, major international technological and scientific projects and field surveys, expeditions, relief efforts, and service teams on every continent, including Antarctica, also have resulted from increased funding.

It was the recognition of the importance of science that led to a national mandate to universities. As World War II came to a close, President Roosevelt requested Vannevar Bush, an MIT engineer who directed the Office of Scientific Research and Development, to consider how science and technology — which had contributed so much to the Allies' success in the war — should be supported in the postwar years so that their public benefits would continue to be enjoyed. Bush proposed the creation of what eventually became the National Science Foundation, through which government support for research could be channeled. His reasoning was that by making such support competitive, and by locating most of it within universities, the link between education and research could be strengthened. Today, the wisdom of that premise has been confirmed by the quality and creativity of American science during the past fifty years (see Chapter 9). The National Science Foundation, with an annual budget of more than $4 billion, is the chief source of support for university research in science and engineering, while the National Institutes of Health provide some $21 billion a year for research in the biomedical sciences.

While these developments have greatly expanded the presence of science on the campus, the influence of science is far wider than actual facilities or research ventures would indicate. Perhaps science's biggest impact has been upon our attitude toward knowledge; its strongest influence has been upon the unconscious epistemology of some members of the campus community. And that influence has been all the more remarkable because it has, I think, been unintentional and often unnoticed.

It is all too easy, for scientists and nonscientists alike, to assume that science produces truth. What it generally produces, however, are models: deliberate in their assumptions, limited in their scope, provisional in their conclusions, and extraordinarily useful for certain purposes. But if we push these models too far, insist on their perfection or totality, or equate them with truth or reality, we invite confusion. Models illustrate certain features; they illuminate certain linkages, even perhaps certain causes. But they are neither perfect nor permanent. The Aristotelian universe lasted more than a millennium before it proved to be inadequate; the concept of ether as a universal substance endured for less than a century. Models are limited, and they are disposable. They assist understanding and encourage explanation. But they are neither exclusive nor exhaustive.

Science is knowledge based on deliberate abstraction. From the wealth of experiences to which we are subject, scientists abstract those experiences that are generally accessible to an appropriately trained observer, are generally numerical, and are, generally again, repeatable. Some experiences are deliberately excluded from science. Observers — trained or not — will not agree on beauty or the value of a sunset, for example. A scientist will be interested in the air temperature, the humidity, the cloud conditions, the atmospheric pollution (or lack of it), the time of year, the time of day, the geographic position, and so on. All these are identifiable, verifiable, numerical, and repeatable (in terms of duplicating the observations). But grandeur, majesty, mystery, remembrance — all things that most of us treasure in a sunset — are excluded from the scientific lexicon, not because they have no meaning, but because they are nonquantifiable, nonuniform, nonrepeatable.

There is a chasm between the scientific attitude and the totality of our human response. Simon Fraser, to the anatomist or the zoologist, is an animal, a mammal, a quadruped, a carnivore, a canine, and so on. But to me, Simon Fraser is my dog — not just a yellow Labrador, but a loving, faithful, inquisitive, intelligent, obedient (more or less) friend.

Science has been triumphantly successful in its results largely because of its reductionism and methodological materialism. But this abstraction has its limits. The most refined scientific analysis of a Shakespeare sonnet — the chemical composition of the printer's ink, the physical characteristics of the paper, the geometric distribution of letters on its surface — will reveal little about the meaning of the sonnet, not because it denies the existence of meaning, but because its abstraction does not include it and its conclusions do not embrace it. Science lives by generalities and abstractions. Literature, art, and life itself also involve generalities, but what give them meaning and substance are the particularities.

If that were all, no problems would exist at our universities. Chemists and classicists, physicists and philosophers could live happily as academic neighbors. And at a personal level, of course, they do. But science can be a troublesome neighbor, especially in the absence of another dominant paradigm or culture. Science all too easily slips over into scientism: an assertion that the scientific description of the universe is exclusive — all there is. A few scientists, including some popular science writers, abstracting even further, become militant imperialists, annexing philosophy and draining the larger human experience of all nonquantitative elements. But the arts, and the art of living, all involve a personal view, an individual interpretation, shareable but still unique, a particular exploration of experience, time and space. We do not ask of art or poetry whether the experimental controls were adequate or conditions uniform or whether we are dealing with an appropriate statistical sample. We sometimes have to admit bewilderment or ambiguity, paradox or contradiction. We require of art, not group verifiability or reproducibility but individual insight; not the possibility of falsification, but the authenticity of viewpoint. We do not "check the data" or "run the numbers," but we are instead confronted and invited to respond. My response to Hindemith's music or David Smith's sculpture or Rostropovitch's cello performance, let's say, says little about the "validity" or stature of any of these creations. A negative response from me to any or all of these things, even if that response is unanimously confirmed by a whole faculty of music, endorsed by another of the fine arts, and ratified by every scholarly academy and professional organization in existence, would still confirm little or nothing that the next century's critics might not well reverse. Remember how the Impressionists were ridiculed and reviled by their contemporaries, and not least by the academicians? At the heart of art, music, literature, and life is a stubborn individualism, a personal viewpoint. Literature, while it seeks to touch experiences that are universal, invites responses that are personal, that depend not only upon the context of the particular culture, time, and place, but also on our particular place in it. We judge art, music, literature, and their "statements" slowly, differently, personally. No two of us, perhaps, share quite the same reaction.

Original scientific conclusions and the literature of science once dealt with such generalities (I think of the readability of Lyell's *Principles* or Darwin's *Origin*). And they still sometimes do, as Stephen Hawking, Stephen Jay Gould, Lewis Thomas, John McPhee, Carl Sagan, and others demonstrate. But generally science is now so organized, so competitive, so complex, so refined in its detail, and its original discoveries are so widely communicated, that rapid confirmation or falsification is usually possible. (Cold fusion is an example of rapid falsification.) That "verifiability" or "falsifiability," often seen as "truth" or "reality," is possible because science is consciously abstractive; most of the things that make life meaningful (beauty, significance, purpose, personal relationships) have been intentionally filtered out. Scientific confirmation involves measurability, repeatability, statistical significance, and "meaningful" data. This is wholly appropriate for science. Indeed, it is essential for science, and its distinctive style and results represent a triumph of human creativity. But to assume, casually or deliberately, that that's all there is to life, that this is an exclusive description of reality, is to drain life and the world of significance, so that the very things that make us human (love, trust, commitment, justice, and truthfulness) have only relative or statistical meaning. Specialization, essential though it is to the progress of science, "is full of dangers, and it is cruelly wasteful," in J. Robert Oppenheimer's memorable words, "since so much that is beautiful and enlightening is cut off from the world."[2]

Yet such an impoverished view of experience has become the reigning paradigm for some in the academy, not by deliberate choice or by considered conviction, but rather, I think, by the vacuum left by the collapse of traditional belief. Discussions of love, or trust, or justice, or duty — even of truth — are rare today, even in literature courses, not only because it is now fashionable to insist that all "texts" represent political statements, but also partly, perhaps, because as a society we have assumed that only the conclusions of science, the hard physical properties, are "real" and that all else is somehow so personal and thus so subjective as to be, if not meaningless, then at least unsuitable for serious discussion.

Science is not a villain in this so much as a victim. Its occasional excesses — like those of other disciplines — would matter less if they were subject to challenge and debated within the learning community. But that community is now a much less conspicuous feature of the campus, diminished not only by growth in the size and inclusiveness of the university, but also by the tendency of many faculty members to regard their own discipline or profession as self-contained and freestanding, in need of neither the assumptions, nor the conclusions, nor the support of other studies and thus exempt from their scrutiny or critique. Science is but one example of this much wider tendency. Perhaps the social sciences come closest to the expansive claims of science. It is worth noting here that some influential social scientists now suggest that a new concern for moral values may be required to renew the vigor of scholarship in sociology.[3]

Community, though it is a threatened species, is far from being extinct. In the best universities, community is still fundamental to the process of discovery, an essential means of learning. No longer the community of conformity of the New England college, the new community is based on engagement rather than agreement. So the question becomes, How can community be restored?

Wistful longing for a bygone, simpler age with clarity of purpose and purity of discipline will not redeem us. Nor should we — even if we could — weaken the influence of the professions (we need them) or limit the scope of science (technology, with all its ambiguous benefits, requires it, and so do we, for we must know ourselves and our world).

There are those who would remove science from the heart of the university, arguing that it is largely unnecessary for professional education, that it promotes a narrow scientism and a shallow concern with inquiry, as opposed to culture.[4] These critics would preserve only the minimum science that is required to provide an understanding of the physical and biological world. I find this separation a desperate solution to a serious but manageable problem. The professions increasingly depend on science, and its findings not only impinge on every aspect of our understanding and culture, but themselves require the scrutiny and criticism that only other fields can effectively provide. Science needs the added richness that comes from other areas of experience, and other areas of experience need the benefits of science and its distinctive viewpoint. Not the least important reason to retain a strong science program and to broaden the responsibility of the scientist within the university is to make the austere beauty of the scientific world more widely accessible, without condescension on the one hand, or authoritarianism on the other. It is too late to unscramble this omelet, and, even supposing we could, it is not desirable to do so. But there are ways in which the community of the balkanized campus can be restored.

Faculty members must affirm that membership in a university — like American Express — has not only its privileges but also its price. And that price is a commitment to common discourse. The fundamental reason for the existence of the university is the benefit of shared dialogue. Without it, the claim to be a university or a collegium is groundless. If dialogue is not restored, universities will be cooperating in a pretense. They will have become an elaborate hoax, an expensive sham. They will have shortchanged the society that supports them.

Dialogue, moreover, must be multidirectional — discipline to discipline, faculty to faculty, faculty to student, student to faculty, campus to community, and public to professional. Universities need to establish new incentives and new structures to encourage such dialogue; in blunt terms, outreach and dialogue must become institutionalized in hiring, contract, salary, and promotion decisions. Campus-wide citizenship and contribution must be recognized and rewarded. With that, the professions will find new perspectives, the disciplines will find new vigor, the individual will find new inspiration, and knowledge will find a new power of synthesis. But unless teaching patterns, degree requirements, curricular design, residential schemes, and faculty appointment and promotion procedures reflect this new commitment, little will change; the dominance of the inward-looking disciplines will continue. Only in community, in dialogue, across the boundaries that now divide them, can universities regain their full effectiveness. Only in dialogue can they fulfill their obligation to the society that supports them.

The campus culture must embrace the human experience in all its richness, breadth, and ambiguity. That means a willingness to admit the limitations of our understanding and to acknowledge our doubts as well as our certainties. That is not always now the case. "Hollow men and moral nomads" are as abundant within the campus as they are without. It is, perhaps, even more difficult for academics than it is for others to express their doubts, to acknowledge the extent of the unknown. Humankind in general and scholars in particular tend to prefer comprehensive and tidy classification, with each new encounter representing a particular instance of a general category already recognized and established. Yet the life of fulfillment is the one open to the unexpected, the novel, the uncategorizable. Malcolm Forbes is reported once to have said that the purpose of education is to replace an empty mind by an open one. Perhaps the most educationally deprived person of all is not the uninstructed, but the overinstructed: the scholar who, exquisitely skilled within the narrowest confines of a discipline, has ceased to engage the larger issues of life. Values have been so privatized that it is sometimes even seen as indelicate to discuss them in public. If the universities can restore dialogue, scholars will cease to lament differences; they will cherish them. And in doing so, they will enrich the life of the campus, enliven professional education, and invigorate the scientific enterprise. They may also point the way to society as a whole, contributing in some measure to healing our divisions and restoring our common purpose.

But how do you go from diagnosis to prescription, from general exhortations affirming the value of common discourse and embracing all the richness of human experience to action? Two things seem to me to be needed. First, if universities see the restoration of community discourse as a goal, they must provide new structures and new incentives. Structures will require extradepartmental opportunities — colloquia, plays, lectures, exhibitions, debates, residential colleges, intercollegiate programs, joint majors, and so on. Incentives will require targeted recognition, compensation, and promotion that reward collegiate contributions and commitment, as opposed to the narrowly based, disciplinary limited, research-exclusive system that is now most common.

There is a second need as well: we shall develop common discourse only to the extent that we undertake common tasks. Common research and scholarship cannot be "managed" or imposed; they must grow from the interests of those who participate, and they are growing slowly. But they could grow much faster if funds were available to support the early development of multidisciplinary initiatives, which often need some preliminary results before they can compete with more traditional research for federal funding.

But the best common task is teaching; interdisciplinary teaching, from the freshman year right through graduate work, can have a transforming effect on the community. It takes effort, time, and creativity to embark on this work, but it should be encouraged and rewarded. It is a powerful teaching method, with major benefits for the students, but perhaps its greatest benefit is to the faculty, whose scholarly interests can be ignited and transformed by this simple opportunity. This is a task for deans. Creative design of the curriculum can be the means of enlivening and challenging the whole university.

The University as Microcosm

The three major changes in the character of the American university over the last half century — growth in inclusiveness, growth in professionalism, and the influence of science — have contributed to the loss of community and have gone largely unremarked by the university's supporters and largely unnoticed by its critics. Yet these three changes reflect parallel and profound changes in the character of American society, and they have contributed substantially to the nation's strength and prosperity. The growth in inclusiveness, for example, with the growth in campus size it has required, has been a major means of both accommodating and empowering the increasing numbers of underrepresented racial minorities and of expanding the role of women in our society. The class of 2004 at Cornell, for example, includes 47 percent women and 29 percent minorities. Fifty years ago, the comparable percentages were 22 percent for women and close to zero for minority students. At every other Ivy League university, the percentage of minorities would have been equally low and the percentage of women would have been zero. Nationwide, women are receiving more baccalaureate degrees than are men.

So also, the rise in professionalism reflects the growing engagement of universities in every major area of American life, from health care to environmental conservation, from human services to communications technology, from manufacturing to management. Universities train each new generation of professional leaders, promoting high standards of professional competence and responsibility, pioneering new discoveries, developing novel approaches and creative solutions to society's needs and problems. Undergirding many of the solutions are the basic science and engineering that support them.

The gains from recent changes in universities have been as immense as they have been far-reaching. They underlie and reinforce every aspect of the prosperity and health of the nation and the incredibly complex and sophisticated technological web on which our society depends. But no change as profound as this comes without cost, and — while the benefits to both the nation and the universities have been great — the cost has also been considerable.

The universities need to manage and monitor these changes, not in order to reverse them, but in order to reduce their negative impact, while preserving both the changes themselves and the substantial benefits they provide. That kind of balance is never easy, of course, but it is essential. And it is not unlike the kind of balance we have to achieve in many other areas of life. Restoring community and rebuilding partnership are tasks for both the university and the nation.[5] The university, in this respect, is a microcosm of the nation. Alfred North Whitehead once remarked that the secret of progress is to preserve order in the midst of change and change in the midst of order. That is the challenge that both our nation and our universities face today.

{ 5 }
TEACHING AS A MORAL VOCATION

Engineering has never been known as the most exciting subject to study in college. There are all those numbers and formulas and, worse, the jokes about the people who do study it, with their perfectly sharpened number-two pencils neatly lined up in their shirt pockets.

What, then, explains the fact that Mary Sansalone's engineering students have been known to cheer so loudly that colleagues have come to her classroom, asking: "Mary, can you please control your class?" Moreover, what explains why this young professor of civil and environmental engineering was the first engineer to be named national "Professor of the Year" by the Washington-based Council for the Advancement and Support of Education (CASE)?

Well, she doesn't do rap. She doesn't dress up as Queen Victoria. And she doesn't practice any of the other antics that some teachers have used in an effort to get the TV generation to listen in the classroom. On the contrary, she is personally unassuming — shy, even — and almost the consummate traditionalist in her teaching methods.

At 9 A.M. one November morning, some sixty freshmen file into Sansalone's classroom for her 9:05 lecture; half of them still look sleepy, perhaps even asleep. She has already set up the room. A window is open in the back; three projection screens are pulled down in front; an overhead projector, a slide machine, and a movie reel are ready to go. Now she is waiting, available for questions from students before class.

A petite, red-haired woman with a youthful look about her, Sansalone wears khaki pants, short brown boots, and a white tailored shirt with the sleeves rolled above her wrists. She could be mistaken for a graduate student. In fact, she has been — at least on the first day of classes. By now, no one makes that mistake.

When all but the most incurable latecomers are seated, she shuts the door and begins. "The last time, we talked about dynamic loads on structures. Today, I want to talk about the force of winds." Engineering, it soon becomes clear, is about understanding the forces of nature — winds, seas, and earthquakes — against bridges, office buildings, and other structures. Focusing on bridges, she clicks on some slides and reviews a history of bridges undone by the forces of nature. After each one, she explains the solutions that were later developed. The pattern of problem-solution-problem-solution constitutes the undergirding to most of Sansalone's lectures, providing a storyteller's approach that is based on experience and illustrates what being an engineer is really about: not writing formulas down in a notebook and memorizing them, but encountering new problems when building new structures and creating new solutions.

Problem-solution-problem-solution-problem: Sansalone flips on the video machine to show footage of the collapse of the Tacoma Narrows Bridge, which was also known as Galloping Gertie. "Oh, my God," a student exclaims. The bridge is swinging in the wind. A car begins to cross — it is a reporter's car, Sansalone points out — but the driver cannot make it go straight. The bridge is swinging too wide, one way, then the other. He gets out and tries running across but is unable to run straight with the pavement moving under his feet. For one black-humor moment, he looks like an ill-fated Charlie Chaplin, but he perseveres and makes it across, just in time to look back and see the bridge collapse into the water, pulling his car down with it.

While the students are still catching their breath, Sansalone picks up the analysis: "Nobody could understand what went wrong. So the engineers conducted a whole bunch of studies and what they found was . . ." She goes on to provide the technical explanation, which they now have a little more reason to be interested in than they were before.

Sansalone speaks with an interest in, attention to, and familiarity with her own material that seem older than her years. And therein lies one of the secrets of her success. Like a movie star who recalls a childhood of Saturday afternoons spent at the cinema, Sansalone remembers a childhood spent traveling with her father, a civil engineer, and her seven brothers and sisters to construction sites.

"My father would pile us into his Jeep, which was full of tools, and we'd drive from one site to the next, checking on the progress," said Sansalone, who now drives a Jeep herself. "Obviously, once we got there, he didn't want us running all around, so he'd put us up on a bulldozer here, a crane there. And over a couple of years, I'd see the whole environment develop: the clearing of the field, the roads being laid, the foundation poured, and the buildings going up."

The fact that she decided to study engineering comes as no surprise. But what did come as a surprise, to her at least, was that she found the classes so boring. "I remember sitting in classes, wondering, 'Why are they making this so dry?' The thinking seemed to be you had to give students all the tools — the mathematics and the physics — before you gave them the big picture. I thought it should be the other way around."

And so, upon becoming a teacher, she restored the real-life feeling of engineering, by emphasizing famous case studies, teamwork, and hands-on experience. The approach earned her several teaching awards at Cornell before CASE named her the 1993 "Professor of the Year."

To one who was riding bulldozers before bicycles, however, this approach seems simply sensible. "The best way to teach is to get students to apply their skills as soon as possible, to give them an early experience with hands-on construction instead of endless numbers." Not only have her students, as a result, designed and built a playground at a local community center, an eighty-foot bicycle bridge over a creek, and a timber frame for a science center, but each student in her freshman course, "Modern Structures," is required to team up with another to build a model wooden bridge that will be tested in competition at the end of the term. It is during this exercise that Sansalone's colleagues complain that her class is uncontrollable.

Half the class meets in the laboratory, teamed up and touting their bridges. Talk of bets on the winner goes around. Then, one team at a time stands in front of the class to have their bridge tested by Sansalone, using a machine that exerts hundreds of pounds of pressure. As instructed, they first predict where their bridge will fail and why, then hand it over. Students cheer, then become quiet, carefully listening for what sounds like the slow start of popcorn popping: the cracking of wood. When it happens, one student grabs another's arm, and Sansalone turns off the machine to save the bridge before it is destroyed, the point already being proven that it would not withstand more weight. "What would you do differently next time?" she asks. Problem-solution. Grades are awarded not by whether the students win but by what they learn.

Later in her office, where she is marking the students' final papers, Sansalone points to the pile of bridges on the floor. "Look at what the design students did," she says. "They all had the same problem, and they came up with thirty-five independent solutions. There is a lot of human element in engineering, because there can be so many different solutions."

And, in the end, a feel for the human element is what makes Sansalone cross the line from a competent teacher to an outstanding one. "It makes such a difference to let students know you are interested in them — especially students who haven't been exposed to this kind of environment before. They can get on campus and be so intimidated. They see other students who have gone to prep schools, and they haven't, and they're beaten before they get started."

Like her feel for engineering itself, Sansalone's feeling for student support also has its roots within. "I first went to Swarthmore and was completely out of my element," she says. "I heard other students talking about their European vacations, and paralysis set in. Suddenly, I was thinking, 'I can't do anything. How can I compete? I haven't been out of Cincinnati.' I didn't last the semester. I lacked for self-confidence and so now can recognize it and instinctively know what to do with students who do [too]."

Since then, she has traveled a long way in a relatively short time. But the fact that she has not lost the feeling for her past is why students line up outside her classroom. It is why she has a reputation for reaching out to women and African Americans. And it is why when her students cheer and someone interrupts to ask her to "control" her class, Sansalone says, politely and proudly, "I am not about to control them." She knows they are feeling the same excitement she felt when traveling to construction sites with her father.

The Teacher as Coach, Guide, and Role Model

The essential quality of a great teacher like Mary Sansalone is not only mastery of, and passion for, the subject, but also personal integrity and commitment. In this chapter, I want to make a few observations, based on my own experience in the classroom, about the characteristics of outstanding teaching; discuss some ways people today think university teaching is falling short of that standard; and conclude with a proposal that universities engage in a wholesale reevaluation of how they teach.

A generation or two ago, a professor at a major university would have described himself as a professor or an educator; today, such an individual is likely to describe herself as an engineer, an architect, or a musicologist, and, if pressed, to say that she teaches at such-and-such university. Universities need to restore pride in the role of the engineer, architect, or musicologist *as* professor. A professor who is not both an expert and an enthusiastic expositor of his or her subject is a contradiction in terms. A professor who regards his or her teaching load — note the term — only as a means of supporting a career in research is an impostor. Any professor worthy of the name must regard teaching as a moral vocation. It is not just courses, after all, but people who inspire, transform, and redeem. In short, professors must be not only instructors but also the following three things: coaches, guides to the territory, and role models.

A professor should be like a coach who encourages, trains, inspires, and prepares the student for the contest; who establishes the goals, initiates the team into both the rules and the spirit of the game, designs and calls the plays, and develops intensity, commitment, and spirit; who instills confidence in the ability and skills of his or her team; and who brings out the best in both individuals and the team, welding the differing skills and the various needs of individuals into an effective, organized whole.

Alexander Agassiz, the great nineteenth-century Harvard geologist and zoologist, was such a coach. He used to give each of his students a fish, with the instruction to observe it carefully. Then he retired to his office nearby, available if needed. After a week of scrutiny, the students would be invited to describe their specimens. Usually, Agassiz would smile and say in a kindly way, "That's not quite right." And back the student would go — to make more observations, sketches, measurements, hours of study, until at last, weeks or months later, the professor was satisfied: the student had become a competent observer.

Agassiz was teaching about more than fish, about more, even, than techniques of observation. He was teaching about learning, about precision, about self-confidence, about the progressive synthesis of knowledge and the satisfaction of discovery. He knew that the best education involves a "drawing out," not a "forcing in," that the professor has to persuade students of their own ability, to instill not just competence but also self-confidence. How much of this benefit would have been lost if, like some of today's professors, Agassiz had given an "easy A" on the student's first effort?

I also see the professor as a guide to the territory of knowledge. There is a world of difference between the platoon commander, leading his troops through the jungle toward a specified destination or target and requiring absolute obedience and discipline, and the guide, familiar with the territory, leading an independent expedition through it. The role of the professor comes somewhere between the two, but nearer to that of the guide, depending to some extent upon the character of the individuals involved on both sides of the learning equation and the nature and level of the subject itself.

The most important thing about the professor's role as guide is that the exploration of the territory be a joint one. But while the journey of exploration is one the student has freely chosen to make, and while all successful learning involves a measure of the student's self-exploration, in no sense should the student be sent off alone. The professor should choose the accessible routes, accompany the expedition, share the hardships of the journey, accommodate the unexpected, and learn along with the student.

It is not enough for a professor to be able to walk into a lecture hall and speak brilliantly for fifty minutes. The professor must be familiar with the whole range and sweep of the field. He or she must be able to organize material, divide it into manageable segments, stress its relationships, introduce its principles, identify its assumptions, explore its ambiguities, reveal its implications, discuss its application, and explain, challenge, answer, interpret, illuminate, and "distinguish between the major features and the lesser," as Newman put it.

I also see the professor as a role model for the student. Whether as thinker and scholar, showing balance, objectivity, and commitment to the subject, or as professional practitioner or performer, the professor becomes the embodiment of the field he or she professes. The professor, consequently, must show both how to learn and how to perform according to the canons of the subject and the standards of the profession. That requires professional integrity, intellectual commitment, social concern, and public responsibility.

There are always dangers of proselytization in the teaching relationship. Even in fields such as economics or management, there is the danger of presenting one's personal views on tax reform or unionization at the expense of others. Certainly, the professor should not serve as an advocate for a particular political program or religious viewpoint. A fundamental commitment to fairness and balance is essential.

That is why the professor provides not only a professional role model but also a personal model. For even in the most formal lecture series, the attitude, commitment, character, enthusiasm, sensitivity, fairness, objectivity, and presentation of the professor will illustrate the personal. In each meeting, through every lecture, he or she serves as a model, either for or against some particular view of personhood and individual responsibility.

E. B. White once described an encounter with one such professor during his student days at Cornell:

I wasn't particularly interested in the Middle Ages but I was trying to get an education and was willing to listen to almost anything. The professor [was] a little old gentleman named George Lincoln Burr. He had white hair, and we students used to see him trotting briskly across the campus carrying a big stack of thick books, taller than he was himself. For the first few days, his class in history seemed pretty much like any other college class. But as Professor Burr talked, something began to happen. Somehow I seemed to be transported into another century [and] I began living in the dark days when a few men who still called their souls free were struggling against tyrants and bigots, struggling to preserve what priceless shreds of knowledge and truth the world had at that time managed to scrape together. . . . My chance encounter with George Lincoln Burr was the greatest single thing that ever happened in my life, for he introduced me to a part of myself that I hadn't discovered. I saw, with blinding clarity, how vital it is for Man to live in a free society. The experience enabled me to grow up almost overnight; it gave my thoughts and ambitions a focus. It caused me indirectly to pursue the kind of work which eventually enabled me to earn my living. But far more important than that, it gave me a principle of thought and of action for which I have tried to fight, and for which I shall gladly continue to fight the remainder of my life.[1]

Current students at Cornell praise Isaac Kramnick, the Richard J. Schwartz Professor and chair of government, for his ability to make them appreciate the often difficult theories of their intellectual forebears, such as Locke and Hobbes, in a classroom that values discovery and intellectual openness. As one student wrote, in nominating Professor Kramnick for the university's highest teaching award, a Weiss Presidential Fellowship, "[Professor Kramnick] had no interest in imposing any of his own views on me; he wanted only to assist me in finding a voice and to make sure I could critically evaluate all kinds of views." And although Professor Kramnick teaches two large lecture courses, he manages to create a vital, intimate classroom atmosphere that involves every student. In addition, he advises upward of fifty-five students a year and is known for his accessibility, his forthrightness, and his ability to listen with respect and genuine empathy to their concerns.

The Role of the Student

All this discussion may suggest that the burden of responsibility for the student's education rests with the professor. It does not; it rests squarely with the student. I cringe when I hear or read that someone received his or her education at this or that university. You do not receive an education any more than you receive a meal: you have to seek it, order or prepare it, and assimilate and digest it for yourself. Andrew D. White told a class of Cornell freshmen a century ago, "You are not here to receive an education. You are here to educate yourselves." He was right.

This is especially true in universities, and perhaps most true in the best ones. A plan is prepared, help is everywhere, advice is abundant, facilities are available, resources are at hand, support is provided, progress is monitored — but education is still one of those do-it-yourself deals. It has to be. A university can no more "give" an education without the student's initiative and effort than a restaurant can give a meal, or a travel agent a vacation. You must assimilate the first and participate in the second. The student has to be an active participant, not a passive customer. You can purchase a portrait of yourself, commission a report, order a suit, borrow a book: all you have to do is pay, or commission, or beg and then enjoy the results. Not so an education. You can no more purchase or order or borrow that than you can borrow a game of tennis or purchase a loving family. Students have to participate, contribute, involve themselves. Education is not a spectator sport; it is a transforming encounter. It demands active engagement, not passive submission; personal participation, not listless attendance.

At some elementary or secondary schools, a student may be hounded along the path of learning, with the teacher providing minute-by-minute supervision. Even at some colleges, a smothering professorial concern and a pablum-like curriculum may require little effort on the part of the student. But not at a university. There, the student will be thrown in at the deep end. There, the student will be challenged to excel, required to perform, tested to the limits. There, the student must be a motivated, talented self-starter. The student must go for it, flat out, top speed. Help, support, encouragement, advice, guidance — all these are at the student's elbow. But he or she must select the goal, must put in the effort, must run the race.

That expectation leavens the student-faculty relationship. The student won't get a test every Friday, won't be given fifteen pages from a highlighted text for homework over the weekend and then quizzed on it on Monday morning. Students are expected to pace themselves, plan their schedules, think for themselves, help themselves, ask for themselves, seek out the professor, assistant, counselor, or dean for themselves. But, once they do, all the vast resources of the institution are available to them, and they flourish. This is a quiet transformation. They will learn to think; they will grow in discernment, develop in leadership, and mature in judgment — even as they think they're only studying physics, or just taking a course in history, or merely playing on a team. It is often only in retrospect that most graduates realize what a transforming influence the undergraduate experience has proved to be.

But if the ultimate personal responsibility for a student's education belongs to the student, the institutional responsibility rests chiefly with the professor, not to guarantee effortless results ("Madam, we guarantee satisfaction or you will get your son back," quipped Woodrow Wilson when he was president of Princeton), but rather to instruct, to befriend, to encourage, and to guide the student on the long voyage of discovery. No one else can make this voyage for the student, but the student is unlikely to derive the maximum benefit without the help and support of at least one concerned and sensitive faculty mentor.

Teaching as a Moral Vocation

Teaching isn't confined to the classroom, of course. Our parents are our first and most important teachers. Many others — siblings, family, neighbors, classmates, friends, physicians, clergy, journalists, authors, public figures, politicians, playwrights — also play a role. Only a small part of learning takes place in the lecture room; but, though small, it is crucial, for the society of tomorrow is shaped by events within the walls of the classroom of today.

But does this elevated description of the role of the professor correspond to the reality of the nation's universities? Not every professor is a star, of course. But most are responsible, passionately committed to their profession, and deeply concerned for their students.

There are some universities and colleges where the faculty and teaching assistants are unionized, and where some aspects of instruction are matters of dispute and negotiation. In California, affiliates of the United Auto Workers now represent some ten thousand graduate student employees.[2] I confess that I find it difficult to reconcile the professional responsibilities of the professor or teaching assistant with union membership. I have had direct experience of unionization and contract negotiations in the case of graduate student teaching assistants and medical interns and residents. Whatever the alleged benefits to their members, I regard such unions as a divisive and destructive influence on the university community.

Others will, no doubt, claim that professional unions (a phrase I regard as an oxymoron) are different from industrial unions. I agree to the extent that, in spite of unionization in a number of institutions, academics remain a relatively mild-mannered group in their dealings with on-campus and off-campus constituencies. This gentility was reflected in the report of a recent union demonstration by British professors who responded to the lack of salary increases by marching on the Houses of Parliament in full academic regalia with signs that read, "Rectify the anomaly." But I still conclude that faculty and graduate student unions are a corrosive campus influence because they promote a narrow view of the teacher's role.

Because of its profound impact upon both the individual student and society, teaching can never be just a job, however demanding; not even just a career, however professional. To the best professors, teaching is a moral vocation. It is moral because it seeks to develop not only comprehension, but also commitment; it influences and shapes not only the intellect, but also the will; it involves the cultivation of not only the mind, but also the heart. Education involves, in Johann Heinrich Pestalozzi's words, "the natural, symmetrical and harmonious development of all our capacities." It is a vocation because it is a calling and not simply a job; successful teaching requires not only knowledge, but also commitment. And it is a priority because everything else in the university depends upon it and follows from it: the education of the nation's leaders, the recruitment of each new generation of professional practitioners and scholars, and even, at a more self-serving level, the existence of the university itself.

Described in these terms, the academic life may seem rather more lofty than the daily round of chalk and talk, rather less prosaic than the Wednesday lab demonstrations and weekly papers. But the two are linked together. The qualities of a great teacher shine through the activities of the classroom, the lab, and the library. It is scholarship pursued in this spirit that not only creates great teaching but also inspires great research. Great teaching still has the power to inspire, to encourage a critical but open outlook, a breadth of interest and a generosity of spirit. And students are challenged and inspired, not by these qualities in the abstract, but by their embodiment in the professor. It is this potential redeeming influence that makes teaching the most noble of all the professions, the most moral of all the vocations, and the most demanding of all careers.

Most faculty members I know are committed to their discipline, care deeply about their students, and regard teaching as a major professional obligation and binding personal commitment. It is also the case, I think, that teaching continues to improve, aided by the adoption of new learning technologies. Possibilities are emerging for wholly new kinds of educational alliances and learning strategies to deliver information on any topic, to any person, in any place, at any time, and universities need to explore how these technologies can augment and enhance the personal transaction between professor and student that is at the heart of great teaching and learning.

Professors Teach Too Little, TAs Teach Too Much

Two complaints are commonly made about the undergraduate experience: that professors are "not teaching enough" and that teaching assistants are "teaching too much." What one does not hear are hard facts. No reports are identified, no numbers presented.

So let me offer a few facts from the campus I know best. In fall 1999, Cornell had 4,116 graduate students (excluding those in advanced professional programs, such as business administration, law, medicine, and veterinary medicine). Of these, 960, or 23.3 percent, had appointments as teaching assistants. Of these, most (except in writing seminars and some language courses) assisted professors only by grading papers or leading small discussion sections. They neither lectured nor independently led a class.

Whether graduate students teach many classes or just a few, the fact that they are in the classroom at all is of concern to some people. Continuing increases in tuition have led to a closer examination of the "product." In addition, teaching assistants have been characterized as unqualified — merely "students teaching students" or "children teaching children." Finally, there is an impression that many graduate students who have come from other countries do not speak fluent English.

Graduate student teaching assistants do lack the experience of senior faculty. But they have two qualities of great value: they are close in age to the students, and they have an enthusiasm for their subject that can be contagious. A leading research university is responsible for preparing the next generation of professors by providing them with an opportunity to develop their skills under the supervision of a senior faculty member. Moreover, by the time graduate students are permitted to teach, they are sufficiently expert in their subject that significant numbers will go on within the very next year or two to become junior faculty members at equally prestigious universities. April's teaching assistant at Stanford may well become September's assistant professor at Harvard. And because they are at the beginning of their careers, most take their teaching responsibility very seriously, spend numerous hours preparing, and develop creative approaches to old problems.

But good teaching requires more than good intentions or even long hours of preparation. It also requires knowledge of grading mechanics, class management, and motivational techniques. My impression is that care is generally taken to provide teaching assistants with this knowledge. They are given intensive training in teaching techniques. Their class presentations are filmed and critiqued. And there is careful planning and monitoring during the course — at the university level, in individual departments, and by faculty members responsible for the course. But this care is not universal, and there are occasional horror stories of faculty neglect of their teaching assistants. Universities have an obligation to make instruction in pedagogy a requirement for all graduate student teaching assistants and to ensure that they receive the guidance and supervision they need to be effective teachers of undergraduates.

The other criticism sometimes made of teaching assistants is that they do not speak understandable English. It is true that many graduate students are foreign-born and speak with an accent, but it is also true they could never get into graduate school if they were unable to speak English. But universities owe it to their undergraduates to screen graduate student teaching assistants for speaking ability and to train those who are deficient. There are comprehensive programs at most universities to do just this, and often these programs go beyond just the teaching of English to address cultural differences — from gender roles to the balance of power in teacher-student relationships — that might affect their ability to relate appropriately to American students. If, after screening and training, there are some TAs who are still deficient in their ability to communicate, they must be weeded out. But part of the reason for this complaint may be that for some students this is the first time they have been exposed to speakers with foreign accents, which — providing the TAs are skillful teachers — may be an education in itself.

There is another side to the complaints we hear. Graduate students may teach too much, but senior faculty are said to teach too little. Some may rarely teach undergraduates. Yet for every faculty "star" who has negotiated a reduced teaching load, there are countless others who regularly teach undergraduates and involve them in their research and scholarly work. Nobel Prize–winning chemist Roald Hoffmann has taught the first-year introductory course to undergraduates every year since he came to Cornell some thirty years ago. So did the late astronomer Carl Sagan, best known for his PBS television series *Cosmos*. So do the vast majority of professors, less well known outside their fields, who carry out the majority of teaching at the nation's universities.

At Cornell, a faculty member will not even be considered for tenure unless his or her teaching has been evaluated with the same diligence as his or her research; and "stars," like all faculty members, readily meet the expectation that they will teach undergraduates. In the Cornell physics department, for example, seven professors are members of the prestigious National Academy of Sciences, two are Nobel laureates, and all perform at least 50 percent of their teaching in undergraduate courses. In the thirty-five-member department of history, one of the top departments in its field nationwide, every faculty member teaches undergraduates.

Teaching, by its nature, is not a public or visible act beyond the classroom. Faculty do not become widely known for it. Most teaching is, and always will be, done by those whose names gain a household familiarity only to students and their parents.

All of this is not to say that professors now spend sufficient time in the classroom. There is no universal rule of thumb here, but it seems to me that the minimum number of courses faculty members in the sciences should teach is two courses per semester, one being an undergraduate course; one course is reasonable only if the course is very large and extensive personal laboratory hours and supervision are also involved. In the social sciences and humanities, an average teaching load of two courses plus a graduate-level seminar is not unreasonable. That teaching commitment is probably higher than that of most faculty members, but it would still leave plenty of time for scholarship and research. Provosts, deans, and department chairs are the ones who need to make sure professors neglect neither teaching nor research. Such a modest change should not produce more courses; the aim should be to produce more course-equivalent contact with students.

In fact, I'd like to reduce the number of courses universities now offer, many of which represent the fragmentation and pulverization of knowledge to a degree inappropriate for undergraduates. I would offer many of these very specialized courses only every second or third year. They would still be available to all undergraduates, though less frequently. And, because in most cases these superspecialized junior- and senior-level courses now enroll only three or four students, they would still be relatively small courses if offered less frequently.

Without increasing teaching loads, reducing the number of courses would free up faculty time for alternative ways of teaching and advising: senior projects, special studies, directed reading, study abroad, field surveys, service programs, and many more. It would also free up faculty time for two other priorities: reducing class size in some of the elementary courses, and team teaching with those from other disciplines, both of which would have a beneficial effect on the quality of course offerings. Teaching fewer courses would improve learning styles, increase collegiality, and would lead, in time, to growing satisfaction on the part of both faculty and students.

Class Size

At Cornell, most courses given in the university's largest college — Arts and Sciences — in the academic year 1995–96 had a reasonably small number of students. Seventy-one percent of all undergraduate courses, or 1,311 of 1,855 courses, had fewer than twenty students; 82 percent had fewer than thirty students; and 86 percent had fewer than forty students.

Many undergraduate students, however, also found themselves in some very large courses. Some 44 percent of student course enrollments were in courses of one hundred or more students. While these very large courses represented only 6 percent, or 107, of all the courses offered, many students were, nonetheless, affected.

While at some public universities large courses have been a cost-saving measure because of funding cutbacks over the past fifteen years, at private universities they have usually been developed to accommodate student demand for a particular course taught by a particular professor. Roald Hoffmann's general course in chemistry, for example, fills a 493-seat amphitheater and requires supplementation by dozens of twenty-two-student laboratory sessions. If a course like this taught by a professor like this attracts so many students, would it be better to deny hundreds of students the opportunity because it means sitting them in a large class? I think not.

Still, some things do get lost in large classes, and that may include the personal element of teaching. Many professors have found ways to compensate through increased efforts to advise students and meet with them individually during office hours, and by the use of teaching assistants as mentors in small group discussion and laboratory sections. Creative uses of e-mail are also proving useful.

The real issue about class sizes is not that some are too large but that too many are too small, because the smaller the class, the greater the cost and the less available the faculty member for other student contacts and instruction. This does not mean that all lecture classes of 30 students should be increased to 100 or 150. But it does mean the number of classes of interest to only three or four students should be reduced, perhaps, as suggested above, by teaching them to slightly larger groups of students every two to three years.

Do large classes inhibit learning? Are they less effective than smaller classes in encouraging student understanding? Various studies suggest that, if learning is defined as retention of information, large classes are just as effective as small. Where small classes do provide superior results is in the manipulation and utilization of knowledge, which is facilitated in smaller discussion groups.[3] This implies that a large lecture class with small discussion sections may provide the best of both worlds. And all classes — large and small — need to be designed so as to maximize the out-of-class interaction between the professor and the students.

Grading

The third issue concerning the quality of undergraduate teaching at research universities is student evaluation or grading. A mark of F (failing) or D (unsatisfactory) is becoming almost nonexistent, and even marks denoting the average, C, are becoming increasingly rare.

The marks of excellence at Harvard, A and A−, accounted for 22 percent of all grades given during the academic year 1966–67. Twenty-five years later, that number nearly doubled, with A and A− accounting for 43 percent of all grades given. At Princeton, the percentage of A's increased from 33 percent to 40 percent from 1989 to 1993. At Brown, where it is official policy to give only grades of A, B, or C, the percentage of A's rose from 31 percent to 37 percent between 1981 and 1992.

At Duke, the mean grade-point average rose from 2.7 in 1969 to 3.3 in the fall of 1996. Nor is the instructor's decision on a grade quite as final as it once was — and still should be. The University of Pennsylvania has a faculty committee that hears petitions from students who feel dissatisfied with their grades. The committee heard about one thousand cases in 1996 and in about half the petitions either raised the grade or allowed the student to drop the course. As if to emphasize the absurdity of much of the grading system, it was recently reported that a "student who used a false transcript to gain admission to Yale University earned a B average there in the two years before he was discovered and expelled in 1995. . . . His average at the community college where he'd started: 2.1" — a grade of C.[4] In the sciences and science-based disciplines, this movement toward more generous grades is much less conspicuous, though there are many exceptions.[5]

One reason grades have become inflated may well be that overall, nationwide student performance is improving, though SAT scores would not suggest that. The best universities and schools have become increasingly selective in admissions, a fact that *is* supported by SAT scores. Most students at our leading universities are extraordinarily able. But the degree of grade inflation is extreme. Some suggest it results from the growing importance of grades for those students who wish to further their studies at law school, medical school, or other highly competitive graduate programs. Another explanation is that this may be a carryover from the 1960s, when failing a student could mean sending him to war.

There is, I think, another reason for improved grades: universities have increasingly seen their task as one of helping the student to succeed in the task of learning. A generation ago, a university president would tell a class of incoming freshmen, "Look to your right, look to your left; four years from now only one of you three will be graduating." This was said with a touch of pride; it was an affirmation of institutional standards. But no more. Given the extraordinary skills of today's entering students at the most selective universities, the prospect of such failure would be unthinkable.

A recent commission on higher education established by three major foundations, whose distinguished membership included former cabinet officers, university presidents, and corporate executives, called for every student to be given not "the opportunity to fail" but "the right to succeed." The *right* to succeed? Think of the consequences of adopting that "right" in a medical school next time you contemplate surgery.

The goal must be to help more students meet rigorous standards, not to compromise the standards themselves. But lowered standards have been the inevitable consequence of the indiscriminate system of evaluation within some universities. How can we defend the status quo when a survey of four-year college graduates purports to show that 15 percent of them "are, for all intents and purposes, 'functionally illiterate' "?[6] Research universities cannot escape some responsibility for these results. After all, they prepare the professors; they provide the model for these "other institutions."

The university must demand higher standards of its students in at least some institutions, and must offer more support in achieving those high standards in all institutions. Universities are in the business, not of "grading" — as though they were classifying eggs — but of evaluating skills and assessing knowledge. The purpose of this evaluation is not only to provide a benchmark, but also to guide and advise the student in reaching it.

Excellence in teaching involves balance; balance between high standards and unreasonable demands, between the joy of learning and the discipline of scholarship, between the autonomy of the student and the direction of the teacher, between the requirement of impartiality and that of personal conviction, between the need for linkage and the danger of premature synthesis. There is no easy formula for any of these, but the excellent teacher, concerned with both the integrity of the discipline and the well-being of the student, will have an intuitive sense of how to present material in ways that are intellectually rigorous and that also offer students a challenge that is at once demanding and achievable.

Physicist Freeman Dyson, who did graduate work at Cornell under Nobel laureate and professor of physics emeritus Hans Bethe, commented in his book *Disturbing the Universe* that Bethe had an uncanny ability to size up a student's intellectual capabilities and the time he or she had available for the work and then select a problem at exactly the right level of difficulty so that it could be solved by the student within the allotted time. In Dyson's case, it had been arranged that he would be at Cornell for nine months, and Bethe assigned him a problem that miraculously he solved within the allotted time.[7]

The fact that universities, including the top research universities, are awarding grades across a smaller range — or grading more and more students alike — creates two other problems. It fails to give those who rely on grades, such as graduate schools and employers, valuable information about greater and lesser degrees of performance. And it risks creating a disincentive for two sorts of students: the worst performers, who can rely on getting a reasonable grade with inadequate work; and the best, who see their peers getting almost the same grades as they do, often with considerably less work.

Intelligent and industrious though today's students are, it is not clear that nearly half deserve to be rated excellent; nearly half cannot, by the nature of things, be at the top. There is as yet no University of Lake Wobegon. Grading with loose standards is harmful not only to public confidence in what a passing grade, or degree, from a university means; it is also a disservice to the social contract undergraduate colleges have with employers and with graduate and professional schools to provide a fair and honest measure of a student's performance. It is harmful, most of all, to the student.

Universities themselves have now recognized this situation, and corrective steps have been taken. Some universities, including Cornell and Dartmouth, provide transcripts that record not only the grade for the individual, but a record of the class size and class average. Dartmouth reports that a year after adopting this practice, grades were generally lower. Stanford has reintroduced the grade of F for the first time in a quarter century. Presently, 90 percent of all Stanford grades are A's or B's. The goal is to return to the grade of C for average work, in contrast to the present situation where only 12 percent of all grades at Cornell, for example, and only 9.4 percent at Princeton, are C's.

Many of us who were educated a generation or two ago can remember receiving a poor grade in at least one course — and how much harder that made us work the next time. We might also remember what it felt like to have someone say our work was excellent when we knew it was not. To learn requires that we be evaluated honestly about our performance. Otherwise, our trust in the belief that good work brings rewards, that good work is worth the effort, is undermined. Accolades for feeble effort and awards for undistinguished work provide little incentive to the student and even less help to the public. They undermine the high standards the universities profess, and they weaken the social contract of certification to which universities have committed themselves. But, most of all, they betray our students in depriving them of high expectations.

Aaron Sorkin, playwright and screenwriter, returning to speak at the 1997 commencement at his alma mater, Syracuse University, reflected:

> As a freshman, part of my core requirement was to take a class with Professor Geri Clark. . . . We read and discussed two plays a week. . . . The problem was that the class met at 8:30 in the morning . . . and all this going to class and reading was having a negative effect on my social life in general and my sleeping in particular. At one point, being quizzed on *Death of a Salesman,* a play I had not read, I gave an answer that indicated I wasn't aware that at the end of the play, the salesman dies.
>
> And I failed the class. And this had consequences. It not only meant I would have to repeat the class my sophomore year, but in the drama department, students aren't allowed to perform until they've completed Freshman Core, and so the F in Geri's class meant I wouldn't be on the stage for another year, and that was seismic. It was the low point in my life. It was depressing, frustrating, and infuriating.
>
> And it was, without a doubt . . . the single most significant event that has occurred in my evolution as a playwright.
>
> I came to my sophomore year, and I went to class, and I paid attention; and we read Aristotle and I paid attention. Something was happening to me in class, and I didn't know what it was at the time, but I was paying attention.
>
> I have stood at the back of the Eisenhower Theater at the Kennedy Center in Washington, watching a pre-Broadway tryout performance of my play, knowing that when the curtain came down I could go back to my hotel room and fix the problem in the second act with the tools that Geri Clark gave me.

Four years ago I was introduced to Arthur Miller at a Dramatists Guild function, and we spent a good part of the evening talking. A few weeks later, when he came down with the flu, he called me and asked me if I would fill in for a day as a lecturer in the City University of New York. The subject was *Death of a Salesman*. . . .

When I give interviews, and the interviewer asks me what my big break was, I tell them it was the day Geri Clark flunked me and said, "Come back and pay attention next time."[8]

The University's Responsibility: Learning about Learning

Universities need to take a long, hard look at their teaching efforts and do everything they can to strengthen their effectiveness, to identify the benchmarks needed to measure that effectiveness, to nurture and reward outstanding teaching, and to give to the undergraduate experience the sustained, campus-wide priority and attention it deserves. What is needed in the university is an institution-wide commitment to a ground-zero evaluation of its own practices. This will require the initiative and support of the university and college officers, but it will be the faculty who must undertake the process. It will not be easy. It will be time-consuming, and it will be divisive. But it must be done. If war is too important to be left to the generals, education is certainly too important to be left to the president, or even the deans. And if the review is time-consuming, it is likely also to prove timesaving. If it is initially divisive, its ultimate impact is likely to be collegial. And if the students will be beneficiaries of this activity, so also will the faculty. It can become one of the most challenging and invigorating events in the life of the university.

A critical area for study and for action is how to help newly appointed assistant professors develop into competent teachers as well as creative researchers, for even the best new faculty members often feel unsure of their roles. The best help universities can offer a newly appointed assistant professor is to establish a formal mentor relationship with a master teacher. When Phyllis Moen came to Cornell, her office was next to that of Urie Bronfenbrenner, a founder of Head Start and emeritus professor of human development and family studies.

"I watched Urie and thought I wasn't productive enough," Moen recalls. So she worked harder. "Urie always says people need maximum support and maximum demand, and that's what he's provided for me."

There is a need to encourage this kind of relationship between junior and senior faculty. Professor Moen now heads the Bronfenbrenner Center for Life Course Studies, where she is carrying on and extending Professor Bronfenbrenner's work.

The whole area of student advising also cries out for attention. Each year I have a few students who ask me to write them a letter of recommendation for an appointment or admission to a professional program. As long as I know them sufficiently well, I happily do so. But among these there always seem to be a small handful who tell me that they do not know a single professor well enough to ask for such a letter. That's after enrolling in forty or more courses, after being at the university four years, and after paying more than $120,000 for the privilege. It may well be that in every case it is the student who is to blame for this lack of contact. But I know from student conversations over the years that that is not the whole story. Advertised office hours are not always faithfully kept by faculty members. Faculty advisers are sometimes absent for the whole period of freshman registration. Some professors brush off students seeking help because they are "too busy just now with an application deadline." Department chairs do not always reinforce the centrality of student advising.

With many praiseworthy exceptions, faculty members too often do an unworthy job of student advising, in spite of the fact that they know it to be a major requirement for student success and satisfaction. There's nothing mysterious about the reasons for this: advising is generally unstressed by university officers, unenforced by chairs, unrecognized by peers, and unrewarded by the institution. It cries for reform, and deans must lead the way.

A third area for investigation is how to help professors to continue to improve as teachers. Even seasoned teachers can profit from candid assessments of their teaching. Edward Ostrander, a professor of design and environmental analysis and a social psychologist, had taught for decades when he joined an experiment to evaluate the effectiveness of his teaching by videotaping his critique of projects made by his design students. He didn't expect to learn what he did. "I've been teaching thirty years, and I was startled by my behavior," he said. He had thought he was giving feedback gingerly; but he discovered he said things like "That stenciling looks like something you'd find down at the docks. Why the heck did you use that?" The method was as likely to be as instructive, he said, "as a student telling me, 'Gee, your class is dumb.'"

Now Professor Ostrander is a good teacher, but what this — like so many examples — proves is that we all need to keep on learning: there is always room for continuing improvement. That is why it is important that we have an ongoing process of self-evaluation, with support and reward from the institution.

It is not only at the personal level but also at the institutional level that there is a need to learn about learning. Universities claim, fairly I believe, that their students enjoy a learning advantage; that is, they can obtain an outstanding education because of their association with teachers who are themselves active scholars. That is undoubtedly true in graduate and professional education. It is frequently, but not invariably, true in undergraduate education. Four things are needed to make it a reality for all students.

First, the cognitive process of learning, as well as the act of teaching, needs to be studied with the same creativity and professional intensity that faculty now devote to research. There is startlingly little study of the university's own work. We need to learn about learning, beginning with the basics of the process of cognition and including such practical matters as effective teaching methods and evaluation procedures. How do students learn? What can be done to experiment with different styles of learning? What is effective teaching? How and when should it be measured? Whose opinions should be sought: students, faculty, peers, alumni, employers, all the above? What can be done to encourage continuous improvement in institutions? What support is needed? Are the findings general in significance, or do they vary from discipline to discipline? How can both cooperation and competition be encouraged?

None of this, of course, will guarantee a successful experience for every student. That will still depend as much on student initiative and motivation as on faculty expertise and commitment. The task of faculty members is to ensure the greatest opportunity for the encounter to be successful, so that the excitement and challenge of learning become lifelong.

Second, universities must be willing to act upon what is learned. It is probable that the answers to some of the questions above will suggest other "delivery systems." The Cornell College of Engineering has had remarkable success in teaching math to freshmen and sophomores through collaborative learning. The college offers optional, one-credit, two-hour weekly workshops designed to help students hone their math skills and, perhaps as important, their communication and collaboration skills. Facilitated by upperclass students, the workshops divide underclassmen into small groups, whose members work together to solve problems that parallel those presented in their math classes. The emphasis is on teamwork and problem solving, not on competition. Students learn from each other, and their learning is facilitated when they can make mistakes in an environment that cannot evaluate them. The workshops have been so successful that they have been extended to students in introductory-level physics, and a three-credit course has been developed to train student facilitators for the workshops.

It is time to reevaluate, not only the process of learning, but also the structures of learning that have long been traditional parts of the university system. We need to know whether the accumulated impedimenta of teaching (credit hours, majors, distribution requirements, electives, and grade-point averages) and the existing patterns of organization (divisions, departments, schools, and colleges) continue to serve us adequately or whether they should be modified. So, also, the responsibility and role of the department chair, the use of teaching assistants, the expectations of the faculty, and allocation of resources will all need to be reviewed in the light of what we learn. Universities must be ready to adapt, invent, discard, and replace.[9] If undergraduate learning is the university's central task, then the integrity of the institution requires both analysis and action. Neglect and inaction would be a betrayal of the public trust.

Third, there is an urgent need to consider how to make more effective use of the new learning technology that has in recent years become available. An encouraging start has been made in computer-assisted instruction, satellite linkages that permit students and faculty from various campuses to engage in cross-campus conferences and courses without leaving their own, and in the vast resources made available via the Internet. Already instruction and practice in everything from fine art to clinical procedures benefit from this new technology, but much more use is possible (see Chapter 11).

The new information technology eliminates distance, not simply by providing a means of personal communication — after all, telephones have existed for 120 years — but also by providing virtually unlimited access to information. The student no longer comes to the library; the library comes to the student. Even the relationship of the student to information is transformed. Once a search for information involved card catalogs, finding an appropriate book or periodical, checking footnotes, scanning a table of contents, running through the index, combing references, each step plodding, time-consuming, dull, and demanding. Such a search often involved locating and scanning a dozen additional books or a score of technical journals, any one of which might not be held by the library and, if it was, might be out on loan. At its best, the process was tedious, inefficient, and slow; at its worst, it was also unproductive. Now the student, wherever located, has sorted, cross-referenced, indexed information available at the click of a mouse. Although at present many of the cross-references in some areas are likely to be irrelevant and much of the indexing may be of little value for scholarly use, this new information technology is potentially transforming in its impact.

So the whole concept of what once needed to be known, and how it was best taught and learned, is changing in ways we don't yet fully understand. It is changing because the new wave of information technology, when it is refined, will give us information on anything under the sun — comprehensive, detailed, up-to-the-minute, exhaustive. In fact, one of the problems with information technology is that we are flooded with information — much of it trivial — and deluged with data — many of them inconsequential.

But information — however comprehensive, however up-to-date, referenced, indexed, sorted, websited, and verified — isn't knowledge. Knowledge is information assimilated, modified by personal understanding, transformed by reflection, ordered and ranked by careful consideration, related and employed by individual judgment. It comes, not from a passive mind, browsing the Web, but from an active, searching, questioning mind, attacking the data, challenging the interpretation, mulling over the meaning of information. And that outlook is better caught than taught.

So the teacher-student relationship is also transformed. No longer is the teacher the lecturer, the personalized tape recorder, dispensing information, but rather the adviser, mentor, guide. Most of all, the teacher is for the student an example of an engaged inquirer.

Oddly enough, in this new information age the residential learning community takes on added, not reduced, importance. It was once said that at a good university the student learns at least as much from his or her fellow students as from his teachers. In an age of electronic learning, the role of other learners, whether teachers or fellow students — discussing, comparing, reviewing, and challenging everything that is learned — becomes of even greater value. In this lively community everything is up for grabs, every item is on the table. The capacity and power of electronic access are reinforced by personal contact and face-to-face discussion. Sometimes the discussion of a novel idea or a more formal, late afternoon lecture or group reading of some new text will be followed by slow, personal contemplation. Sometimes contentious debate will follow the presentation of a paper, or there will be a heated argument at coffee time over a novel hypothesis, or spirited exchanges of contrary viewpoints will be sparked by the presentation of a new art exhibit or a new performance, or there will be quiet, intense, professional discussion on grand rounds about the most appropriate treatment for a patient who is gravely ill. In all these ways and more, the campus community supports the individual as random information is transformed into useful knowledge. That is the greatest value of the scholarly community, the real significance of the university.

Fourth, effective teaching must be recognized and rewarded, not only by the institution, but also by professional societies and other groups, including the public. All the kudos at present flow the other way. From Nobel Prizes to salary increases, it is research that attracts the rewards. Institutions have to create some balance in this, not by denying or reducing the value and significance of scholarship but by linking it to effective instruction. The best teaching can itself be one kind of scholarship. We need to assure those who devote their creative efforts to teaching that they will not go unrewarded. One of the unchallenged myths of academia is that everyone teaches and everyone produces research. The practical situation is very different. We must redress the balance, not by assigning teaching and cognitive research to the less productive researchers, but by recruiting the creative energies of the most outstanding researchers for the imaginative consideration of the learning process.

Effective teaching is more than the successful transmission of information. Tapes by mail and electronic courses would long ago have replaced faculty members if that were the case. Effective teaching involves the personal engagement of teacher and pupil, the challenge of group discussion, the excitement of teamwork in research, the cultivation of values and outlooks. It is, in current jargon, both cognitive and affective.

That is what happens in Mary Sansalone's engineering classes. It is also what happens in the history classes taught by Walter LaFeber, the Marie Underhill Noll Professor of American History at Cornell. On a recent day, it was so foggy outside the window of Walter LaFeber's classroom that you could just barely make out the outline of an oak tree not three feet away if you concentrated very, very hard. But none of LaFeber's students were looking out the window. They seemed, rather, to be obsessed with the conversation indoors, which, as it happened, was about the outside world of politics, history in the making, and that trendy American political sport of "Japan bashing."

LaFeber, an American historian whose interests have traversed a series of current issues — the Panama Canal in the 1970s, Central America in the 1980s, Japan, Michael Jordan and global capitalism in the 1990s — was seated at the head of the table, looking the mature professor and acting the elder statesman. His hair is gray and beginning to thin. He wore a gray tweed jacket, a striped shirt, and green tie. His manner was serious: not gregarious, not garrulous, but generous.

As a student presented an essay that would be followed by a debate and defense of it before his ten peers, LaFeber listened with one hand pressed against the side of his head, the other scribbling notes. Statements of fact, interpretation, and analysis flowed from the student's lips — and then an unsubstantiated impression. LaFeber zeroed in. With the politeness of one who has power, and need not fully exercise it to know it, he asked for the student's sources for that impression. There were none. The impression was discounted. The lesson was clear: analysis of history was welcome, but not without the facts to support it.

After thirty-five years of teaching American history, the most striking thing about Professor Walter LaFeber is that he has not lost a glimmer of his love for his subject, and he still finds the birth of a similar passion in his students a cause for celebration. "It's the best thing about teaching," he said. "You see them livening up in class. You see their interest take off. And you sit there, thinking: Is this going to be the next Secretary of State?"

LaFeber has seen his share of students go on to important political posts. Here are two: Eric Edelman, Cornell class of 1972, was assistant secretary for defense under Richard Cheney, and is now serving in the U.S. Embassy in Prague; and Thomas J. Downey, Cornell class of 1970, who was a U.S. congressman from New York. Also a close friend of former vice president Al Gore, Downey called LaFeber to ask whether his former professor thought Gore should debate Ross Perot about the North American Free Trade Act (NAFTA). (LaFeber did, Gore did, and NAFTA passed.)

How has LaFeber succeeded in inspiring students to so love history that they enter government service? The answer lies in his own early experience of grappling with the significance of the topic. In the late 1950s, LaFeber was in graduate school at the University of Wisconsin, Madison, where his wife, Sandra Gould, was studying English. He was also on the verge of giving up. He thought it was nice to study history, he recalled, but he could not see why the world needed another historian. He considered returning to his hometown of Walkerton, Indiana. "I was utilitarian at the time. I thought, I can read history on the side and make more money working in my father's grocery store," he said.

But to help him think through this decision, LaFeber invited a professor to his apartment. They talked until three o'clock in the morning, and when they finished talking, LaFeber was convinced that history was something more than a nice thing to study. He discovered it was something one could use to change society. "That didn't occur to me before then," he said. "I was pretty parochial."

Not anymore. Since then, LaFeber has found a way to impress this sense of the power of history upon his students and to work with them in a way that makes scholarship and teaching become a two-way street. "With the exception of my first book, which came out of my dissertation, every book I have written [nearly twenty] has come out of a teaching experience," he said.

"I find the best way to test an idea is to say it aloud to students to see what they say, how they hear it. It makes you be very precise and clear. You can have a lot of discussion that you can't have in a think tank. And you get a very different perspective than you get from jaded professionals," he added.

And yet LaFeber also treats students like professionals. He gives them a topic, tells them to read everything they can about it, has them review their reports before they present them to the class, then turns them loose for a debate among their peers. "If you have Cornell students," he said, "you're crazy if you don't let them do that kind of work."

The two-way street characterization is not the way every professor would describe his or her teaching techniques. But it is the style that describes the best professors, who are actively engaged in research or scholarship, at the best universities. It reflects the distinction between instruction, which is limited to imparting knowledge, and education, which is about the drawing out of a student's own abilities, about making the student a partner in exploration and discovery. And it respects a student's potential to experience the greater thing. It is the distinctive characteristic of the research university at its best.

{ 6 }
UNDERGRADUATE EDUCATION
RECAPTURING THE CURRICULUM

Every institution needs a focus; no institution can prosper if it neglects its core business. Industry has lately recognized this, and the benefits have been dramatic: well-designed products, on-time delivery, zero defects, a motivated workforce, satisfied customers, economic competitiveness, and financial benefits for employees, shareholders, communities, and society at large. A university is not a business; not a factory or a mint, as John Henry Newman once wrote, "but an alma mater, knowing her children one by one."[1] But the need for focus, for concentration on the core activity — whether manufacturing refrigerators, curing disease, or nurturing children — is the same, whatever the institution. Distraction of attention reduces effectiveness, and dilution of effort, sooner or later, produces decline.

What, then, is the core business of the modern research university that is engaged in multiple tasks — the education of undergraduates, the training of graduate and professional students, the pursuit of original scholarship and research, and service to communities, government, business, and society at large? I believe the university's core business is learning, and the most basic part of that learning is the education of undergraduates. But to make that unambiguous statement at a faculty meeting is to be aware of a growing restlessness — a subtle unease, an exchange of knowing glances, a preparation for dissent. It is not outright disagreement, but respectful (mostly) qualification, carefully phrased alternative wordings. And those qualifications I understand and respect. But I am unmoved: the core business of the university, while other tasks and needs are important and require emphasis, is learning, and the most fundamental aspect of that learning is the education of undergraduates.

Universities were invented because of the need for students to be taught. Without students, they would not be *universities* — institutes, academies, research centers perhaps, but not universities. Undergraduate education occupies more time, involves more people, consumes more resources, requires more facilities, and generates more revenue than any other activity. Almost everything else universities do depends on it. Other vital functions — graduate education and research, for example — are supported, in part, by it. Undergraduate education also has a huge impact upon society. It supplies the future generations of research specialists and professionals, and it replenishes the supply of teachers. It is in undergraduate teaching that many of the best aspects of our culture are transmitted. It is here we educate the nation's voters and leaders who will determine the future well-being of society in general and of the universities in particular. Here many of the future leaders of other nations are taught. Here the greater part of the public encounters the university. Here the harshest criticism is concentrated. And it is here, above all, that universities must examine their efforts. It is here, in other words, that universities must ask — as former New York mayor Ed Koch once did — "How are we doing?"

My own experience, as student, professor, dean, provost, and president, now extends over fifty years in five different universities. Based on that experience, prolonged involvement with the major national educational associations, and countless conversations with students, faculty, parents, trustees, critics, and champions over the years, I would give America's universities a collective B, maybe even a B+, or perhaps, in that fine-tuned English style, a β+–?. (That's better, incidentally, than a β+?. And a lot better than a β–+?.) But a respectable passing grade will not do for institutions that demand excellence in their students, in their scholarship, and in their professional services. A B-level surgeon in a medical school will soon see patients migrating elsewhere. A B-level application by a university scientist for federal research support has no prospect of success. A B-level manuscript is unlikely to find a reputable publisher. "B" means good: it does not mean excellent.

Curriculum as Potpourri

So why a B and not an A? One profoundly important reason is the lack of an effective curriculum. The curriculum, the compilation of courses offered by a university, means, literally, a running track. It is the path or route by which faculty and students jointly achieve their educational goals.

Today's students encounter the curriculum in the form of a course catalog that may be almost two-inches thick and offer a choice of two-, three-, or even four-thousand courses. It offers enormous — even daunting — freedom of choice but precious little guidance to the individual student, who is more or less left alone in designing a meaningful path through the maze of undergraduate studies and courses. Students come to the campus, one supposes, seeking education and understanding. They are offered hundreds and thousands of courses. What they are rarely offered is any overarching, meaningful statement of educational goals and intellectual purpose within a larger coherent framework. I would almost advocate a printed statement in every college catalog that declares, "Courses without goals may be hazardous to your health."

There is another danger in the thoughtless expansion of the curriculum. It suggests to the student that informed and discriminating choice is unimportant; that one thing is as good as another; that there is no hierarchy of importance or value. But success in any venture requires concentration and demands some limitation. Proliferation of effort produces dilution of effect; lack of selectivity invites distraction. Uncritical accumulation of information provides, not enlargement of understanding, but clever ignorance. A smattering of this and a touch of that are the marks of the dilettante. The "wisdom of the heart," as Santayana has called it, comes from reflection in depth.

That universities have a problem in this area has been widely recognized. In recent years, for example, the curriculum has been called "distressingly faddish, a quixotic mishmash of courses";[2] "a cafeteria with little indication of which are the entrees and which the desserts";[3] and "Dante's definition of hell, where nothing connects with nothing."[4] The predicament reflects the disconcerting fact that at the beginning of the twenty-first century, society's agreement about what defines an educated person — about what should constitute the blueprint of essential knowledge and common discourse — has essentially collapsed. Should all students share a common body of knowledge, skills, and values? If so, what should it be? How should universities best prepare graduates for a future in which the average American will change jobs, and even careers, six times; where specialized knowledge has a half-life as short as five years; where societal and ethical questions are deeply entwined with technical ones; and where relentless self-learning over a lifetime is a prerequisite for professional and personal success? All these important matters remain open questions.

Universities, meanwhile, are too busy with courses — thousands of them — to have much time for such broad educational issues. Yet universities are assumed by a trusting public to embody some significant educational values of their own. Most universities do have such values, though they tend to be implicit rather than explicit, but they are rarely reflected adequately in the curriculum.

Indeed, perhaps the only common educational principle that the typical curriculum reflects is the value of student choice within a broad distribution of fields, and competence within one chosen area. The problem with this principle is that, in practice, the prevailing fashion of distribution and concentration requirements can easily lead to a smattering of this and a glancing acquaintance with that. How useful is it, we might ask, to require a selection from 150 courses in the humanities to satisfy some vague distribution requirement? How useful is a course based on a PBS television series, or attendance at half a dozen foreign movies, in exposing students to the overarching issues once raised in the humanities? Even the new so-called core curriculum adopted by many institutions is not really a core curriculum at all, but a potpourri of student-selected courses having little in common.

This frantic proliferation of courses occurs in virtual isolation, for the American university is now organized in a way that effectively minimizes meaningful conversation with those outside the academic fold and even with those outside the comfortable insularity of the department. Each department is an island continent, each course a self-governing entity, rarely having any relationship or connection other than geographic proximity to its neighbors. The educational cost of this separation is great. For the faculty, it represents an intellectual loss of enriching perspective and of clarifying external challenge; nonsense disguised by the language of academic mumbo jumbo is less likely to be challenged when it is shared only within the comfortable confines of the converted.

But there is also an educational loss to the student, for the arrangement of the curriculum increasingly fails to reflect the way in which scholarship is pursued. What has not been captured within the old wineskins of the departmentally based, course-by-course curriculum are not only the overarching questions of life but also the exciting, full-bodied new wine of interdisciplinary research partnerships that already exist in many areas.

There is also a serious financial cost in the present curricular fashion. It involves significant duplication, as well as substantial division of the student body into small, specialized classes, and growing isolation of the professor from his or her colleagues. How much gain there would be from some modest coordination, combination, and cooperation between related courses, with their teachers and students interacting, comparing notes, and clarifying and challenging their various suppositions!

The challenge, of course, is how to encourage this creative dialogue. It is not, I hasten to add, how to create agreement. Dialogue will admit disagreement; it will accommodate debate respecting the differing convictions it reflects. Disagreement is to be seen, not as a tragedy, but as an opportunity, as Whitehead observed long ago. Where discussion resolves differences, all will gain; where dispute persists, it should be incorporated as a fact of life, a positive feature of the curriculum. It is not the task of the teacher to shelter his or her students from debate, dilemma, and uncertainty; it is to prepare them for these experiences. After all, we live in a dissonant society, in which ambiguity and disagreement are a daily experience. The student needs to be engaged in, not only exposed to, the formative debates that are now inhibited by the fragmentation and laissez-faire isolation imposed by the curriculum.

Recent critics of undergraduate education have shared several general concerns: the lack of a coherent educational philosophy or curriculum, the lack of attention to undergraduates, the imposition of political correctness, and the triviality of much contemporary scholarship. While the complaints are frequently anecdotal, it would be perverse to deny — as some of the universities' defenders have — that there is cause for concern in these areas. Not the least disappointing aspect of these criticisms has been the intemperateness with which they are voiced, sometimes matched by the vituperativeness of the response. In both criticism and response, there is a frequent absence of recognition of the extraordinary variety of educational institutions, the growing diversity of their membership, and the fact that from the time of ancient Greece the development of the curriculum has involved a measure of contention. Indeed, the very nature of the university involves an inherent tension between the tasks of the conservation of learning, on the one hand, and its modification, on the other; between its transmission and its transformation; between tradition and novelty.

It is mistaken to demand that we choose between these tensions as either-or, true-or-false dichotomies. The university prospers to the extent that it embraces the tension and holds each element as a creative opportunity. Even in the most recently publicized tension — between those who regard knowledge as a cultural construct and social commodity and those who regard it as the exploration of an independent reality — there is an element of complementarity in the two views.

But if the literature of complaint has been extravagant, the scholarly literature on the subject of the undergraduate curriculum has contributed little of practical value to the debate. Exquisitely footnoted but excessively cautious, exhaustingly inclusive but elegantly inconclusive, it seems to confirm the very lack of imaginative engagement of which its critics complain. It is learned but lifeless, knowledgeable but superficial, analytical but arid.

But while these controversies could lead us to think that something has only now gone terribly wrong with the curriculum, in fact controversies about what students should study have always existed, as the nature of society and its expectations of education have changed.

Over the last half of the twentieth century, the curriculum was intensely influenced by growing diversification, specialization, and professionalization, as we have discussed in previous chapters. The material aspects of our culture have come to dominate the philosophical, ethical, and aesthetic ones, and students have tended to specialize in practical fields that would further their professional lives, rather than pursue studies that would provide a broad education. Perhaps undergraduate education lacks a coherent theme because our age lacks any coherent, unifying worldview. Unlike earlier centuries, our own time is marked by a host of competing worldviews, including several that maintain that any such view is meaningless. But to shelter behind that fact as an excuse for inaction would be an abdication of responsibility on the part of the professoriate. After all, those who earn their living by charging undergraduates a substantial price for four years of intensive instruction must surely be able to offer some coherent account of their educational purposes and instructional goals.

Recent Reform Efforts

Among those concerned about the state of the curriculum in the late twentieth century, university leaders were the first to call for changes. Harvard College spearheaded curriculum reform in the late 1970s, for example, by restoring structure through newly required general education courses; many other colleges and universities soon followed suit.

Then in the 1980s, the late Allan Bloom, author of *The Closing of the American Mind,* and former U.S. secretary of education William Bennett made the debate a more public one, voicing charges that the curriculum had become incoherent. Employers also expressed concern about the decline in liberal arts education. CBS, for example, donated $750,000 in 1985 to the Corporate Council on the Liberal Arts to sponsor research exploring the influence of liberal arts education.

In the same year, three major reports on the curriculum were issued by a committee of the Association of American Colleges, by the National Institute of Education, and by the National Endowment for the Humanities.[5] Their major charges were that the curriculum failed to provide a solid liberal arts education; that the faculty had abdicated responsibility for design of the curriculum; and that many universities seemed willing to allow marketplace popularity to dictate their educational policies, by surrendering to pressures to provide more professional and vocational courses.

In its report, the National Endowment for the Humanities issued the results of a survey that showed it was possible to graduate from 78 percent of the nation's colleges and universities without studying the history of Western civilization; 37 percent without studying any history at all; 45 percent without studying American or English literature; 41 percent without studying mathematics; 77 percent without studying a foreign language; and 33 percent without studying natural and physical sciences.[6]

The call for reform that followed these reports tended to echo the secondary school's "back to basics" theme. It stressed a core and encouraged the best faculty to teach core courses and to give special attention to the freshman year. More than half of all colleges and universities responded almost immediately. For example, 28 percent of academic officers said their colleges changed their programs as a result of the reform movement, and an additional 27 percent said they were planning changes, according to an American Council on Education survey.[7] There was also an increase in interdisciplinary courses, renewed interest in foreign languages and literature, and a stabilization of the earlier decline in the number of degrees in the arts and sciences.

But the debates continued about the extent to which the curriculum should emphasize Western civilization and the extent to which it should introduce more multicultural courses. Meanwhile, there have been renewed calls for a return to a core curriculum and repeated rejections of that proposal. There have been calls for more language requirement, more quantitative reasoning, more computational skills, more rigorous learning. In short, more of everything.

The irony in some recent criticism of the universities for failing to devote more attention to Western civilization in the curriculum, as Derek Bok has pointed out, is that the critics — William Bennett, Allan Bloom, and Lynne Cheney among them — would be the last to advocate the more centralized control that would be needed to impose this requirement. The kind of concentrated "Western civilization" system they advocate — the great books of Western literature — has long existed and is still offered by a small handful of institutions. But it is not generally regarded as the cure-all that its advocates proclaim and, short of creating a regulated, monolithic system of higher education — a *real* system — it seems unlikely to be more widely adopted. In the free market of educational approaches, where professors by their selection of material and students by their choice of course and of institution each have a hand in shaping the curriculum, it has gradually languished, not because it was not useful, but because it has proved insufficient as an exclusive pattern. To blame this change on some scholarly lapse or moral deficiency on the part of the faculty is grossly to oversimplify the complex processes by which the curriculum gradually develops.

Any curriculum that omits serious consideration of the heritage of Western civilization is likely to be impoverished, but that consideration will be meaningful only to the extent that it is freely selected, thoughtfully designed, and creatively linked to every other aspect of the curriculum. To argue for its uniform imposition is to invite ineffectiveness. I would be reluctant to translate any educational goal — as some critics do — into a single requirement or uniform model. Its expression must always be the product of local institutional expertise and purpose, of local debate and local design. To hanker for more uniformity than that seems to me to invite not breadth but narrowness of outlook, not freedom of learning but imposition of orthodoxy.

In my judgment, those who urge the inclusion of more courses on Western civilization have strong arguments on their side. But so do those who advocate more skill in foreign languages, and those who urge the importance of international studies. After all, we live in an increasingly interdependent world. And so do those who, in an increasingly technological society, stress the need for more attention to quantitative reasoning and increased scientific understanding. And so do those who demand greater writing skills or more awareness of other cultures, ethical understanding, environmental awareness, or economic insight. Who could argue that each of these would be beneficial? And that is precisely the difficulty that confronts the faculty of any university or college. How do you reconcile so many competing demands, all of them praiseworthy, with the limited time that each student has? It is not only Pogo who was confronted by "insurmountable opportunities."

The Obstacles to Reform

There have been three major obstacles to curriculum reform during the past decade. First, as some proposed a return to a core curriculum, others debated the *content of the core,* arguing that it was biased to presume that the history

of Western civilization reflected the history of all Americans. They called for
more diversification through a multicultural curriculum.

The second obstacle was *student demand*. With more students seeing college as the pathway to a job, there has been a tendency to enroll in narrow vocational majors that will translate into a job instead of pursuing the more
general liberal arts degree. For example, students graduating with a baccalaureate degree in arts and sciences plummeted from 47 percent of all B.A. degrees in 1968 to 26 percent of all B.A. degrees in 1986.[8]

Third, reform efforts have been slowed by the *fragmentation* of the university community. Lacking a commitment to common educational goals, faculty members have added courses that reflect their own, increasingly specialized, interests, while students stagger under the burden of thick course
catalogs and the requirement to pick one of this and two of that, with precious little guidance about setting priorities.

The rapid spread in most universities, including my own, of freestanding
programs, centers, and even departments devoted to specialized studies, as
well as a host of cultural issues ranging from poverty, peace, and urban issues
to race, ethnicity, gender, and sexual preference, has also tended to compart-
mentalize knowledge. These latter fronts, for example, are one of the most
rapidly growing fields of scholarship in the humanities, as a glance at the catalog of any university or scholarly press will emphasize; books devoted to
these "cultural studies" now substantially outnumber new books on conventional literary studies. Each of these cultural studies will have its own concentration or major, its own participating faculty, its own advocates and adher-
ents, so that what was once a unified field of literary or historical study will
now be divided and subdivided into specialist groups, often sharing few common interests and concerns. There is no easy remedy for this fragmentation
of what were once unified fields of inquiry. It is, perhaps, no more realistic to
expect such studies to be integrated into a single department of English or
history than it is to expect all the sciences to be reunited in a single department of natural philosophy. But it is reasonable to expect the university to
value and encourage discourse across the boundaries of all these studies.

Failure to promote that discourse reduces the very benefits the university
community was established to provide — benefits based on the conviction
that knowledge itself is best pursued and tested in a community of discourse
and that for all our differences we share a common humanity. It is not our diversity that makes us human; it is our common membership in a single
species. Our most basic qualities, our most fundamental characteristics, de-

rive, not from our racial, ethnic, or sexual differences, but from our common ancestry. Certainly, we should cherish the richness and celebrate the variety of cultures, but to promote the primacy of differences at the expense of human unity is to diminish, rather than to enlarge, the very qualities that make us human. The function of education is to develop humanity in all the richness of its various capacities and in all the fullness of its many expressions. Our differences are a part of that richness, but they are not its source; they are a part of that fullness, but they are not its sum. It is not our differences but the great commonalities that underlie them that we properly call human nature.

The public often seems to recognize this inclusiveness more readily than does the campus and to express more interest in its educational implications than does the faculty. That is why there is little public patience for the academic rigidities and intellectual compartmentalization of the university.

Indeed, little has changed in the century that has passed since Horace Mann declared that to disperse an angry mob, all that would be necessary would be to announce a lecture on education. Every dean knows that the way to guarantee the absence of a quorum in a faculty meeting is to announce that there is to be a discussion of the curriculum. All that is needed to convert the convivial atmosphere of the faculty common room to a chill, uneasy silence is to suggest the need for a major curricular review. Nothing so unnerves the most dedicated professor as the prospect of a debate on the curriculum. Eyes glaze over; tempers shorten; people of generosity and goodwill become intolerant, and those of sound judgment and thoughtful balance become rigid, hard-line advocates. Changing the curriculum, it has been said, is like moving a graveyard; it is a solemn undertaking. It is not that it never changes, but that it never shrinks; it always grows.

To develop a new curriculum one has to agree on a few essentials: What qualities does one seek to nurture? Which knowledge is most important? Which skills are most essential? And the moment those fundamental issues are confronted, narrow scholarly competence can no longer shield faculty members or limit the terms of the debate. They are face to face with fundamental issues, ones to which they are required to respond, not only as seasoned professionals but as human beings, their nakedness no longer covered by the protective armor of their disciplinary expertise.

But faculties must tackle this question, like it or not, for unless they can agree on meaningful educational goals, universities can never fully succeed. The trouble with having no goals, it has been said, is that you may achieve them.

Recapturing the Curriculum

So what should the universities do? Simply stated, faculty members must recapture the curriculum. They must collectively determine a list of educational objectives and then design an effective way to achieve them. That is easier said than done. It will require critical rethinking, rather than finetuning. With few exceptions, the faculty is more devoted to input than output. "It is like a black hole," legal scholar Jack Barcelo has remarked. "A tremendous amount of matter and energy goes into it but nothing ever comes out."

Faculty members shy away from establishing priorities. They have been reluctant to suggest that subject X is more valuable or significant than subject Y in undergraduate education. The end result is that they have replaced requirements by electives, have substituted excessive numbers of undergraduate courses for any critical assessment of their relative merits. Don't misunderstand me: I believe student choice is an essential part of a successful undergraduate experience. But student choice, unguided and uninformed, through a course catalog over one inch thick can be both frustrating and unproductive.

If university faculties are to recapture the undergraduate curriculum, it will mean facing again the difficult and divisive questions about goals, priorities, and requirements. Trustees, presidents, provosts, deans, and all the rest neither can nor should prescribe the curriculum. That is the role of the faculty, but the university's leaders must encourage and facilitate the debate. They should be ready to describe, though not impose, their own preferences, as I have done in this chapter. But the goal should be clear: to equip graduates for both employment and life as motivated self-starters, with a thirst for understanding and the discipline and skills to satisfy it.

There is no one-size-fits-all model curriculum available for all institutions. A successful curriculum, like a successful life, is strictly a do-it-yourself job. It needs local agreement; it depends on local resources; it is conducted by local faculty members; and it benefits local students. It cannot be exported; it cannot be imported. It has to be a homegrown product. Models may exist elsewhere; consultants may give advice; campus presidents may exhort; students may demand. But in the end, the curriculum is the responsibility of the local faculty.

And this responsibility should not be a burden. The greatest privilege a faculty member can have is to design and support a curriculum. All the riches of human experience are there. All the teeming problems and the noisy issues of our society are there. All our capacity and all our hopes for the well-being of our planet and our people rest there. How can the faculty shirk the challenge and the opportunity this presents?

Toward an Identification of the Qualities of an Educated Person

I believe in the need for local institutional design of the curriculum, but I also believe it is useful to discuss objectives, because if universities can reach agreement on these, the most difficult and divisive part of the discussion is over. The curriculum then will almost take care of itself, because many of the remaining issues are operational rather than philosophical, pedagogical but not metaphysical.

The best way I know to do this is by considering, not what courses universities should require, but what qualities universities should seek to nurture in their students.

I believe an undergraduate education should provide an introduction to general knowledge, some critical capacity and disciplined curiosity, and some specialized skills. Its purpose is to develop a person of judgment, discernment, commitment, and balance, with some chosen professional competence. The graduate will not only be well-informed; he or she will be knowledgeable, having a sense of the relatedness of one area to another, prepared, as John Henry Newman wrote a century and a quarter ago, "to fill any post with credit, and to master any subject with facility." Of course, Newman may have remembered his Oxford days with more affection than realism, but his hopes for a liberal education still inspire — and challenge. A liberal education should include "the great outlines of knowledge, the principles on which it rests, the scale of its parts, its light and its shades, its great points and its little, so that it produces an inward endowment, a habit of mind of which the attributes are freedom, equitableness, calmness, moderation, and wisdom."[9]

That lofty Victorian aspiration, commendable as it is, is enough to produce either cynicism or despair in our own day. So let me be more specific. I believe there are seven qualities essential to the development of an educated person. Others would certainly express them differently, but I think most people who send their children to college, or who hire new graduates or admit them to professional or graduate school, would probably settle for a list that looked something like the following:

1. an openness to others, with the ability to listen, read, observe, and analyze with comprehension and to speak and write with clarity and precision;
2. a sense of self-confidence and curiosity, with the skills to satisfy both;
3. a sense of proportion and context in the worlds of nature and society;
4. a capacity for delight in the richness and variety of human experience and expression;
5. a degree of intellectual mastery and passion in one chosen area, with an awareness of its assumptions, substance, modes of thought, and relationships;
6. a commitment to responsible citizenship, including respect for and ability to get along with others; and
7. a sense of direction, with the self-discipline, personal values, and moral conviction needed to pursue it.

Before discussing each of these qualities — and providing illustrations of how they apply today — let me respond to three possible concerns with this list.

First, some will argue that, even if less pious than Newman, it sounds rather like a list of virtues from a nineteenth-century tract. Perhaps it does. But does that make these any less significant qualities, especially given their shortage in today's society? Are they not, after all, the qualities a civilized society must nurture? If the alternative is thought to be other values, what are they? If the alternative is thought to be no agreement on values, what purpose is education assumed to serve?

Second, it will be claimed, these qualities are the fruits of a lifetime rather than of four years. So they are. It is true that universities are not charged with certifying fully mature characters at age twenty-two. But they can establish a climate in which these qualities will be nurtured, by providing not a set of prescribed courses or a list of academic requirements but day-by-day contacts, the give-and-take of campus life, high expectations, richness of experience, a wealth of example, and the vigor, enthusiasm, and curiosity that abound in the campus community. For these intangible qualities are contagious; they shape and influence the growth and development of the undergraduate and, through individuals, are carried out into the larger society. That is why the debate on the curriculum is a legitimate topic for public debate. It shapes the society we are and that we hope to become.

Third, some will assert, these qualities represent a return to the liberal arts and a rejection of professional studies. But surely this is not so. By specifying goals rather than requirements, outcomes rather than inputs, we give faculty members the greatest freedom to select the means of achieving them. I believe several of the goals I have described can be achieved through professional courses as well as through the more traditional liberal arts. Universities must achieve their results through their students' career goals, not in defiance of or instead of them. Indeed, what we need is not the elimination of professional education but its enrichment as a vehicle for liberal learning. There is a world of difference between the purely technical vocational undergraduate course — narrow in purpose, restrictive in scope, oblivious to questions of larger moral purpose and social significance — and the professional course, infused with a spirit of liberal learning. The difference lies in the attitude and skills of the professor. Universities must address the larger questions of social purpose, moral values, and human benefit by providing liberal education *through* professional education. Certainly, universities should aim to produce superbly competent engineers, for example, but they should be engineers who practice their profession with some sense of the larger environment in which they operate, and with a sense of proportion, aesthetic taste, and understanding of the economic costs, social benefits, and environmental implications of the systems and products they create.

The qualities I describe are a mixture of cognitive and affective attributes, as they must be if education is to engage the student as a whole person rather than a disembodied mind. Nor do I pretend that these qualities should be defined in exclusive operational terms or expressed as measurable objectives, however much the public paymasters of education may urge such a course. Quantification of character is a hazardous operation.

With this said, let me now discuss each of the seven proposed qualities in more detail, demonstrating why they are important and how they can be developed at the university.

1. *Openness to others, with the ability to listen, read, observe and analyze with comprehension and to speak and write with clarity and precision.*

There are really three related qualities here: openness, comprehension, and communication. The second and third will be of little value without the first. After all, communication that never reaches beyond the household or the village will be less inclusive, less informed, and less influential than communication within a larger cosmopolitan community. But openness is not achieved by courses on openness. It emerges most readily, I think, in those with a sense of self-confidence as they live in a widening circle of individuals from other backgrounds and persuasions, as they begin to discover and compare the treasures of other traditions, as they develop an ability to communicate, and as they observe others — professors, coaches, advisers, fellow students, authors, artists — who are themselves open to others. Openness, then, should be a by-product of the classroom, the playing field, the library, the residence hall, and the generous and inquiring climate of the campus.

But openness alone is not enough. The ability to communicate effectively has never been more universally important — or more at risk — than it is today. Recent studies have found the rate of illiteracy in America to be shockingly high.[10] It is estimated that one out of every five American adults is functionally illiterate, with reading skills below the eighth grade level. Among unemployed adults, 50 percent to 75 percent have minimal or no literary skills. Employers have reported a decline in the ability of their employees to express their thoughts in writing, even in forms as relatively straightforward as a brief letter or memorandum. Those who study the effects of television have issued warnings over the past twenty-five years about the decline in the ability of young people who watch seven or eight hours of television a day to communicate through speech or writing, and to concentrate on words without the benefit of fast-moving pictures for extended periods.

At the same time, as we move further into the information age and the age of global competition, the ability to communicate — to listen and speak, to read and write, to think effectively — has become a factor of growing importance. William Brock, the former senator and U.S. secretary of labor, has forecast, "The things that are changing in the world are all related to the mind, and we're going to compete or participate based on our cognitive and our interpersonal skills. Mostly, production is not going to be related to substance but ideas, competencies — software, if you will."[11]

The need for college graduates to be able to communicate effectively is also a result of the fact that knowledge is now growing so rapidly that an undergraduate education can no longer be expected to provide all, or even most, of the information needed in a typical professional lifetime. Rather, it must serve as an excellent introduction to a lifetime of learning, by honing the skills necessary for continued learning. The first step to achieving that goal is developing the ability to communicate: to listen, speak, read, and write effectively.

Every part of the student's program is an exercise in comprehension: formal lectures, assigned reading, oral presentations, plays, exhibits, student societies, the student newspaper, practice with the team, conversation at dinner. As comprehension grows, so too will discernment and the ability to communicate ideas, to compare and contrast, to challenge, to assert, to support, to confirm, to illustrate. All this is part of an expanding area of shared experience and conversation. And much of it — probably most of it in the best universities — will be the result of student-to-student exchanges.

The basic ability to listen and read with comprehension and write and speak with precision and grace will generally, though not always, be developed in the schools. In some colleges and universities — though in very few of the research universities — inadequate school preparation has led to the development of extensive college-based remedial programs. My own view is that this task is better done elsewhere. Universities perform it with little enthusiasm, with no greater success than others could achieve and at greater cost. To offer remedial programs in college is an expensive and often ineffective approach. Universities should help the schools do a better job, working with them in developing and offering effective programs. All school students — college-bound or not — would benefit from this.

In contrast, the typical freshman writing program will take already competent students and will develop their existing reading and writing skills with imaginative assignments. At Cornell, for example, most freshmen take two semester-long seminars, taught in discussion sections no larger than seventeen. Students select their top five seminar topics from a list of about 125, ranging from Greek tragedy to jazz and from global warming to global economic competition. Most are assigned to one of their top choices.

The seminars help students learn to write good expository prose while also gaining a greater understanding of topics of interest to them. Continuing students, usually juniors and seniors, can develop their writing skills further through the Writing in the Majors Program, which incorporates a strong writing component into upper-level courses in specific fields. Sophomores, as well as juniors and seniors, may also choose a more general expository writing course to further refine their skills.

The ability to read with comprehension and to write and speak with precision is crucial to success and fulfillment in any career, indeed in life itself. So there is no opting out of this requirement. This is something for everyone, and completing it in the freshman year provides a foundation for all that follows.

2. Self-confidence and curiosity, with the skills required to satisfy both.

Self-confidence tends to emerge from growing personal competence in selected areas, from growing experience in widening groups, from successful completion of assigned tasks, and from high expectations and consistent encouragement by those whom we respect — parents, colleagues, teachers. The same is true for a lifelong sense of curiosity. So these, too, will be by-products of a satisfying university career, but they will emerge only if students are known to the faculty members who teach them. Production-line graduation is a failure, whatever the technical competence of those who graduate. The university is an alma mater, a mother of learning, and mothers — whatever their differences and whatever their shortcomings — know their children one by one.

The best universities have an overall faculty-to-student ratio of 1:10 or better. The biggest state universities have a faculty-student ratio of probably twice that, say 1:20. It is eminently reasonable for each faculty member to know twenty students *well* — not casually, but well. It will be argued that this ratio is uneven, that some departments — English, government, biology, perhaps — are overwhelmed with numbers, while others are not. If so, the chair, the dean, and the provost must make adjustments, reassign responsibilities, reallocate resources. The positive qualities universities seek to impart to their students are not simply cultural adornments to personal lives and professional careers; they are the basis of the future well-being of our society. Neglect that, and all the administrative committees, research proposals, conference papers, and scholarly books in the world will not save us.

Faculty members, whether in undergraduate or graduate courses, have an obligation to know their students. In large courses, this will call for unusual efforts and special arrangements. And the need in professional school is every bit as great. Let me introduce you to Professor O. Wayne Isom, M.D.

Dr. Isom arrives in the operating room, scrubbed and covered head-to-toe in hospital blue. A seventy-five-year-old man is on the table, awaiting open-heart surgery. A former union leader, the patient was turned down by several hospitals a decade earlier; he was, they said, too ailing and elderly to survive an operation. Then he went to Isom, who operated successfully — so successfully that the patient outlived the replacement heart valves Isom implanted. This is what has brought him back for a second operation — optimistic, though the risks are higher than ever.

Already prepared by an assisting resident, the patient's chest has been shaved, washed with an antibacterial agent that has left a yellow stain, and cut open, right down the middle. Julian Nieves, a third-year medical student, stands by the table waiting to see what he will learn by watching the chief heart surgeon at one of the best hospitals for heart surgery in the nation.

"Come stand close to me," says Isom, a middle-aged Texan with blue eyes and a quick, perfect smile. "I want you to see what we're doing." From above the mask that covers his mouth and nose, Nieves's eyes dart from Isom to the anesthesiologist to the nurses to the heart monitors to the patient. What he is witnessing is not something one forgets: the heart pumping in its own pool of blood.

The resident suctions the blood surrounding the heart, like a dentist suctioning saliva from a mouth, as Isom hooks the patient up to a heart-lung machine. The machine pumps oxygen throughout the body, essentially taking over for the heart while it is operated upon. "You see this?" Isom says again to Nieves. "Lean over. You see what we're doing? This ought to make a little more sense to you now than it did in the books." This machine, Isom tells the student, came out of a "stupid idea by a general medical student" who got the idea while observing in the operating room.

"There are two main things I want to instill in these students," Isom explains later. "One is some basic scientific questioning about what we're doing so they can think of ways for us to do things better. The other is an obsessive-compulsive behavior toward patients — toward excellence."

Third-year students, who observe in this and other divisions on two-week rotations, know of Isom's own record of excellence before they meet him. Originally from Lubbock, Texas, a flat, dry farming town of five hundred people, Isom has virtually a zero mortality rate. As head of the hospital's Cardiothoracic Surgery Division, he also oversees an annual caseload that has more than tripled, from 400 to 1,500, since he took over in 1985. Among the responsibilities of this job are supervising a staff of eight hundred, counseling young doctors, seeing patients, operating, and teaching — something that seems more second nature than work.

Before the students come to his division, Isom also knows something about them. He looks up their background and interests in the school records and puts notes about them, along with a thumbnail photo, on index cards that he keeps in his coat pocket. Then when he sees a student, he can recognize him or her by name or sneak a look at the cards and say, "Hello, Julian," before the student has any reason to expect it. It surprises them every time. So do the questions during surgery, "How's the tennis game?" or "Have you had the chance to skate lately?" Isom credits his small-town past with teaching him this: "If the professor knows the student's name, there's a certain accountability."

Back in the operating room, Isom carefully removes the stitches holding the patient's first faulty valve in place and, once undone, holds it between his clamps to show Nieves how it has calcified, thickened, and begun to tear. Then he begins to sew the new replacement one in, explaining, "If I don't put the stitches in at the right place, I might as well take a gun to his head." A William Faulkner fan, Isom often speaks in metaphors and similes, giving technical descriptions a memorable image. The heart valve, he says, works like a kitchen swing door, the oxygen is pumped around the heart like a horseshoe, the blood-level monitor is like a tachometer in an airplane: "You can fly without it, but it sure is nice to have it."

For two hours, he continues working on the first valve while narrating his steps for Nieves's benefit (and throwing in the occasional question), until at 11:45 A.M., he pauses to stand up straight, take a deep sigh, and check the time. Noting that the operation is running late, he asks the anesthesiologist to call his office and tell someone to update his noon-hour patients.

Turning his attention then to the second valve, Isom tells Nieves to stand on the other side of the table and hold the heart back with a retractor so he can better get to the valve. "Hold the retractor with your left hand," Isom says. Nieves holds it with his right. Isom lets a brief, forever-long moment pass. Almost anyone, even a lay visitor, might have fumed: "Left hand! Hold it in your left hand!" But Isom merely repeats himself, matter-of-factly: "Left hand." And to everyone's relief, Nieves gets it this time.

Isom's handling of that moment left a mark on Nieves. He later recalled with a nervous laugh that another doctor would have devastated him for his mistake. "Some people in surgery tend to look down on medical students, we're the bottom of the totem pole, we're not supposed to say anything. But Isom, a man of his stature, he is one of the nicest men I've met in my life. He is really considerate of how we feel — how intimidated we feel — and he takes the time to teach. It seems like he has never forgotten what it is like to be in our position."

Isom knows how important precision and calmness are in surgery, and it is because of this that he tries to build confidence instead of criticizing students before they know all that they are supposed to know. "That old image of the professor of surgery yelling and throwing things and intimidating students in the operating room is to me just a sign of insecurity," he says.

Finally, three hours after beginning, the second valve is stitched into place. Isom sews the heart back up and calls to the anesthesiologist, "Ventilate the lungs." He does. He calls to the nurse, "Shock," meaning give the heart a jolt. She does. Nothing happens. She does it again. Still nothing. Tension, for the first time, seems palpable in the O.R. After all this fine work, this calm teaching, everyone wonders, is the result to be failure? Just then, the heart jumps and begins beating again.

"All right!" Isom cries.

No medical student ever forgets his or her experience with Wayne Isom. A six-week clerkship leaves a lifelong impression of meticulous concern, superb professional skill, and an extraordinary interest and caring for those around him. It is as much a model for life as an induction into surgery. And if Wayne Isom can achieve all that in a brief six weeks, why not every professor in the more extended contact of the typical course? Every faculty member has an obligation to know his or her students. Every faculty member has the privilege to personify his or her discipline or profession and embody its values.

Self-confidence and curiosity will be by-products of this type of teaching and of an active life in the university community. But what of the skills needed to justify self-confidence and satisfy curiosity? Some of these will also be by-products, though one might reasonably argue for a course in logic as a general requirement. The skills most frequently lacking in our graduates, however, seem to me to be those in formal quantitative reasoning: in proportional thinking, analytical comparison, and a quantitative approach and apprehension.

But why should a student who plans to major in English be required to study computer science or statistics? Why should a French major be obliged to appreciate physics or philosophy? Quite simply, because university graduates must be more than skilled specialists or technicians in their fields. Students of the sciences must master quantitative and formal reasoning; it is a necessary step on the path to the discipline of science. But nonscience majors must also be able to reason in quantitative and formal terms, because it is a necessary step toward being an informed citizen.

More than half of the issues before the U.S. Supreme Court and the Congress in an average year are in some way science-related, as Edward O. Wilson, the two-time Pulitzer Prize–winning biologist from Harvard, has observed.[12] To understand such issues, even as a layperson, requires some understanding of the kind of thinking that underlies them, and that, at some point, involves quantitative and formal reasoning. But this kind of thinking is needed not only for scientific issues. Consider how frequently opinion polls are presented and relied upon in this country, or how frequently businesses rely on surveys to bolster their claims. And then consider how easily numbers can be used to represent, or misrepresent, any alleged facts one wishes. It is clear that even to be able to read critically what appears in the daily newspaper, to draw inferences from it, and to judge its implications require some understanding of quantitative and formal reasoning. How this understanding is to be achieved must reflect local resources and local discussion. But, however it is to be pursued, the goal itself — the cultivation of self-confidence and curiosity along with the necessary analytical skills — seems to me to be an essential part of the preparation required for a meaningful existence.

3. A sense of proportion and context in the worlds of nature and society.

If some understanding of quantitative and formal reasoning is necessary for one to function as a citizen, then it follows that some understanding of humankind's place within the natural world and the larger society should also be considered basic goals for the college graduate. The responsible citizen, as well as the competent professional, needs increasingly to draw on an appreciation of the natural world if he or she is to make sense of the policy issues that are most important to us today.

Genetic screening, for example, is one of the most hotly debated issues of our time. Yet how can we think through and form opinions about the issue — to decide, for example, whether it is appropriate to screen fetuses for the gene that causes muscular dystrophy, to counsel mothers not to carry such a fetus to term, and to provide this information to an insurance company — without some understanding of basic biology? How can one responsibly consider whether to support NASA funding without some understanding of the significance of its programs? And how can one even begin to consider environmental concerns such as the greenhouse effect without some grasp of physics and chemistry?

Undergraduates are going to need some exposure to the natural sciences in the university. Simple exposure, however, is not enough. The typical science course, which is often rigidly sequential, heavily mathematical, and strongly laboratory-based, is unlikely to appeal to most nonscientists. Universities need to make these courses user-friendly for nonscientists — as well as scientists — if they are to prepare all students to be citizens of the world. I believe this can be achieved, not by diluting the content of the course, but by incorporating aspects of the history of discovery and the work of individual scientists; the critical assumptions and underlying philosophy of science; the great debates and controversies; the false starts and discarded theories; the working methods; the application and the implication of these subjects. This is not to imply that universities need to develop additional courses in Physics for Poets or Chemistry for Composers. The goal, it seems to me, is to provide an introduction to, and an appreciation of, the natural sciences within the context of human societies, rather than studying each in isolation. Everyone — scientists and nonscientists alike — would benefit from such expanded and enriched courses.

In addition to "humanized" basic science courses, an appreciation of the natural world can be gained through courses in such areas as astronomy, geology, and oceanography because of the larger issues they raise, their dependence on and linkages with other sciences, and the fascination of firsthand fieldwork and observatory experience.

When I was a professor of geology, I used to take my students on one or two extended field trips a year. These varied from a weekend camping trip in the Appalachians to a six-week field survey camp in Wyoming. Another field excursion involved a group of thirty or so beginning students who traveled to Britain for three weeks to explore the geology of that country, where so much of the initial work was done to establish the formal scale of geologic time. Our focus was the immensity of geologic time, based on the rocks, structures, and fossils we studied. Our focus was scientific, but each student was required to present two papers on the influence of geology and landscape upon some other major topics: the Roman invasion, the development of scenery, the location of industry, the novels of Hardy, the poems of Wordsworth, the paintings of Turner, the sculptures of Moore, the pattern of agriculture, the location of breweries, the building stones and architecture of cathedrals, the changes in climate, the components of the industrial revolution, the form of cities, and so on. The study of geology in the field was enlivened and enriched by this wider set of interests and relationships. Any course, anywhere, offers comparable possibilities for linkage and enrichment. Experiential learning and linkage are among the most powerful and enduring methods of creative understanding.

But the natural world is only one part of the context in which we live; we are also part of a social web of great complexity. I believe all of us need some comprehension of this social web, but we need more than a formal course in sociology. We need to understand our own foundation and the context of our own society, here in this place at this time.

The values, ideas, and goals that have shaped our society permeate all we do, often unrecognized and unacknowledged. We need to understand them. It was Whitehead who once declared that the real bigot is the person who fails to acknowledge any personal values or assumptions. Effective education requires some exposure to these great themes of human aspiration and hope. The "best that has been thought and the best that has been done" clearly have a place here, however we define them, but understanding the tensions of competing values in the long quest for meaning, purpose, and justice undergirds the convictions that make us human. This sensitivity requires a lifetime of experience for its development, but programs in history, philosophy, literature, and religion can do much to pave the way. So, too, can lectures, plays, study abroad, and the community itself, where priorities and goals will be matters of spirited debate, whether political or philosophical. National concerns such as poverty, crime, and drug abuse are embedded in questions of ethics, economics, politics, and the law. We need to understand the problems both through the particular prism of the social sciences and also within these social contexts. Only armed with this knowledge can anyone make any meaningful analysis of the societal issues we confront. Only equipped with these perspectives can anyone offer effective recommendations for reform or cast a vote with understanding.

But even as we grapple with these problems, we always face the tendency to assume that we are the first society to confront them or the first to experience them with this degree of intensity. That is why I believe some understanding of a time and culture other than our own is one of the components of any balanced view and any sense of proportion. Language and literature courses, area studies, history, art, and anthropology — all these can provide ready insight. So can other means beyond traditional courses: exhibitions, movies, lectures, societies, volunteer activities in the local community or elsewhere, and many more. The presence of international students on the campus benefits everyone in this respect, and the option of a junior year abroad or a summer research or service project abroad offers rich opportunities. In some universities, foreign language skills are a graduation requirement. In others they are not, especially in the professional baccalaureate programs. In some institutions, noisy debates on the role of Western civilization have deflected attention from the more basic issue of the need for comparative understanding of other times and cultures. *How* such understanding is achieved will be a local decision, varying greatly with the aims and resources of each individual institution. *That* such understanding should be achieved seems to me a desirable expectation for all institutions.

4. Delight in the richness and variety of human experience and expression.

Literature, art, religion, music, dance, and drama are the records of personal experience and encounter. We need to explore the human experience, in all its richness and ambiguity. The university years offer golden opportunities for this exploration, but one real challenge is simply to marshal the richness of campus resources so that the arts are appealing rather than indigestible to busy undergraduates. The aim, it seems to me, should be, not so much to develop a smattering of understanding of all the arts, but to develop a taste for and curiosity about some: better an enthusiasm for Mozart and Monet than uninspired A's in forgotten courses on baroque music and impressionist art. What we must do is excite and interest, whet the appetite, invite a lifelong intimacy. That is why the use of the whole campus is so valuable. Chance visits to an exhibition or a play and the enthusiasms of friends and roommates — whether for E. M. Forster or Andy Warhol — are all fruitful influences. Courses, at their best, also can provide a matrix within which other interests may be developed. They can be especially helpful, for example, in appreciating other cultures and in identifying tastes, interests, and insights across lines of difference and periods of time. On campuses that are becoming increasingly preoccupied with technology transfer, entrepreneurial centers, and new revenue-producing activities, universities must reassert that the humanities are central to the curriculum, that the values they embody remain of vital concern to every discipline and profession. Whatever the critical methods of the current fashion, universities must be unapologetic for the sweeping range of issues and concerns the humanities embody and their implications for all human experience.

And what is true for literature is true for art, in its widest sense. Plato insisted that art should provide the basis of all education. It is not now and never has been some frill added to the garment of human experience. It is, instead, a basic expression of human understanding. It is no accident that art is ubiquitous and influential in every culture worth the name, from ancient Egypt and Greece to Renaissance Italy. It has been in the most literal sense the embodiment of insight, an assertion of the human spirit. Education, unleavened by the sense of beauty and luminosity that art can provide, is a wasteland. The most sophisticated skill — whether technical or academic — is barren without the insight art provides. As in other attributes, so in this; the aim of education is to encourage the imaginative encounter, the reflective experience that can enrich every aspect of life.

5. Intellectual mastery and passion in one chosen area, with an awareness of its assumptions, substance, modes of thought, and relationships.

An intensive study of one field of knowledge, with particular emphasis on its foundations, linkages, and implications, is the motive behind the selection of a major. Pursuing a major is often the crowning experience of the undergraduate years. But in some cases it provides something of less value: at its worst, it is a string of unrelated courses, each of interest in its own way, but all leaving unexamined the critical methodology and principles of the discipline. That defeats the overriding purpose of the major, which is not the accumulation of a mountain of particulars, but their generalization. It is not the acquisition of information that matters most, but rather its digestion and integration. The marks of an educated person are not the mere possession of knowledge but its comprehension, not its volume but its significance. If we neglect this greater comprehension we shall become like Bette Davis's father: "Daddy, in his infinite wisdom, always saw the roots and not the flowers," she wrote. "He took the watches of the world apart and never knew what time it was."

In general, I believe universities perform well in the requirements they impose for the major, but most could do better. Double majors help, demanding, as they do, comparison and synthesis. Thesis topics are of immense value because they require the assimilation and utilization of extensive information, whether obtained from books or from firsthand observation. Expert guidance and mentoring help, even at a rather simple level: "Have you thought of this?" "Have you ever read that?" "What would happen if . . . ?" And so on.

The major should be the undergraduate's capstone experience, and the preparation and presentation of a thesis should be the introduction and bridge to a professional career. It is here that everything comes together, that all the skills and insights of four years are brought into play. This means, of course, that the thesis topic should not be overly restrictive, that it should require a broad approach, and that it should be related in some appropriate fashion to other areas of significance. A student mapping the geology of an area of Nevada with silver deposits, for example, may be required to examine the balance between mining opportunities, economic trends, and market prices, or might alternatively be required, as part of a related history project, to study the impact of silver mining on the economy and social structure of ancient Greece. A student working on the genetics of *Drosophila* might be required to demonstrate an understanding of the contemporary issues — scientific and ethical — of gene therapy or the macromutation-evolution debates of the early twentieth century. A student writing a thesis on Mozart's early chamber music might be required to have a chapter on the technical development of eighteenth-century stringed instruments, or the physics of the cello, or the composition of court audiences, or the economics of ecclesiastical patronage.

What is needed is a faculty adviser who is attentive, creative, and committed to the joint discovery between teacher and student that a good thesis will involve. But what is also needed is a faculty adviser who knows the student, knows his or her colleagues in other disciplines, and takes a lively interest in the larger community of learning.

6. A commitment to responsible citizenship, including respect for and ability to get along with others.

The great untapped resource of the American university is the campus community. Here the disciplines reinforce one another; here professional practice both draws on and contributes to basic knowledge; here students encounter those of other backgrounds and other convictions; here they learn to respect and understand those who think otherwise. It is here that responsible citizenship is developed, here that leadership is encouraged, here that team-work is required.

"You can't live in the twentieth century without realizing people out there think differently from you," Kenneth McClane, poet and professor of English at Cornell, has said. The multicultural debate of the past fifteen years has demonstrated that. As the population of college students and faculty has, like our country, grown more diverse, the calls for an understanding of other cultures have become stronger. Yet we must strike a balance, and in recognizing the braided channel of cultural streams that have influenced our society, we must also recognize the watershed and headwaters from which the nation arose.

In the United States, our rich mix of cultures, religions, and political persuasions is a source of strength and creativity, but it is also the source of major division. We stress freedom and diversity, but we have not yet learned how to encourage both freedom and responsibility, both diversity and unity. Beyond a few precious goals we as a people hold in common — the provisions of the Bill of Rights, a commitment to truth and tolerance, a respect for others — there are few common social goals. We are a nation of pragmatists, but even pragmatists need some light to live by. I believe we can develop that understanding and sense of direction only in active debate in the wider community.

In the candid and noisy debate of cosmopolitan campuses is a national experiment in understanding. Ideally in these supportive communities, disagreements can take place without those involved being disagreeable. A difference of opinion is not a misfortune but an opportunity for further understanding. It is here where one interest or persuasion competes with another, and one skill or approach complements and enriches another, that freedom of inquiry flourishes.

Yet in practice, many campus communities define themselves in terms of groups or factions. It is not group identification that is at issue here, but group segregation. Of course there will be groups: geographic, disciplinary, ethnic, service, scholarly, athletic, musical, residential, religious, political, and many more. It is not association but separation that weakens the university community and limits the exchange of ideas. That is why isolation and separation on the campus, however laudable the motives, are inconsistent with the purposes of the university and will have a limiting effect upon the free exchange of ideas that is the foundation of the university community. That is why any attempt by one group or discipline to impose its own restraints or methods on other areas restricts the freedom that is vital to the work of the university. Those in universities have to learn to live together, not concealing their convictions, disguising their differences, or minimizing their concerns, but sharing them, step by step, forging a larger community that unites them in their humanity.

There is a world of difference between the energizing, demanding climate of such a community and the sheltered passivity and intellectual timidity of a fragmented campus population.

Perhaps the best way to mobilize the campus as a vital experimental site for a national demonstration in community building is to link it more deliberately to tackling a selection of challenging issues in its own neighborhood. Student volunteer efforts, research studies, development models, business plans, environmental proposals: in all these and more a compact between the campus and the neighboring community yields substantial benefits for both.

Universities need all their members if they are to prosper. The fragmented university community needs study, experiment, honesty, and patience. The university must remain a place of openness, tolerance, and inquiry. It must be a place, not of suppressed concerns and timid conclusions, but of open inquiry, robust debate, generous spirit, and welcoming inclusiveness. Universities have worked hard to bring both intellectual and cultural diversity to their campuses. To negate that goal would be to squander our most precious national resources: the talents and vigor of all our people.

7. A sense of direction, with the self-discipline, personal values, and moral conviction needed to pursue it.

Fifty years ago President Harry S. Truman appointed the Zook Commission with the basic charge of providing students with "the values, attitudes, knowledge and skills to live rightly and well in a free society."[13] Few faculty members today, I think, would accept that charge as wholly appropriate for universities. There would be careful editing, selective deletion. I can almost hear the complaint: " 'Knowledge and skills,' sound right; but 'values and attitudes . . . to live rightly and well . . . ,' that gives me some problem. That seems inappropriate for a university. Too directive. Too paternalistic."

What is reflected in such an attitude is the triumph of superficial cultural sensitivity and narrow disciplinary preoccupation over any realistic sense of larger societal needs. There is no inconsistency between a high regard for the individual, respect for his or her racial or ethnic heritage, cultural tradition, and religious persuasion, and commitment to equal opportunity in our open and diverse society, on the one hand, and, on the other, a conviction that society can continue to provide rights and freedoms only when we acknowledge that we share common interests beyond our individual differences and a common responsibility — which is itself created by our rights and freedoms. They are not given; they are earned. And they are earned, not by the endless assertion of individual rights, but by the faithful discharge of common responsibilities.

That is why this particular educational goal will not commend itself to all members of the faculty. "My job is to teach chemistry," it will be argued by some. "All moral convictions are relative," will argue another. "The institution can't have any precise moral agreement on most issues," will argue a third. All are right, at least to some degree. But I want to argue that universities have some responsibility for the moral well-being, as well as the intellectual development, of their students. That is, after all, why most universities were founded. I do not argue that universities have the sole responsibility in this, or even the major responsibility; home, church, temple, school, the media, entertainment, reading, and friends exercise a huge influence, for good or ill. But I do argue that a concern for intellectual development cannot be separated from a concern for the moral issues in which this development and our communities are all embedded.

The rhetoric of college catalogs and university announcements gives expression to the issue. Consider this statement, taken from the University Announcements of Cornell University: "By their nature, the liberal arts emphasize reasoning in different modes, clear and graceful written and oral expression, organizational ability, tolerance and flexibility, creativity and sensitivity to ethical and aesthetic values . . ." In admission decisions, the university gives full consideration to those "intangible, but important factors that form good character and an effective personality," to which I am tempted to shout "Bravo!" I believe that statement is not a pious platitude. I believe it reflects the general view of most members of the faculty. The problem, I think, is not lack of assent to the general proposition but, rather, a lack of any agreement as to how to go about forming a good character and effective personality. The situation is aggravated by the extent to which the analytical abstraction and critical techniques, which are the faculty's scholarly stock-in-trade, shake the foundations and unsettle the convictions of students. This is, of course, neither unexpected nor wholly undesirable, but if universities succeed only in questioning assumptions or destroying convictions, while not encouraging students in their attempts to rebuild or refine or replace them, they leave students deprived. There are intellectual, as well as moral, problems with such a process, for it tends to weaken critical judgment and devalue thoughtful discernment and discrimination. A sense of proportion and a search for relationship become less valued than narrow technical competence. All professions depend on the cultivation of responsible personal values.

The great purpose of liberal education is freedom. This involves freedom from ignorance, with the fear, prejudice, and irrationality that accompany it. It involves freedom from the isolation of one's own self, time, and place, which can be gained by experience of the diversity and strength of continuity and community. It involves freedom from meaninglessness and destructive nihilism, which can be gained by the discovery of meaning and relationship at every level of experience. And it involves freedom from inhumanity, which can be gained by the realization that all knowledge is grounded in individual understanding and experience.

But the goal of freedom is informed commitment. If it encourages rootless abstention or an indefinite suspension of judgment, then students will become bystanders and spectators rather than participants in life. Their last state will then be worse than their first.

Some values are implicit in the work of the academy. These include open-mindedness, intellectual integrity, tolerance, a respect for the evidence and for the varieties of evidence that are appropriate in given fields of inquiry, a respect for others and for personal freedom of inquiry and expression. Most of these values are implicit in what those in universities do, rather than inscribed across the portals of their buildings. That they should be implicit makes them no less important. Perhaps all scholars need to identify the unexamined, unadmitted values that lie below the surface of their methodologies.

It may be argued that the student is free to absorb values by osmosis, but that values should not be openly recognized or discussed. I would argue, however, that it is, in fact, impossible to teach without imparting values. Faculty members will stand for something, whether deliberately or by neglect, and that stance will permeate their teaching. Whether we like it or not, the teacher is a role model for his or her students.

The reason for the urgency and priority of the present task is that society depends upon its distributed values. I should like to say that society depends upon its common values, but in the fragmentation of our present age, it is not easy to identify many values that we hold in common. If universities are to reaffirm their commitment to examining values on their campuses, there seem to me to be three necessary guidelines. I believe, first, universities must recognize their limitations in this area. Psychologists conclude that perhaps 90 percent of all learning takes place in the first five years of life. This means that the influence of universities is likely to be limited, and probably less than that of other institutions — the family, the place of worship, the community, and so on.

I believe, second, that universities must respect and preserve the autonomy of the student, the integrity of the disciplines, and the integrity of the institution. Students, the disciplines, and the position of the faculty member will all be threatened if universities use them as a basis for proselytizing or for cheap moralizing. Universities are committed to strive for rigorous objectivity, however unattainable it may be in practice. But one component of that objectivity is that we should acknowledge our assumptions, as well as accept a common responsibility for accuracy and integrity. Universities must also insist that any exploration of values must clearly and deliberately leave the fundamental freedom and responsibility of choice to the individual student. That involves a steady determination to preserve varying influences and viewpoints and an honest attempt to explore and examine all competing solutions and alternative schemes. The faculty-student, faculty-colleague, and faculty-administration relationships may be violated by partisan advocacy of particular value systems. Indeed, the integrity of the values themselves will be destroyed if universities attempt to indoctrinate or to moralize at every turn. Vacuous moral generalizations are as dangerous as empty neutralism. Moral development ought to be a by-product, rather than the purpose, of teaching. Universities exist neither to indoctrinate activists, nor to create saints. They exist to educate students, but this has to involve more than the mere credentialing of narrow technical competence.

The integrity of the institution must also be safeguarded. I submit that the institution should not be an advocate for particular causes over and beyond those clearly expressed in its catalog. It will best benefit society by serving as a place for independent exploration of the human condition. As such it shelters debate, it encourages criticism, and it seeks synthesis. The only issues on which it can legitimately take a corporate stand are those vital to its mission of scholarship and service. This view of institutional neutrality on all but the most fundamental issues is easily misunderstood, but it is basic to the freedom and responsibility that universities need to survive. This neutrality is a self-imposed duty, a considered position, rather than a cowardly abdication or a careless omission.

In recognizing the need to grapple with questions of values, universities will align themselves with their past. "Knowledge is virtue and virtue knowledge," declared Socrates. And, if more recent critics have been more skeptical, they have generally recognized the link between knowledge and virtue. When Will Rogers observed, "A simple man may steal from a freight train, but give him a college degree and he will steal the whole railroad," he shared a common assumption with Socrates, even though he reached a rather different conclusion.

Ultimately, however, it is not the curriculum, not courses, but people who matter most in education. It is people who transform and redeem; the mode of learning may be every bit as important as its content. Style may have as much influence as substance. The curriculum, no matter how broadly conceived or expansively developed, will not, by itself, guarantee success. Universities must put their trust, not in courses, but in people. Courses do not give coherence; requirements do not lead to wisdom. But both provide a vehicle for the development of those qualities. They provide a platform for their demonstration, a setting within which the professor may exemplify the enthusiasm, openness, impartiality, fairness, rigor, and integrity on which sound learning depends and by which competing claims and conflicting interpretations can be analyzed and evaluated. It is those qualities that can enrich a life with meaning and significance.

Will these steps produce results? I confess I am not sure, for they must overcome current apathy and self-indulgence.

Are these steps worth the effort? Of that I have no doubt. John Gardner has a passage in his book *No Easy Victories* that describes the kind of institution that I have in mind. "I like to think," he writes, "that no matter how much the university becomes entangled with the world on its outer fringes, the inner city of the university will be above the battle in some quite distinctive ways. I should like to believe that it will, to borrow some lines from Bernard Shaw, 'stand for the future and the past, for the posterity that has no vote and the tradition that never had any. For the great abstractions, for the eternal against the expedient; for the evolutionary appetite against the day's gluttony; for intellectual integrity, for humanity, for the rescue of industry from commercialism and of science from professionalism.' I like to think that it will stand for things that are forgotten in the heat of battle, for values that get pushed aside in the rough-and-tumble of everyday living, for the goals we ought to be thinking about and never do, for the facts we don't like to face and the questions we lack the courage to ask."[14]

For research universities, that is no mean goal.

PROFESSIONAL AND GRADUATE EDUCATION

Two things distinguish the American research university from all other institutions of postsecondary education: a sustained institutional commitment to research and the substantial presence of postbaccalaureate graduate education and professional training.

Professional Education

Although many colleges, once devoted exclusively to the liberal arts, now offer some undergraduate professional programs, all the doctors, lawyers, city and regional planners, veterinarians, dentists, and most of the recruits to senior positions in other fields — business, engineering, architecture, conservation, and so on — receive their professional preparation in doctoral and master's degree programs at research universities. The studies they pursue combine intensive specialist training with a solid intellectual foundation of associated disciplines and fields. In these programs intensive professional training is also linked to the inculcation of high professional standards and the cultivation of personal responsibility.

The New England colleges, as we have seen, offered divinity, Greek, Hebrew, and Latin as a preparation for professional careers in church and state. From the mid-seventeenth century to the early twenty-first, professional preparation has been a major task of the American university. Even those fields such as medicine that in this country developed beyond the campus as apprenticeship systems were subsequently entrusted to the universities a century or so ago.

And the range of professional graduate programs continues to increase. In the last decade or so, such diverse fields as gerontology, communications technology, health policy, and real estate management have become areas of formal professional training on several campuses. Though the more traditionally minded may turn up their noses at master of professional studies degrees in hotel administration or international diplomacy, such training is valuable in preparing future practitioners for the range of complex issues they will confront on the job.

The popularity of professional programs is beyond dispute. The Cornell Medical School, for example, admits a class of 100 students each year from over 7,000 applicants. Most of these individuals submit multiple applications, so this does not mean that 6,900 fail to gain admission to *any* medical school; but competition for admission is intense, as is competition among hospitals to "employ" their graduates as residents. In Cornell's Johnson Graduate School of Management, well over 2,000 applicants compete for 260 places. By no means are all of these only domestic applicants; the Johnson School receives more applications from Tokyo than it does from New York City.

Four questions emerge in considering the place of professional education in American life.

First, how good are the products of the present system of graduate and professional education? There is no simple overall index of quality here, but by any measure I know, the results are superb. The success rate for first-time candidates from the research universities in the independently administered medical and bar association boards, for example, runs in the high 90 percent category. A recent study of success rates in passing the state bar exams illustrates the point: there is a conspicuous gap between the pass rates of graduates of the leading research universities and those of other institutions. Yale graduates, for example, had a pass rate of 97 percent, Harvard and Cornell 96 percent, Columbia 93 percent, and Pennsylvania 91 percent, in comparison with an average of 78 percent for all schools in their state. The University of Michigan had a pass rate of 89 percent (vs. 70 percent for all schools in the state), Chicago 97 percent and Illinois 90 percent (vs. 87 percent), and in California, with an all-school average of 73 percent, Stanford had 91 percent, Berkeley 90 percent, and UCLA 89 percent.[1]

The success of newly minted M.B.A. or M.Eng. graduates in finding immediate employment in multinational corporations is impressive. International students clamor for admission to U.S. graduate and professional degree programs, often returning to their own countries to areas of major responsibility. The large and growing number of governmental leaders from both the industrialized and developing countries with advanced degrees from U.S. universities is a striking tribute to their international currency.

The most important quality test, of course, comes not from statistics but from personal experience. All of us, willingly or not, are at some time patients, clients, customers, users, colleagues, employers, or observers of the American professional. In my own view, subjective and unrepresentative as it is, the professional skills and personal responsibility embodied by these services are superb.

They are not perfect, of course. But there are professional review boards to consider complaints, stringent continuing education standards, renewal of licensing requirements to insure updated skills, and a free and open system of competitive practice, where the client can shop for the best services. The universities can take substantial credit for the remarkable quality of our professional services, and the nation can take both credit for the demanding standards on which it insists and comfort in the benefits of the quality they promote. I know of no other nation that enjoys such a consistently high standard of professional services.

Second, what about supply and demand? In certain fields, medicine for example, supply seems adequate, although physicians may not be distributed optimally among the specialties or among the nation's geographic regions. In technical areas such as engineering and computer science, good jobs are going unfilled for lack of people competent to do the work. In other fields, law for example, some would argue that we have too many professionals and should limit the number of graduates in such fields of oversupply.

Yet in view of the uncertainties of future supply and demand, any command economy in professional recruitment seems to me to be as uncertain in its consequences as it is undesirable in concept, for it is never desirable to limit the range of human creativity and choice.

Let me give two examples of the difficulty of even the most informed and careful projections. In 1989, Bowen and Sosa published a study of the pattern of projected faculty retirements and student enrollments in the 1990s and concluded that a growing demand for academic employment would outstrip the supply of graduating Ph.D.s.[2] What they did not predict — and could not have foreseen — was the impact of two external factors: legislation that required the ending of mandatory retirement for faculty members and severe financial constraints and consequent downsizing that affected most universities.

Equally careful projections by the National Science Foundation and other knowledgeable observers of supply and demand for scientists and engineers in the 1990s also suggested serious shortfalls.[3] The Policy Division of the NSF predicted a shortfall of 700,000 engineers and scientists by the year 2000, but failed to foresee the impact of extensive corporate takeovers, mergers, and downsizing (435,000 engineering jobs were lost in the early 1990s), the effects of recession and recovery, decline in defense funding and federal investment in science, and the virtual demise of the great corporate research centers at such companies as RCA, IBM, GE, and AT&T. All these trends — inevitably unforeseen in the 1980s — had a severe effect on employment in these fields, although this trend by the late 1990s reversed itself again and technical jobs went begging.

Every past national projection and master plan of which I know has proved unreliable, and the integrated workforce planning of socialist countries has proved most unreliable of all. That doesn't mean that we should not make prudent projections and responsible local adaptations. But it does mean we should be suspicious of "national plans" that limit individual choice and personal access to careers.

The forces of the marketplace, while imperfect, continue to be the best arbiters of supply and demand. Universities are unlikely to devote their resources to producing large numbers of unemployable professional graduates for very long. And talented individuals will not for long devote years of demanding learning and large sums of money to programs that prepare them for nonexistent careers, not least when they could have devoted those same years and that same money to pursuing careers in other more lucrative fields. The market operates in this realm too, even though there may be a lag of a year or two in the response of supply to demand.

Third, given the quality of services required, are the length and costs of professional training reasonable? For an M.Eng. degree, a student typically spends one additional postbaccalaureate year in school, then moves into an attractive corporate position. For an M.B.A. degree, the requirement is typically a few years' responsible employment and then a two-year professional degree. In some cases, course work is sandwiched between further periods of internship, and in some universities the M.B.A. and other master's degrees may be a longer, part-time course for those in full-time employment. That degree length and flexibility seem to most knowledgeable observers — employers, for example — to be about right, though other patterns are already emerging. There is now, for example, a one-year plus summer term M.B.A. course for those with specialist degrees in economics or business or with advanced degrees in science, engineering, and mathematics. There are also a few institutions that give credit for specialized employment experience.

In law, the typical professional degree requires three years of study. A J.D. graduate has the bar exams — no mere formality — and then the job market

— crowded now, but still attractive and very rewarding. For some others, especially M.D. and many D.V.M. graduates, the professional degree is not the end. For the young thoracic surgeon, for example, there will be five more years of residency training under brutally demanding conditions and at a modest salary, and generally five further years of fellowship training before full-time practice begins; that adds up to eighteen years of demanding post–high school education and training. It is training for which admission requirements are stringent and increasingly competitive at each successive level. And it is training that leads to a level of personal performance that is regularly checked by independent professional board reviews and examinations. Such are the intellectual and technical requirements for many areas of professional practice.

The costs of the various courses of study are substantial, typically $25,000 a year for medical school tuition in a private university, for example, plus room, board, books, and supplies, for a total annual cost of about $39,000; scholarships and loans are normally available. Tuition costs for other professional schools are similar, with the public universities — because of their state subsidy — typically being substantially less expensive than the private schools.

A recent study by the Education Resources Institute estimated that 1995 medical school graduates had an average debt of $64,059, including loans for their undergraduate education. For law school graduates, the debt was $40,300, just for law school. The result of this level of debt is that few such graduates are able to contemplate low-paying public-service jobs. Law school graduates working in a legal aid clinic, for example, would have to devote up to one-fourth of their income to repaying student loans.[4]

Yet there are good reasons that such education is expensive. Almost all this postgraduate professional training involves intensely personal instruction and one-on-one supervision. That is why the professor — whether of surgery or of architecture, of engineering or of music — must also be a practicing professional, meeting the same professional standards as his or her advanced students. And that, in turn, is why universities not only encourage but require a high level of professional practice by their faculty — whether in clinics, concert halls, factories, research labs, conference rooms, or design studios. Professional education requires professional practice; each benefits from this dual role.

The extraordinary demands of professional service and the complexities involved in say, the design and manufacture of a new jet aircraft, or a new power plant, or a new pharmaceutical drug — as well as the sweeping conse-

quences of error — call for the most comprehensive and professional education and training. Generally, both the length and the demands of such education seem appropriate.

Fourth, what about the relationship between professional education, public policy, and professional practice? Some argue that it should be closer: that
universities should be directly involved in creating public policy or professional standards. In several important respects, they are. They are the sole
source of new recruits to each profession, and with those new professionals
comes the influence of their mentors, in technical skills, personal character,
and professional standards. Their individual faculty members serve on every
conceivable professional council, public body, corporate board, and society
committee. They serve, not as institutional representatives of the university,
but as individual practitioners and expert advisers. In addition, their individual faculty members are particularly active as members of professional bodies
that accredit university professional degree programs, license individual professionals, and certify hospitals, clinics, and similar institutions.

That, it seems to me, is a significant level of responsibility; it is also, I believe, as far as such influence should go. To have universities and their faculties, who teach and certify the students, have more control than that over
their subsequent professional practice would represent an imbalance of public, professional, and academic oversight. The public deserves the judgment
of others less intimately involved in the educational process in overseeing
professional practice and in developing public policy.

Graduate Education

Graduate education is as old as the university. The medieval university had as
one of its chief purposes the education of masters and doctors, who were
qualified to teach anywhere *(in docendi ubique)*. Graduate education today
involves the advanced preparation of students for teaching, scholarship, and
research, and increasingly for professional practice.

THE MASTER'S DEGREE

America's universities award about 380,000 master's degrees every year;
that is about a third of the number of baccalaureate degrees awarded annually
and about ten times the annual number of doctorates. The degree itself is not
easily defined. It may be — and often is — a rather focused technical preparation for a professional career in management, drama, chemical engineer-

ing, forestry, social work, computer systems, bacteriology, hydrology, international law, public health, museum conservation, city and regional planning, journalism, or scores of other professions. It may be a more general degree — in the humanities or social sciences, for example — with emphasis on broad understanding and individual scholarship. It may be an alternative to the Ph.D. for a student who, voluntarily or involuntarily, does not complete the doctoral degree.

The master's degree is both a graduate degree and also, in many cases, a terminal professional degree. The distinction between the two, based on whether the degree is awarded by the graduate school — comprising the whole university — or by a single professional school or college, is not very meaningful here.

Just as the nature of the degree differs from field to field, so also do the requirements. Typically, the degree involves a one- or two-year program, often with a thesis, which may range from a substantial work of independent scholarship to an extended essay or literature review. Off-campus assignments or internships are sometimes required, and part-time and remote electronic study are becoming increasingly frequent.

Does this variety of styles and requirements call for more standardization? I think not. Given the vast range of knowledge, skills, and experience required in the various professions, differences in degree requirements seem to me to be not only inevitable, but also desirable. The different educational requirements for, say, public administration, epidemiology, geophysical exploration, gerontology, demography, aerospace engineering, international diplomacy, tropical conservation and agriculture, and Portuguese literature make any notion of standardization inappropriate. What does matter here is quality of "product" — the effective, self-motivated graduate-practitioner — rather than uniformity of process.

Given the growing technological complexity of society, it seems inevitable that the demand for high-quality specialist master's degree recipients will increase, both in this country and elsewhere. Already, international students make up a substantial portion (more than half in some technical fields) of the master's degree students enrolled in American universities. This is a pattern of international cooperation that has reciprocal benefits and that contributes not only to improved professional services and robust international development but also to growing international understanding.

The master's degree represents the American university at its best — consciously scholarly in its foundation; deliberately analytical in its approach; unapologetically practical in its purposes; international in its membership and vision; attuned to societal needs; responsive to public priorities; having its academic sleeves rolled up and intellectual feet firmly planted on the ground. This is a degree that embodies education linked to life, public tasks informed by learning, technical skills enhanced by professional standards, and social purposes advanced by knowledge. What better example could there be of the role of the university in contemporary society? It is a program that deserves to be studied as an effective model by universities as they contemplate the deficiencies of the Ph.D. degree program.

DOCTORAL EDUCATION

Doctoral education is one of the most distinctive and important activities of the contemporary research university; it is also one of its most recent, variable, vulnerable, and wasteful features.

Doctoral education is one of the most important of all the tasks of the university because it is the foundation for the nation's research and development enterprise. It prepares the scientists, mathematicians, and engineers on whose skills industry, public health, government, biomedicine, agriculture, conservation, communication, and other areas of life depend. It educates scholars, who contribute to the arts, humanities, and social sciences, and it provides the future faculty of the nation's — and many of the world's — colleges and universities.

Two statistics illustrate its larger significance. Of the Ph.D. recipients of 1995, 44 percent of graduates in the physical sciences and 62 percent of those in engineering received industrial appointments.

Of the 42,705 Ph.D. recipients in 1997, 27 percent were foreign nationals, down from 32 percent a year earlier, a decline that now seems to be a trend. In earlier years in some fields — especially science, engineering, and some social sciences — their numbers exceeded 50 percent. Whatever its shortcomings, the U.S. Ph.D. program is the gold standard for the rest of the world. Of the same 1997 cohort, 41 percent were women and 8 percent ethnic minorities.

The doctoral degree is the apex of the academic enterprise; it takes longer to achieve than any other degree, and it occupies more time than any other activity for those who teach and supervise research within the program. In spite of its ancient lineage, and the prominent part doctoral education now plays, both directly and indirectly, in the life of the university, it is of comparatively recent origin in the American university. The first graduate programs appeared at Harvard in 1872, and were reinforced in 1876 by the founding of Johns Hopkins, with its major emphasis on research.

Doctoral education is one of the most variable activities of the university because it is often only loosely structured, highly specialized, and intensely individualistic. It varies not only from discipline to discipline and college to college, but also from faculty member to faculty member, reflecting both personal idiosyncrasies and the prevailing departmental culture — or lack of it — to a much greater extent than do other degrees. Consider, for example, the differences among doctoral studies of the ecology and preservation of tropical rain forests, medieval history of the Baltic region, Mozart's early keyboard music, nuclear physics, privatization in the former Soviet Union, the pathology of osteoporosis, and the nondestructive testing of concrete structures. To describe such studies — each the topic of a Ph.D. dissertation — as highly individualistic is not a criticism; it is a tribute, an acknowledgment of the precisely defined and essentially personal nature of any scholarship worthy of the name.

Doctoral education is vulnerable because its support depends on funding from many sources — state, federal, industrial, foundation, university, personal, and others — which vary in magnitude, duration, continuity, and availability, as well as in function. Some funds support research assistance, others provide teaching support for undergraduate courses; some are fellowships, others loans; some have strings and obligations, others have none.

And doctoral education is also one of the most wasteful of all the activities of the university; over 50 percent of those who enroll in Ph.D. programs fail to graduate. The comparable attrition rate for doctoral programs in law and medicine is less than 5 percent.[5]

In the light of these features, it might be tempting simply to urge universities to "shape up," to require faculty members to "get their act together," to "get serious about this." But any attempt to legislate universal expectations or requirements for the Ph.D. is likely to be counterproductive, in part because the successful Ph.D. graduate is "handcrafted" and the individual style and method of the supervising faculty member need to be respected, and in part because of the major differences among disciplines. But one must also acknowledge that though there is considerable room for improvement, resistance to change is strong. Narrow training, overproduction of graduates, using students to meet instructional priorities, and inadequate mentoring are frequent complaints.[6] To the extent that they are real, they can be corrected only at the department level. Neither heavy-handed "re-engineering" nor campus-wide "reforms" are likely to improve the situation. What is likely to be useful is to identify the issues that need to be addressed and suggest directions that might be beneficial. Administrative imposition will not solve this problem. Departments must reform their own programs, and the university's officers must see that they do.

THE PH.D.: ITS PURPOSE

The Ph.D. is one of the most ambiguous activities of the university. Although it is acknowledged as the crowning product of the academy, there is precious little agreement on the function it serves. Some see it as primarily a form of preparation for the future university teacher, whatever the discipline, a rite of academic ordination, as the late Kenneth Boulding once described it. Others see it as training for and initiation into the conduct of research, wherever the "researcher" is employed. Others view it as a work of independent research, a direct and substantial contribution to the general pool of knowledge and scholarship, and still others see it as a means of producing "trained minds" to meet the fundamental needs and address the larger issues of contemporary society.[7] Ideally all these functions may converge, or even coincide. In practice, they rarely do; to foster scholarship only coincidentally promotes citizenship that addresses the needs of society. To develop skills in some exquisitely refined area of research may contribute little to the large-minded view of knowledge that a university teacher should exemplify.

Nor is there agreement on the relationship of graduate education or training to the baccalaureate degree. Should there, for example, be a sharp discontinuity between the two? Or should promising graduate students be selected early — in high school, or during their early undergraduate years, beginning their graduate preparation in their senior year of college?[8] Is the Ph.D. a vocational and professional qualification, even in nonprofessional areas such as the humanities, or should it instead be a "liberal" degree, for university teachers, with emphasis on the broad intellectual and social context of a given field or topic? Should it even be encouraged for future scholars and teachers, given the dangers of stifling creativity and narrowing insight by heavy doses of courses in "method"? Boulding, perhaps one of his generation's most gifted university economists, declined to take a Ph.D. "I went to see my adviser, Professor Jacob Viner, at the University of Chicago," he wrote, "who advised me to take a Ph.D. So I said, 'What do I have to do?' When he explained the rigors of this ordeal, I said, 'If I do all that, I shall be a broken man,' much, I think, to Viner's disgust."[9]

John Passmore has expressed the same concern; arguing that the special excellence of graduate education is training in research, broadly interpreted, he asks whether an undue insistence on scholarly technique may discourage true creativity. "The English historian, A. J. P. Taylor, after a bachelor's degree in medieval history at Oxford, suddenly found himself plunged into the Austrian diplomatic archives. He had no training as a diplomatic historian; he wasted time, he made mistakes. But he came out of that experience with a quirky, but still important, book, *The Origins of the Second World War.* Had he gone to graduate school would he perhaps have said to himself 'I have not been trained to do this work; it would be unprofessional of me to attempt to do it'? I hope not; I fear so."[10]

That concern raises some of the most troublesome issues of graduate education. Even granting that the age of the gifted amateur is over, must advanced expertise come at the expense of versatility? Furthermore, is the university the only appropriate place, or even the best place, for advanced study? And what of costs? Are the universities justified in devoting so much of their effort to the production of Ph.D. graduates, in fields for which there is little or no employment demand, at the very time the public complains of inattention to the needs of undergraduates? Why encourage students to enroll in a Ph.D. program in order to pursue "alternative careers," when other methods — shorter, less costly, and more effective — are available?

And what of the substantial differences between degrees? What does a Ph.D. degree represent, anyway? In many Commonwealth countries, there are still no course requirements — the candidate is a "research student" from the day of registration. The typical U.S. university, however, requires substantial course work and a qualifying examination before the graduate student even becomes a candidate for the degree. And just how does all this training contribute to the capacity for independent work? What is the role of the faculty supervisor in all this? Should he or she provide daily supervision in the lab on a precisely defined experimental project, or are the faculty responsibilities limited to the occasional provision of "a little polite conversation and a pale sherry?"[11]

What role does the dissertation serve in this process? Must it be a work of original scholarship on a topic of genuine importance, or is it primarily a contribution to the intellectual development of its author?[12]

These questions, fundamental not only to the nature of doctoral education but also to the establishment of university priorities and the deployment of faculty time, are rarely addressed, either within the various disciplines and fields or by the university as an institution.[13]

The laissez-faire attitude, which assumes that because scholarship is intensely individual, no institutional norms or positions on graduate education are desirable or even possible, has been too long unchallenged. The differences in purpose and goal, the variable length of programs, and the striking differences in quality and scope of dissertation topics cry out for review. In too many areas, there is vagueness of purpose, woolliness of requirements, ambiguity of expectations, and laxity of supervision. The best programs remain superb, unambiguous in their purpose, explicit in their expectations, consistent in their quality. They must become the benchmark for all. The future of a university's Ph.D. programs, especially the purpose, role, and requirements of the Ph.D. degree, requires the urgent attention of the faculty. It is the responsibility of university presidents to make sure that it receives that attention. Several particular issues require review: the number of Ph.D. students; quality, supply, and demand; the institutional purpose, role, and requirements for the Ph.D. degree; attrition and time to degree.

THE PH.D.: THE NUMBERS

The Ph.D. program affects every aspect of the research university and influences the larger educational system far beyond the boundaries of the campus. The typical major research university will have a graduating Ph.D. class of 400 or 500 students, representing, perhaps, eighty or one hundred fields of study. In 1900, there were 400 new Ph.D. graduates for the nation as a whole. Twenty years later, the number had increased only to 600. In 1997, there were 45,876. That compares with a total of about 1.64 million baccalaureate degrees and about 406,000 master's degrees awarded by U.S. colleges and universities.[14]

The total number of Ph.D. degrees underwent explosive growth in the 1960s, from 10,000 at the beginning of the decade to over 30,000 at its end. What accounts for the pattern of remarkably rapid growth of these numbers? It has been suggested that the high demand for college teachers increased federal support for fellowships and traineeships, and the draft deferment of graduate students during the Vietnam War accounted for the extraordinary rate of increase in the award of Ph.D. degrees during this period.[15] After a stable period from the early 1970s to the mid-1980s, Ph.D. production accelerated again to its present level.

This increase in the total Ph.D. production resembles the situation in other professional fields. Between 1973 and 1985, for example, the number of M.B.A.s awarded more than doubled (from 31,007 to 67,527), the annual number of law degrees (J.D. and LL.B.) increased by more than a third (from 27,205 to 37,491), and the number of M.D.s increased by more than a half (from 10,307 to 16,041).[16] This growth reflects, one supposes, the increasing dependence of our society on trained professionals in every area of daily life.

The fields covered by Ph.D. degrees are as varied as the university itself:

mathematics and physical sciences, life sciences, education, and social sciences each produce 5,000 or 6,000 new Ph.D.s a year; engineering and the humanities each produce 3,000 or 4,000 a year; while business and various other collected fields each produce about 1,000 every year. Numbers of degrees awarded in the humanities have fallen by about a third over the last two decades. This "flight from the humanities" seems to be part of a more general trend away from the arts and humanities toward professional and applied fields at both the undergraduate and the graduate level.[17]

In a typical year, women account for more than a third (38 percent) of all Ph.D. recipients, though they earn more than half (56 percent) of all baccalaureate degrees. Their distribution within the various fields is remarkably uneven. They receive more than half (57 percent) of the degrees awarded in English, for example, but only 12 percent of those in physics and 11 percent of those in engineering. Minority groups, other than Asian Americans, are underrepresented among doctoral recipients. African Americans currently account for about 4 percent, Hispanic Americans about 4 percent, and Asian Americans about 5 percent of all degrees. Recent enrollment trends show no substantial change in the pattern of underrepresentation of African American, Hispanic, and Native American students. Again, distribution of these groups within the various fields is uneven. Asian Americans typically earn almost 20 percent of all degrees in engineering, for example, while over 40 percent of the degrees awarded to African Americans are typically in education. Among non–U.S. citizens there is an equally striking unequal representation by field.

THE NUMBER OF PH.D.–GRANTING INSTITUTIONS

Just as the numbers of students have grown, so also has the number of institutions offering the Ph.D. degree. The six hundred degrees in 1920 were awarded by only 14 universities. Today, some 470 institutions award the Ph.D. degree. Many of these more recently established programs remain small, awarding only one or two Ph.D. degrees a year. Just why there has been such an increase in the number of programs has been widely debated. My own view — deeply impressionistic — is that the flood in the 1960s at the rapidly growing, newer universities of newly minted Ph.D.s from the established graduate schools into vacant faculty positions led to a replication of the graduate programs in which the new Ph.D.s themselves had been incubated. What else did a professor do? They had come to believe that this was the noblest academic calling, and it had substantial practical advantages, not least the access it provided faculty members to inexpensive and capable assistance in their own research and teaching.

The aspirations of institutional leaders often coincided with this faculty goal, and state legislatures were broadly sympathetic to the need to provide access to "new graduate programs in the southwestern corner of the state for our fine young people." At the federal level, there was sympathetic support for these aspirations and a marked tendency to assure the "equitable" distribution of the substantial federal funding that became available in the 1960s. So the Harvardization of scores of "Southwestern Teachers' Colleges" and "Central Normal Schools" rapidly transformed the educational landscape.[18] The newly created programs did provide new access; they did create some useful and imaginative new programs; they did increase the standing and prestige of their parent institutions; and they did, one presumes, assist their faculty in teaching and research. But they did so at a price. Because these new institutions often lacked the substantial range of faculty expertise, library resources, and laboratory facilities required for successful graduate programs, few developed offerings of significant breadth or high quality. With few exceptions they occupy the second or third tier of quality rankings.[19] As federal funding dwindled and in some fields all but disappeared, these new programs also deflected institutional funding and professorial attention from the crucial needs of undergraduate instruction. These "newer" Ph.D. programs have, however, proved remarkably resilient, resistant alike both to closure and to reduction in student numbers; they now account for about one-third of all Ph.D. degrees awarded. Whereas the longer-established doctoral programs have — responsibly, I believe — deliberately reduced enrollment in the light of the reduced academic job market, the newer programs generally have not.

THE PH.D.: ATTRITION AND TIME TO DEGREE

These newer and generally smaller programs do, however, have one redeeming feature: they have much lower attrition levels than do the larger programs. The degree completion rate for those enrolled in the smaller programs is up to 50 percent higher than it is for those in the larger, reflecting, perhaps, the greater care and attention of faculty mentors in smaller programs.[20]

The high student attrition in Ph.D. programs is one of the unacknowledged weaknesses of the graduate scene; more than 50 percent of those who enroll in Ph.D. programs never complete them. And this is true despite the fact that these students are the cream of the undergraduate crop: high GPA, magna cum laude, dean's list, Phi Beta Kappa, and all the rest. Some of the "best" programs, and also the largest, have the highest attrition rates. William G. Bowen and Neil L. Rudenstine report that among students in the larger Ph.D. programs in economics, history, and politics, 25 percent drop out before the start of the second year; of those returning, a further 30 percent drop out before completing the required course work, and of those who do complete it, a further 25 percent drop out without completing the required dissertation.[21] A Ph.D. student in English, history, or political science in one of the better "smaller" programs (Cornell, Harvard, Princeton, and Stanford, for example) had almost twice as high a probability of completing the degree as a student in one of the better "larger" programs (Berkeley, Chicago, and Columbia).

Some attrition is inevitable in any program, not least in one as demanding as the Ph.D. Family situations change ("I decided to get divorced"); personal interests mature ("I just couldn't contemplate spending the next fifty years writing learned footnotes on the relationship of sixteenth-century economic development to marriage and kinship in the western cities of the Hanseatic League"). But, even allowing for the inevitability of some such changes, an attrition rate of 50 percent is extraordinary. It is also unacceptable; neither the maintenance of scholarly standards nor the heavy demands of particular disciplinary research can justify it. How can they, given the intense competition for admission, the elaborate screening procedures, and the stellar qualities of those accepted for enrollment? Attrition arises, not only for the personal reasons just discussed, but also for other reasons: some students wilt and drop under the intellectual burdens of the program, but others drop out in frustration at the time required, and still others in dismay at the lack of faculty encouragement, attention, advice, and direction. Many Ph.D. programs are the least structured, the least scrutinized, and the least supervised within the university.

All too frequently, Ph.D. students are allowed to drift, neglected by the faculty, while serving them in useful but lowly functions in teaching and research. The intellectual wastage, individual frustration, and personal financial loss this attrition involves are a personal tragedy and an institutional reproach that cries for amendment.

For those survivors who do complete the Ph.D. degree, the time required to graduate has become unreasonably long, and it is increasing. A typical sequence for a Ph.D. student will be two or three years of instruction in courses designed to provide both background and particular research skills in the chosen area of scholarship, including whatever language or other technical skills may be required; a comprehensive qualifying examination in all aspects of the chosen fields; the selection and pursuit of an appropriate dissertation topic; and the writing of a thesis and its oral defense in a public setting. This task, supervised either by an individual faculty member or by a faculty committee, represents a lengthy apprenticeship, ranging from an average of almost six years in mathematics to over eight years in the humanities. In certain fields — education, for example — it is even longer.[22] Within the sciences and engineering, time required to degree tends to be within the lower range; in the humanities and social sciences, within the higher. The professional areas fall somewhere in between. During the course of this long indenture, many graduate students are supported for one or two years as part-time teaching or research assistants. Others are supported by fellowships, scholarships, or loans, provided from a variety of sources. A few support themselves. This existence as a junior scholar within a congenial academic community is not without its attractions and even enchantments, but it is very, very long. For many students in scientific and technical fields, it is made even longer by the expectation of two, three, or more years of further postdoctoral study.

I believe that this pattern of ever-longer Ph.D. enrollment is simply too much. The additional years may expand the scope and perhaps improve the substance of the dissertation. They may provide time to acquire particular technical or language skills or to conduct extensive fieldwork, exhaustive archival study, or elaborate experimentation. But eight, nine, or ten years of intensive study is an unreasonably long time for the development of scholarly competence in a particular field. Twenty years ago, the comparable median times were generally 10 percent or more shorter than they are today. And when financial incentives for early completion have been introduced, either provided as a carrot or withdrawn as a stick, time requirements have been reduced. The Mellon Fellowships are a case in point.[23]

In spite of the success of these financial incentives, it is unlikely that any single measure will correct the lengthening enrollment in all Ph.D. programs. But much can be done by deans of graduate schools, department chairs, and directors of graduate fields and programs to correct the aimless drift that seems to afflict so many. Charting and monitoring the progress of individual students (and faculty supervisors!), setting reasonable scholarly goals, with the identification of "soluble" or manageable dissertation topics, and dealing with faculty members guilty of neglect, passivity, and inattention would provide a useful start. Faculty members must be held accountable for the progress of their graduate students. A written annual progress report, signed by both student and faculty member and discussed by both with the area director of graduate studies, would provide a healthy and much-needed stimulus. The need for review and reform is urgent; the deans of the nation's graduate schools have work to do.

THE PH.D.: QUALITY, SUPPLY, AND DEMAND

Given the lengthy time requirements imposed by these programs, one might suppose the results — both the scholarly preparation and training of the student and the dissertation itself — would be correspondingly strong. By almost any measure, they are. A recent ranking of 3,600 programs in 41 fields at 270 institutions was based on the reputation of programs with respect to such different criteria as the quality of the faculty, the effectiveness of the program in educating research scholars, and changes in program quality in the previous five years. Of the 3,634 programs reviewed, more than 60 percent were rated as "distinguished," "strong," or "good." The nation's 60 leading universities — members of the Association of American Universities — although they represent only 16 percent of the nation's Ph.D.–granting institutions, graduate more than 50 percent of the nation's Ph.D.s and provide 83 percent of the 418 programs ranked in the top ten of their disciplines by the National Research Council.[24]

One test of their standing is the attractiveness of these Ph.D. programs to students — often self-financed — from other countries. Recent analyses reveal a healthy export market in graduate studies. In 1995, approximately 400,000 foreign students were enrolled in U.S. universities, making up about 3 percent of total enrollments, with nearly half of them concentrated in advanced degree fields of science and engineering. Most of the rest of these students were undergraduates. It is estimated that they contribute some $6 billion a year in payments for tuition and living costs.[25]

What of supply and demand? Alan Hale was the co-discoverer of the comet Hale-Bopp, but his Ph.D. in astronomy still left him without professional employment, and there are anecdotes of Ph.D.s in medieval history driving cabs in Manhattan.

Reliable employment figures for Ph.D.s are patchy, being readily available in only a few areas, chiefly the sciences and engineering. In all areas unemployment is low; recent doctorate recipients (individuals who completed their degrees in the previous five years) had an overall unemployment rate of 1.4 percent in 1997, for example.[26] The rates varied by field, being highest (3.2 percent) for the humanities and lowest in the sciences and engineering (1.5 percent). Rates of continuing employment remain high. The comparable unemployment rate for the entire U.S. population was 4.9 percent at that time.[27] By and large, then, *un*employment is not a major problem for Ph.D. recipients, but *under*employment may be a serious predicament, about which there are few meaningful data. Many universities and colleges — though not the major research universities — are replacing full-time tenured faculty, for example, by adjunct, part-time, and temporary instructors, and in some cases young Ph.D.s may find themselves with part-time appointments in several institutions at the same time. Others are employed in fields far distant from their own, performing tasks for which the lengthy Ph.D. apprenticeship is generally poor preparation.

A Call for Correction

Ph.D. programs defy easy characterization, but we can summarize a few general features by way of conclusion. The established programs are generally of high quality, have extremely competitive admissions, provide supplementary teaching and research assistance to the university, are attractive to international students, and produce graduates who are in high demand in science, engineering, and some associated technical and professional fields. On the negative side, the attrition rate for many programs is unreasonably high; the length of time required to achieve a degree often unreasonably long; the more recently established programs, though they account for about one-third of new graduates, include many of lesser quality; and there are limited employment prospects for graduates in some fields, including the humanities and some social sciences.

What can be done to preserve the best qualities of the existing programs and correct their deficiencies? A variety of actions seem to me to be required.

The Ph.D. is in urgent need of the same rigorous review and comprehensive scrutiny by members of the faculty as those they apply in their own scholarship. The most appropriate and best-qualified people to provide this review are the graduate faculty, but if they don't, others are likely to do it for them. The first issue to be addressed by each university is the arguments for and against the continuation of Ph.D. programs, in light of their quality, size, scope, support, and cost.

In light of that study, each university, graduate school, and field of study must define and articulate the purposes, goals, expectations, requirements, content, and time norms of its programs. These should be explicit and should become the central part of the graduate catalog. There is now a widespread view that Ph.D. programs should be made "broader in scope" in order to produce more generally skilled, versatile, and widely employable graduates. This suggestion deserves serious discussion, but the Ph.D. may be an expensive and ineffective route to general employability. Wrongly used, this plea may become an argument for the overproduction of Ph.D. graduates in order to satisfy the need of faculty members for teaching and research assistance.

Each college, program, field, and department should develop a rolling, comprehensive plan of graduate enrollment targets, based on available financial support, faculty numbers and expertise, facilities available, and a responsible assessment of the "job market." This is a topic for urgent discussion within and between graduate institutions and their supporters.

This planning should apply to both doctoral and master's degree programs. Creative reinvention and greater use of the master's degree could add to the richness of graduate study and make a significant contribution to societal needs.

Though some graduate programs are well designed and carefully structured, the content of others reflects chiefly the cumulative interests and "intellectual inclinations of individual faculty members." Every program should be the expression of a systematic faculty discussion of the comprehensive needs of students in their chosen field, rather than serving primarily the self-interests of faculty members and their institutions.

There is evidence that both the smallest and the largest doctoral programs may be inefficient, though there is probably no optimum size for a program.[28] Program size, however, should be reviewed.

The states have a responsibility to review the use of public resources to finance new or existing graduate programs in the absence of demonstrated need for them. California and New York, among others, have used program approval authority to regulate the number of doctoral programs supported by their public universities.

Admission interviews and selection procedures must be both rigorous and realistic, with a roadmap developed for each individual student's program.

Multiyear financial arrangements for each graduate student should be planned, specified, and committed, in writing, at the time of admission, subject only to satisfactory academic progress by the student.

Teaching and research assignments and assistantships should be incorporated, explained, and committed as part of this financial package.

Faculty advisers must be held accountable for the oversight and supervision of their graduate students both in their own studies and scholarship, and in the teaching and research assistance they provide. Annual reports on the progress of each student should be required. A faculty advisory and supervisory committee for each student, in contrast to a single faculty adviser, has much to commend it.

Systematic, sustained mentoring and support in professional development, career guidance, opportunities, and planning should be provided for each student.

The faculty community of each graduate field should develop programs to provide professional encouragement, cultural support, and intellectual challenge to its graduate students.

Incentives should be provided both to encourage shortening of the time required for a degree and to support multidisciplinary, interdisciplinary, and highly personalized programs and areas of study, including those with societal linkage and potential benefit.

The role and authority of the dean of the graduate school must be strengthened. This deanship is typically the only one in the university with no authority to appoint or replace faculty members, no budget, and no power to assign tasks or designate responsibility.

Rethinking the nature of the Ph.D. is important to the wider future of higher education in the United States and elsewhere. Ph.D. holders from the ninety or so major research universities fill the vast majority of the faculty vacancies and thus become the dominant influence at the other 3,900 institutions of higher education in this country and a significant number elsewhere. Yet only a handful of the institutions to which they are appointed play a substantial role in the research enterprise; the preoccupation of most of them is with teaching and learning, and it should be. So there is a dislocation between the specialized scholarly training and interest of the newly minted professor and what he or she wants to teach, and the expectations of the students and what they need to learn.

The faculty often tacitly accept their graduate institutions as the model for what their new employing institutions should become. The long years of graduate training produce a love and zeal for specialized scholarship, but fail to prepare the faculty members for the realities and needs of service in a very different type of institution. The student seeking — and needing — not just knowledge, but also some larger sense of its significance and encouragement for critical thought and inquiry, is offered instead, at best, fragmented courses taught in isolation from one another, or, at worst, watered-down versions of the faculty members' specialized scholarly interest. The end result of this encounter is all too often frustration for the faculty member and disappointment for the student.

It is not easy to offer a simple solution to this dysfunction. A Ph.D. holder from Harvard or CalTech is still likely to have the edge over a master's degree holder from a middling regional state university in seeking a teaching job, even at a community college. Perhaps they should have such an advantage, though the reasons why are not self-evident. Yet we can hardly hope to change the aspirations of search committees at four thousand fiercely independent institutions. What can instead be done is to change the nature of the Ph.D. — though this is almost as difficult — acknowledging that most recipients will no longer be employed in highly specialized research roles. The innovative — and unpopular — doctor of arts degree, for example, was designed for teachers in nonresearch colleges and universities, but it has produced little enthusiasm and has had few takers in the quarter century of its existence.

Perhaps a newly designed program might include a sequence of three stages: a one- or two-year instructional program in a given field, including appropriate internship and independent study and scholarly opportunities, leading to the master's degree; a further two-, three-, or four-year (perhaps fixed time-to-degree, depending on the field) program of supervised and mentored research in a well-defined area, leading to the Ph.D. degree. For those who contemplate a research career, there might be a further three years (fixed period) of intensive postdoctoral research in a chosen area, leading, perhaps, to a new degree (doctor of the university or doctor of science/ arts/social sciences) that would become the professional degree for university faculty and others in highly specialized research roles. Both the master's and Ph.D. degrees would then continue to serve as terminal degrees, appropriate for those intending to pursue less research-intensive careers. James Duderstadt, former president of the University of Michigan, has proposed a broadly similar program, but it has yet to be widely embraced.

In spite of the relatively small numbers of students involved, it is difficult to exaggerate the importance of the Ph.D. in the life of contemporary society. The quality and range of the degree provide the foundation for much of the nation's research, including scientific, medical, and technical areas. Through its enrollment of substantial numbers of international students, the Ph.D. degree contributes significantly to the needs of both developing nations and other industrialized societies. It plays a major role in the development of public policy, both in the provision of data, analysis, policy options, and modeling, and in the training of public servants. It produces each new rising generation of university professors, whose attitude, scholarship, and instruction have, in turn, a profound influence upon the pattern and character of the one million or so new baccalaureate graduates each year.

The Ph.D. degree, representing the university's highest scholarship wedded to its most personal instruction, wields an influence of major importance. It would be tragic if the universities failed to provide the attention, oversight, and structure required to make a good and important program even better. At graduation, each new doctor of philosophy is welcomed "into the society of educated men and women." Universities have a moral obligation constantly to justify that claim.

{ 8 }
THE COST
OF HIGHER
EDUCATION

"If you think education is expensive," Ann Landers and others have remarked, "consider the cost of ignorance." It is a telling phrase; a useful reminder.

There is no guarantee, of course, that spending on education will reduce the spiraling costs of ignorance, but the comparisons are sobering. Already, California and Florida spend more to incarcerate their criminals than they do to educate their college-age populations. The number of prisoners in California has grown from 19,000 two decades ago to 150,000 today. In the last twenty years, the state has built twenty-one new prisons but added only one university. The share of the state budget devoted to the university system — once regarded as the best in the world — has fallen from 12.5 percent in 1990 to 8 percent in 1997. In the same period, the share devoted to corrections has increased by 4.5 percent to 9.4 percent, an amount equal to the loss in university funds.

Though this is not a direct trade-off, Barry Munitz, the former chancellor of the California State University system, declares, "To me, you pay now for college, or you pay dramatically more later for prisons for people who don't get an education and wind up committing crimes. The state sends us $6,000 per student, but it pays $34,000 a year for a prison inmate."[1] That may be too simple a correlation, but there is no disputing the correlation between lack of education and joblessness and crime.

When I speak with parents of college students, they usually tell me they are very happy with the education their sons and daughters are gaining. A significant number will pause, and add, "What I can't understand, though, is why it is all so much more expensive than it was when I was a student." These are not people who undervalue education; what they struggle with is not whether it is "worth" it but rather why its costs have increased so rapidly as to threaten to put it beyond the reach of all but the most wealthy.

Indeed, it is a question that few parents can help asking, when they hear that the cost of tuition, room, board, and books at some of the leading private universities has risen to more than $30,000 a year — or more than $120,000 for a four-year undergraduate degree. It is also a question universities have been asking themselves.

I want to explore the reasons for rising tuition. I shall argue that colleges and universities must take several specific steps to come to grips with the rising costs if we are to keep a college education affordable for all Americans. And I shall try to explain that a few widely held misperceptions about college costs have caused many parents and their children some unnecessary anxiety.

Who Actually Pays $120,000 for College?

Let us begin with what is often taken to be the bottom line: the "news" that parents and students now face a price tag of $120,000 as the cost of a four-year degree, an amount equivalent to the price of a house in some parts of the country. It is, on first blush, a shocking figure. Fortunately, it also is wrong.

Most parents do not pay $30,000 a year, over four years, for their children's education, for one simple reason: most colleges and universities do not charge that much. Indeed, only 7.2 percent of the full-time students were enrolled at four-year universities that charged tuition and fees of $20,000 or more during 1999–2000. Most students, 71.7 percent, were enrolled in institutions that charged $8,000 or less. To clarify those numbers further, 50.9 percent of the full-time students were enrolled at four-year institutions with tuition under $4,000; 20.8 percent, $4,000 to $7,000; and 6.1 percent paid $8,000 to $11,999 for tuition and fees.[2]

Another way to understand this, taking into account the costs at both two- and four-year institutions, is by considering the figures in the table on page 138. The $120,000-plus figure that has been bandied about as the current cost of a four-year college degree, in other words, is the cost for only a small number of students at a small number of leading private universities. Most pay far less. If two-year and four-year colleges are considered together, 81 percent of all undergraduates in 1996–97 attended institutions where the average tuition was less than $3,000.[3] The difference between the tuition levels of public and private institutions arises, of course, because of the high level of state subsidies in the former. The actual "costs" — as opposed to "price" — are not very different in the two sectors.

Average Cost of Tuition and Fees for Undergraduates (1999–2000)

Institution	Cost	Percent of All Undergraduates
Public 2-year	$1,627	43.1%
Public 4-year	$3,356	37.8%
Private 2-year	$7,182	1.8%
Private 4-year	$15,380	17.3%

Source: Percentages (1996–97) from the *Chronicle of Higher Education, Almanac Issue* 44, no. 1 (August 1997): 48 and costs from ibid. 48, no. 1 (September 2000): 48.

Even within the four-year institutions, relative enrollment provides an important perspective. Because "higher-tuition" institutions enroll a relatively small proportion of the total student population, relative size and enrollment must be considered when the overall impact of tuition levels at various institutions is discussed. Stanley Ikenberry, president of the American Council on Education, has pointed out that at the University of Illinois at Urbana, tuition and fees were $3,150 in 1995–96, and at Ohio State University, they were $3,300. "Taken together, these two schools alone enrolled 20,000 more undergraduate students than all the Ivy League combined, but that is not the story one typically hears," comments Ikenberry.[4]

But any discussion of price must also involve the question of quality and value. It is easy to overlook the fact that the higher-tuition institutions frequently offer a competitive advantage to their graduates. Thus the average starting salary of recent graduates of a typical member of this group — the University of Pennsylvania — was 57 percent higher than that of a high school graduate. The comparable salary of a graduate of a public university was 32 percent higher than that of a high school graduate.[5] That doesn't represent an institutional guarantee, of course, but it does express the reality of value-added in education, as in much else.

The facts, in other words, demonstrate that "high-cost" private universities exist within a large, amorphous nonsystem of higher education, where competitive market forces operate. Their tuition — contrary to the charges of some of their critics — represents, not what the market will bear, but what they believe an excellent education requires, ranging from outstanding faculty members, extensive libraries, state-of-the-art laboratories, and supportive student counseling services, to reasonable housing accommodation and athletic facilities. Moreover, many students and their families clearly agree with them, for these universities constantly find themselves able to admit only a small fraction of those generally outstanding freshman students who apply (ranging from about 1 in 5 to 1 in 10).

Let me give one specific example. Harvard has roughly 1,600 places in its freshman class, for which it received 18,184 applications in 1996. Of these, 2,905 were high school valedictorians, the best in their respective schools. So Harvard could fill almost two freshman classes with students, every one of whom would be a valedictorian. Of Harvard's applicants, 9,448 had a Scholastic Aptitude Test score of 1,400 or better.[6] The leading universities could, if they wished, in the light of such strong competition for admission, easily increase tuition and still fill all their places with superbly qualified students, all of whom could pay their own way. They choose not to do so because of the conviction that the diversity of the class contributes to the learning process and that a class should be made up of the best-qualified students, regardless of their ability to meet the costs. That is why two-thirds of the students attending private universities pay *substantially less* than the advertised tuition costs; they receive financial aid packages (which include grants, loans, and work-study income) that colleges provide to make the price of tuition affordable in the light of a family's ability to pay. These universities have a dual sense of social obligation: to offer the best possible education in their various fields and to make it available to those students most likely to benefit from it, whatever their financial situation.

The leading private universities — the "high-priced elite" group — have long chosen their students on a so-called need-blind basis. Those who make the admissions decisions literally do not know at the time of selection whether or not any particular individual is able to pay the costs of tuition, that is, whether they have "financial need." After a positive admission decision is made, the university will put together a financial aid package to enable the student to attend. The fewer assets the student's family has, the more financial aid it is likely to receive — and, therefore, the lower the tuition it will be charged.

A small, and dwindling, part of this financial aid comes from the federal and state governments; most of it comes from the university itself, partly from designated gifts and endowments from grateful alumni, some of whom were themselves the recipients of financial aid in earlier years, and the rest from the university's general funds. This represents a major financial commitment for any university. At Cornell, for example, in 1999–2000, the total university contribution to student financial aid was over $69 million. About 70 percent of students at Cornell receive some form of financial aid.

But even rejecting the myth that the average cost of college is more than

$120,000, and the further myth that most students at "high-price" institutions pay the full cost of tuition, there remains a question that is deeply troubling to those contemplating college costs: Why is it that so many parents are convinced that tuition costs have risen faster in recent years than ever before?

The answer is: They have. One recent calculation suggests that "the average middle-class breadwinner must now work 95 days to pay for a year of private college tuition. Twenty years ago it took slightly more than half as long to pay for the same education."[7] Over the same period, in contrast, the workdays required to buy a new car stayed about the same, and the days required to pay for milk, a refrigerator, and even a gallon of gasoline went down significantly. Even for a middle-income family, the relative rise in tuition has been steep. Only health care costs rose faster than college costs, and we know the consequences for that industry.

Yet tuition has risen much more steeply than inflation for most of the past century. So why does it seem to have risen faster only during the past decade? One reason is that until the last decade, family incomes were rising faster than tuition. From 1965 to 1980, private college costs, when considered as a percentage of median family income, actually declined from 29 to 25 percent, even though tuition itself was rising steadily. So alumni parents in those years didn't sense a great difference from their own college days. But from 1980 to 1990, tuition costs rose from 25 to 35 percent of median family income. In other words, the increase during the 1980s was 40 percent — a very palpable hit.[8]

But the fact that family income levels failed to keep pace with their pre-1980 levels does not tell the entire story. In recent years, for example, when administrators were asked why universities were so expensive, they usually cited academic costs that have been rising faster than general inflation, and argued that tuition, therefore, must do the same. By exceptional academic costs, they meant computerization of the campus, increasingly sophisticated and expensive scientific equipment, foreign books and scholarly journals for the library, faculty salary increases to make up for earlier subinflationary increases, compliance with government regulations, costly maintenance of generally older buildings, rising employee health care costs, reduced government research support, and student financial aid costs that were ballooning because of government retrenchment.

One of the most careful studies of costs yet published is that by Charles Clotfelter,[9] who studied cost increases in arts and science departments at three research universities (Harvard, Chicago, and Duke) and one liberal arts college (Carleton). Clotfelter found that over a fifteen-year period (1976/77 to

1991/92), mean tuition and fees increased at a real annual rate of 4.6 percent. For the decade 1981/82 to 1991/92 the rate was 5.3 percent. In seeking to explain these cost increases, Clotfelter showed that faculty salaries grew in real terms (compensating for a decline in the 1970s), that financial aid rose sharply, and that capital investment, especially for computers, new construction, building renovation, and equipment, increased significantly. While these expenditures did not generally give rise to new programs, they did frequently lead to improved performance and increased activities, partly in response to surging demand for their services, pressure from competing institutions, changes in federal support, and new compliance requirements and partly in response to the insatiable appetites and "unbounded aspirations" of the universities themselves.

This study, though confined to four institutions and inevitably generalizing various trends and pressures, seems to me to reflect the experience of most research universities, for whom these are all real cost problems; I have cited them myself. But what we must now realize is that these costs and others like them are not unique to higher education, nor are most of them systemic, long-term costs. Citing them, therefore, does not really justify the sharp increase in tuition costs, nor does it prepare us to grapple with the issue. So let us look a little more closely at this issue of costs, some of which are "inherent inefficiencies," as it were, in the nature of the university and others of which can and must be better managed.

Reasons for Rising Tuition Costs

The continuing increases in college tuition costs reflect the interaction of half a dozen different factors:

CUTBACKS IN FEDERAL FUNDING

In 1980, the federal government began to cut back dramatically on its direct financial support to students. Prior to 1980, a full 80 percent of the financial aid the government awarded to students was given in the form of grants and scholarships that did not have to be repaid; 20 percent consisted of loans that students were required to repay with interest. But since the early 1980s that proportion essentially has been reversed: 25 percent of the financial aid awarded by the government now takes the form of grants and scholarships that do not have to be repaid; 75 percent consists of loans that must be repaid with interest.

Universities, concerned that the prospect of such a significant debt burden would cause many able potential students — especially those of modest means — to skip college, responded by greatly increasing the grants, scholarships, and other funds they provided to students. As a result, while tuition has risen more steeply than general inflation, colleges and universities have increased their own financial aid awards at a rate *twice as fast as the rate of increase in tuition.*

Let me illustrate the impact of that reduced federal funding on Cornell. In the period 1987–88 to 1997–98, federal and state government funding for undergraduate financial aid grants was essentially flat (it actually decreased a little) in inflation-adjusted dollars, while Cornell's use of unrestricted funds for financial aid tripled to more than $40 million and its use of funds from gifts more than doubled to $20 million. Total funding for undergraduate financial aid at Cornell in 1997–98 was $185 million, with $44 million coming from the federal government ($33 million of it in loans), $5 million from the state government, and $64 million from Cornell.

This has set up something of a paradoxical relationship between tuition and financial aid: As tuition has become more costly, universities have had to offer more financial aid to needy students. Yet to provide that aid, they must make tuition even more costly. This is a dangerous equation, which universities must now reconsider. A system that amounts to secondary taxation — however worthy — has its limits. And in some universities, more than 20 percent of every dollar received from tuition is now earmarked for financial aid.

TECHNOLOGY STASIS

A second reason tuition has increased at a rate higher than price increases in other industries is that, unlike other businesses, universities have not yet applied new technologies to reduce instructional costs. Major corporations routinely use worldwide electronic networks to improve efficiency in every aspect of their businesses. Universities also make brilliant use of computers to advance science, to manage their business affairs, and to provide access to data banks; but, in their basic business of teaching resident students, they have not diverged much from the methods of Socrates, except that most faculty members have now moved inside. And student demand for e-mail, personal Web pages, Internet access, on-line databases, and electronic communication with their professors has actually increased costs. Still, as described in Chapter 11, information technology has the potential to increase access, improve quality, foster new partnerships, and reduce costs.

But most faculty members, most universities, and most professional practitioners are not yet prepared for the transformation that distance learning will bring. Almost all universities are already testing new ways to apply technology to teaching; however, part of the reason why college costs regularly outpace inflation is that massive change has not yet begun. The social interactions and intellectual cross-pollination of the campus, which are essential components of any meaningful undergraduate education, are not easily replicated in cyberspace.

HUMAN SCALE

The third reason for the rising cost of tuition is related to but distinct from the question of technology. The university educates its students one by one. Its production is limited by what a person — either student or professor — can produce. The scale of campus life and the intimacy of the learning relationship can be stretched only if the main purpose of universities — to educate individuals — is not weakened. The most effective learning at the university level — whether the subject is philosophy or molecular biology — involves a personal teacher-student interaction and cannot progress without the student's personal engagement. This complex learning process is not confined to the classroom. It depends on other settings — the library, the laboratory, and the field, for example — and it demands time outside formal lecture hours. It is expensive, but it is also important, for it inspires the student to move beyond rote learning to more comprehensive understanding; at its best, it cultivates personal insight and creative application.

In theory, Mary Sansalone, whom we met in Chapter 5, could teach engineering to millions of people via satellite. The transfer of information would be no problem, but good teaching involves time to explain, to analyze, to synthesize, to review, and to listen — especially to listen. Students need the personal attention of a teacher-mentor to kindle the spark of inquiry; and, since they are often grappling more with concepts than with facts, they learn at different speeds. To the extent that faculty members sometimes fail to make this personal connection possible, they undermine and negate the essential nature and purpose of the university. But even if some fall short, personal interest and individual concern remain the essential foundation for effective instruction, the proven means of harnessing the creative energy and developing the talent of the new generation. And these limit traditional "cost-efficiency."

THE PRICE OF TOP TALENT

For many positions, particularly positions on the faculty, universities seek to hire the people who are the world's best at what they do. Such people are expensive, and universities often compete for their services with profit-making businesses. Because business knows that top talent will eventually benefit its bottom line through improved efficiency or better management, it can expect to more than recoup its investment in high salaries. A university's bottom line, however, involves not revenues or profits but how well it pursues its work of instruction, research, and service. It is excellence in these areas that determines success, and, while that excellence does also benefit students and the world, it does not defray the cost of top talent. (See salary details later in this chapter.)

SOCIAL BENEFICENCE

A fifth costly difference between universities and business is that universities, especially the private ones, consciously undertake expenses for no other purpose than their social benefit. More specifically, universities do not *have* to offer hundreds of scholarships of more than $10,000 a year, for example, but they believe the nation benefits if they keep their doors open to any able student. They do not *have* to backfill when fiscally strapped states cut funding for students. They do not *have* to perform research when the government consistently reduces the level of reimbursement of their overhead costs for conducting that research. A principal reason universities do these things is that they believe they serve the public interest, and they accept this service as a fundamental role of the university. But playing that role is expensive.

When a corporation funds charitable activities, it may do so with money that would otherwise be paid as taxes on profits; and even then, it often chooses projects with an eye to the good name or long-term interests of the company. Support for local schools or hospitals in the communities where plants are located is a good example. When universities provide scholarships from their general revenues, the money is simply subtracted from the operating budget that pays for other critical items such as salaries, libraries, or building maintenance. And, I assure you, there is no public relations benefit. Some — especially financial aid recipients — complain that universities are too stingy. Others — especially non-financial-aid recipients — complain that they are too generous.

THE EXPLOSIVE GROWTH OF KNOWLEDGE

One of the major factors in rising tuition has been the habit — developed in the buoyant days from the 1960s to the 1980s — of adding worthy academic programs. Among the new curricular areas added in the last thirty years have been computer science, operations research, biotechnology, environmental science, manufacturing engineering, Asian languages, human genetics, immunology, and cognitive science. For all the benefits these new areas have brought, the add-on habit — well-meaning but impossible to sustain — has been overtaken by a new sense of financial constraint. Universities are now compelled to restrain costs as well as promote new knowledge. Their future growth will have to be by substitution rather than addition. They have already become far more selective in the new areas of study they support, and over time this must continue.

Although administrators can — and must — reduce costs and contain cost increases in every corner of the university, as most are already doing, the impact of such better management is likely to be limited. Price inflation arises largely from causes that are inherent in the university — "inefficiencies" in its nature rather than in its management.

Price, Cost, and the Market

Continuing concerns about college costs are reflected by a 1997 report from the Council for Aid to Education that predicts that, if present trends continue, colleges and universities will face a catastrophic $38 billion shortfall by 2015,[10] as well as by the appointment by the House Committee on Education and the Workforce on July 16, 1997, of a special congressional commission to study the rising cost of attending college.[11]

No one would suggest that the sharp rises in tuition costs since the 1980s must simply be accepted as the new status quo, a fact of life in American education. Nor would most people accept such an answer if anyone did suggest it. But besides anguished analysis and gloomy talk of federal regulation, another force is at work: competition in a free market. This competition already exists among traditional universities and colleges and now seems likely to intensify as institutions in the same market sector cap or reduce tuition and offer targeted financial aid packages that resemble car dealers' discounts. One recent report suggests a growing proportion of upper-income families are now sending their children to less expensive, public universities.

There is also another type of competition that is growing: for-profit institutions that offer competitive alternatives to traditional colleges in selected market niches. Perhaps the best illustration of this is the University of Phoenix, which in 1998 enrolled 40,000 students in ten states, employing just 45 full-time and 4,500 adjunct faculty members.[12] It offers associate's, bachelor's, and master's degrees in business, information technology, health care, and education, operates seventeen campuses and forty-seven smaller learning centers, and aims at the older (average age thirty-four), employed (average thirteen years) student. Tuition averages $6,310 a year, but many students are reimbursed by their employers.

Two things make the Phoenix approach competitive: its well-defined, targeted student pool — working adults, who study on a part-time basis — and its method of instruction. Unlike traditional colleges, it franchises its instruction to a part-time faculty, all of whom are also employed in the fields they teach and who follow a prescribed, standardized, centrally developed, sequential curriculum. Phoenix has close ties with industry, gives credit for "life experience" and offers no "frills," such as athletics or dormitories. This is truly a "stripped-down" institution.

Does it "work"? Well, it seems to, in spite of the ridicule and skepticism of some more traditional academics. Its parent — the Apollo Group, a public company quoted on the NASDAQ Stock Exchange — is profitable. With an enrollment of more than 75,000 students in 2000, it is the largest private university in the United States. Its students and their employers seem enthusiastic and satisfied. It is accredited by the North Central Association of Schools and Colleges.

What Phoenix and other nontraditional colleges offer is a different approach to knowledge: knowledge as a transaction, information as a commodity. It is an approach that fills an important need, and it is one that will be amplified and extended by the growing use of technology. What they do not offer is the value added to that knowledge that comes from membership in the traditional residential community of the research university. That value is what research universities must cultivate and reinforce. And as they do, and face growing price competition in doing so, society will be the beneficiary.

Considering the Alternatives

Many alternatives to and proposals for change in the traditional residential research university have been put forth, by the general public, business leaders, the media, government officials, and universities themselves. In this section, I consider the most commonly heard alternatives.

OPTION 1: CUT FACULTY SALARIES?

To some who remember when a schoolteacher earned $5,000 a year, it may seem simply profligate that his or her successor may now earn $50,000. Yet these same people may casually accept salaries in the millions of dollars for midlevel sports and film stars, senior business executives, surgeons, or bond salesmen.

A world-class professor pursuing research on the frontiers of engineering, physics, or chemistry, who teaches undergraduates based on that research, leads a large graduate research team, and trains tomorrow's professors and scientists for government and industry, may earn $125,000 to $175,000. Is that a lot for someone whose discoveries may provide major benefits for society? Is it a little?

A top humanist — author of a dozen or so definitive books, directing the thesis work of four or five graduate students — may earn $125,000. Is that a lot for someone who, perhaps, sets the terms of public debate, advises the federal government on policy issues, and helps students contend with the great, overarching questions that most of us have no time for? Is it a little?

Social scientists tend to be on the lower side of that spread; professors of law, business, and medicine on the higher side. (A significant number of clinical professors in medical schools earn salaries in the range of several hundred thousand dollars, but these are paid from their private-practice patients' fees, from which a substantial amount is also contributed to the schools' general budgets.)

But the figures I have mentioned are for world-class people — Nobel laureates and those of comparable stature — at the very top of their careers. The average 1999–2000 salary for a senior professor at a private research university was around $103,700 and at a public university around $82,500. A new assistant professor, the entry rung of the faculty ladder, will begin at a salary closer to $49,000 at a public university and $58,500 at a private university, even though he or she is probably around thirty years old and holds a Ph.D. degree. Liberal arts colleges, even the best, pay substantially lower salaries, on average, than research universities. The average 1999–2000 salary for a professor at a public, four-year institution was $66,657 ($71,574 at a private); for an associate professor the comparable figures are $53,143 and $53,144; and for a new assistant professor $41,963 and $44,836.[13]

In setting salaries, universities respond much as Hollywood, professional sports, local school districts, business, or government does. They are guided by the market. When they hire clerical or maintenance employees, their "market" is defined by what such positions command locally. For midlevel management jobs, their market is local or regional, occasionally national. For most faculty or senior administration positions, the market is national and international.

In the case of scientists and engineers — and to a lesser extent social scientists or humanists — salary is only one part of the competitive package. It is not uncommon to have to find half a million dollars for a specialized lab to recruit a promising young scientist, even as an assistant professor. There may also be other negotiated, nonsalary benefits that help the professor establish his or her work, including short-term funds for graduate student research assistants.

Is such compensation excessive? I do not believe it is if one compares it with compensation in other areas: medicine, law, business, sports, entertainment, or investment, for example. To argue that it is, is rather like saying that professional baseball salaries are too high. Enforcing such an arbitrary judgment would keep some of the best people out of universities — or baseball — and open the way to grateful second-stringers. The effectiveness of the university depends on its ability to bring together a constellation of the most accomplished and promising scholars across the arts, sciences, and professions. It can do that only by paying the "market price."

OPTION 2: INCREASE FACULTY WORKLOADS?

Workload is perhaps the area most cited to illustrate alleged waste. It's a tricky question. Part of the question concerns faculty time devoted to research, which, as I already argued, is fundamentally intertwined with student scholarship at research universities. But as a strictly financial question, universities have to recognize that teaching is labor exchanged for payment. Since payment (typically some 70 percent of it) comes from student tuition, the payer/student is entitled to substantial direct return, including the personal interest and attention of his or her instructors. The question is just how much of each professor's classroom time a student is entitled to. Responsible administration, professional judgment, and personal commitment are the only meaningful guides in this.

But granted the difficulty of standardizing teaching duties, should there not at least be some minimal university guideline or requirement for formal classroom teaching? I have suggested elsewhere that most research university faculty should be able to discharge their several duties and still meet at least four one-semester classes a year (see Chapter 5). What is overlooked, however, in making that "requirement" is that some classes have three students and some three hundred; the teacher of the latter class quite literally "earns" for his or her department one hundred times more revenue from tuition than does the former. Some classes have extensive laboratories, studio requirements, or fieldwork assignments. Here, as with the question of closing programs, each case is best considered separately in light of its "economic viability" and intellectual significance before deciding either individual teaching assignments or whether a course should be eliminated or continued.

But could a university not reduce costs by further increasing teaching loads? It could, but that would come at a cost that must be weighed. If universities had arbitrarily driven up workloads twenty-five years ago, there might have been no biotechnology today. That is why I pose the two-course-per-semester workload as a very rough guide. But even a rough guide is better than none; and requiring a renewed faculty commitment to teaching has more than financial benefits for the university.

Perhaps the best way to approach the issue of faculty "productivity" is not classroom hours but student credit-hours taught per full-time faculty member. That way the number of students paying to attend each hour of class can be factored in. If Professor Jones continues to teach two classes but increases their enrollment, he increases revenues without increased expenditures. Adopting such a measure, together with a two-course-per-semester class assignment as a norm, would lead to a significant increase in teaching "productivity" and over time to a reduction in the rate of tuition increase. There will, inevitably, be faculty complaints, especially from those in the sciences and economics, where teaching loads are conspicuously lower, but deans and provosts have an obligation to address this issue in light of the university's larger social responsibility.

OPTION 3: STRIP DOWN OR SPLIT UP?

Some have argued that it is wasteful for universities to compete and that they should split up and share fields of study. Undoubtedly they should, but I confess that I am as unenthusiastic about a planned and regulated academic market as I am about a planned and regulated national economy. I prefer to use the market as the mechanism. If there were no competition at all — with a handful of universities, for instance, becoming the *only* ones offering physics — universities could reduce their collective costs for both professors and equipment. But they would undoubtedly lose the best minds to competing industries and institutions, both here and abroad. And you simply cannot teach engineering or chemistry or astronomy or geology or biology — not to mention medicine, agriculture, and other professional areas — without offering instruction in physics. Indeed, a medical school alone must offer a full range of basic sciences, from anatomy to biochemistry, neurology, physiology, and cell biology. And today's engineering education must offer — besides a full range of the physical sciences — biological and environmental science, economics, and management. Surely, there can be cooperation in teaching — increasingly across campus borders — but the very interconnection of fields of knowledge renders unworkable the idea of limiting disciplines to certain campuses. This kind of model has been tried; it was developed by the Russians and later copied by the Chinese. It was based on ultraspecialization of some universities; they established universities devoted exclusively to telephone technology and railroad engineering, for example. The results have been singularly unimpressive.

Yet times have changed. A new realism about costs — and the public obligation to restrain them — has made most universities question whether they should continue those programs or departments whose work is not prized and whose classes are sparsely attended. Cornell closed its nursing school after a century of service because of declining federal support and duplication of the program in other universities. Columbia has closed its library school, geography, and linguistics departments; Rochester, its doctoral program in mathematics; Georgetown, its dental school. Meanwhile, other universities across the nation have phased out departments or reassigned the budget lines of retiring faculty to new fields so that new appointments can be made without net additions to the faculty. Indeed, it is now individual retirements or reduction of programs and departments that provides the funds to establish the new and vital programs. This approach is healthy only as long as it is not pursued simply as a cost-cutting exercise without making educational judgments.

Should universities close down departments of classics and music, for instance, because they do not draw enough tuition-paying students to cover their full costs? I don't think that answer is easy, even when we acknowledge that all universities must gain better control of costs. My own view is that America needs to maintain a small group of truly world-class, comprehensive universities, even if they carry some "money-losing" programs. There surely comes a time when some departments should reconsider their focus or should be reduced in size; but research universities should be slow to eliminate all faculty positions — and all possibility for undergraduate study — in a discipline that has been in our bones for centuries. A society that traces many of its values back to Greece and Rome should think carefully before it severs its links to those civilizations. A society facing intense economic competition from the countries of the Pacific Rim should think twice before dismantling Asian studies. I was once at a lunch in Chicago when a proud father told me his daughter had recently graduated from Cornell with a joint major in economics and Japanese studies. "That's the weirdest combination I ever heard," observed another table partner. "Maybe so," replied the father, "but she had real problems choosing between three different job offers in Tokyo. She's now over there with a major U.S. bank." That's the benefit of linkage.

But suppose America's leading universities set out to reduce their costs at all costs. Suppose they appointed less qualified (and therefore less expensive) professors, eliminated some course offerings, reduced library book and journal purchases, deferred building renovation or laboratory modernization, limited health or other student services, became commuter schools, and cut out financial aid. Most would regard that, not as a brave step forward, but as an irresponsible step back. The leading universities are great institutions, faithfully established over the years. Supported by generations of benefactors, they are among the world's greatest centers of learning. In a world increasingly dependent on expert knowledge, critical skills, new discovery, and highly educated people, such actions would represent an abdication of responsibility.

Some critics cry for just this "stripped down" university. But to reduce the nation's leading institutions to the "stripped down" version — scores of which already exist — would be an act of moral abdication. Such new cut-price, discount, no-frills institutions would offer not only fewer courses, less student support, and less professional training; they would be open only to the wealthy. Then the charge of elitism might be justified. Nor is it just the promising youth from lower-income homes, underrepresented minority families, and inner city neighborhoods who would be denied the benefits of the best education there is. The nation at large would lose the expert leadership, critical skills, professional services, and new knowledge on which its future depends.

OPTION 4: ELIMINATE TENURE?

There is one other popular suggestion for reducing costs: *eliminate tenure.* Tenure "perpetuates deadwood," "rewards incompetence," supports "overpaid and underworked" professors. It produces inflexibility, reduces accountability, and increases costs. That's the way the arguments go.

On the other side, the arguments are equally strident, for tenure has its passionate defenders. It is to many faculty members what the divine right of kings once was to kings: inherent in the nature of the professoriate, essential to impartial scholarship, vital to academic freedom, and obviously beneficial to the community.

To question it is, to such people, an act of high treason. To challenge it is to threaten the bulwark on which the integrity of the academy depends. These assertions are not frivolous, nor are they entirely self-serving. Nor are they applied only to the academic profession. The impartiality of members of the Supreme Court, for example, is guaranteed by just such tenure, and its public benefits are great. The freedom of governing boards of public universities — whether elected or appointed — is reinforced by long-term appointments of their members, typically for eight years. Such long-term appointments not only provide protection against external pressures — political or academic — but also encourage long-term thinking and responsibility.

It is not the benefits of tenure that are in question, but rather its liabilities, and especially the institutional inflexibility to which it leads and the lack of individual responsibility and professional accountability it sometimes allows. If university leaders and faculty advocates have been quick to defend the benefits of tenure, they have been slow to address its liabilities. Both require consideration.

But why does tenure continue to be such a contentious issue? After all, only about 25 percent of the nation's 1.2 million college and university teachers are tenured, and even that tenure is seen by many to be withering under its own economic weight. Of the current full-time untenured faculty, for example, only about 40 percent are eligible to be considered for it, down from about 60 percent two decades ago. And almost half of four-year faculty and 65 percent of two-year faculty are part-time![14] So if tenure is eroding, why the continuing public complaints that tenure undermines accountability and limits productivity, and why the attempts by boards of regents of some large state universities to end or modify the system?[15] I think there might be several reasons. One is that the academic community has done a poor job of explaining not only why tenure exists, but why it should be preserved. To the standard response that tenure is essential to defend academic freedom, some ask why the 75 percent of the teaching force who are untenured are denied the same protection. And anyway, they add, isn't the existence of the First Amendment adequate protection for everyone who teaches, without the need for tenure?

Another reason for public concern is that the so-called elite universities, though not all the so-called elite colleges, are heavily tenured and show few signs of changing that arrangement, being unmoved, it seems, by the trend to appoint part-timers. The typical Ivy League university, for example, may have as many as 80–90 percent of its faculty tenured. In the best public research universities, the ratio is also generally high, much higher than the figures quoted above may suggest.

So how do these universities and others defend tenure? Perhaps it was never easy to defend it. Certainly, it is less easy now that the federal government has removed the possibility of mandatory retirement at some fixed age: 65 or 70, for example. Effectively now, tenure at, say, age 35 offers a guarantee of lifelong employment. It offers even more, its critics add: it offers faculty members both freedom and support to select a narrow field of study, to provide the most modest teaching services, and to please themselves about their hours, their job, their vacations, even the most basic responsibilities for which they are paid. In short, tenure entitles faculty to do anything they please, with congenial colleagues, a country-club-like campus environment, a reasonably generous salary, and benefits that range from reduced tuition for their children to subsidized concerts, plays, and athletic facilities.

How can one possibly defend such a system? I do so with some difficulty. I also admit that for the reasons I've just discussed, it may be a system whose time has passed. But let me explain why, on balance, I still prefer a mixed system of appointment that would include the option of tenure. Over the years, tenure has proved a remarkably effective way to support and retain the work of the best minds in the world. I want to keep Wayne Isom, Mary Sansalone, John Hsu, and Walter LaFeber in the university. And I want to keep them because in this setting they can share their skills with younger scholars, expand their own expertise, and increase human understanding by their practice, scholarship, and research. Wayne Isom could triple his salary in private surgical practice. John Hsu could prosper as a concert performer and musical director. Mary Sansalone could leave tomorrow for a successful professional career in civil engineering. Walter LaFeber could have a brilliant career as a full-time author, professional lecturer, and consultant. But we need them to share their gifts with the rising generation of younger scholars and professionals. A tenured appointment provides the stability and security to ensure that. If you don't keep Wayne Isom in the university, where do you turn for the next generation of cardiac surgeons? If Mary Sansalone devotes herself to private practice, who will ensure the competence of bridge designers in thirty years' time?

But doesn't tenure also shelter the less eminent, even the lazy? Yes, it does, in some cases. But not, I think, in very many, and I'd pay that price to keep the future John Hsus and Walter LaFebers. I admit that's a judgment and not all will agree. I also admit that the tenure system illustrates that universities are not efficient places, in the sense in which that term is used in industrial productivity: they are not "operated" in a structured and direct way. They're more like an orchestra than a factory. Perhaps even more like a jazz band, with its improvisation. That lack of direction is deliberate. You don't obtain fresh insight by command; you don't dictate new discovery by executive decision. Universities, and the teaching, discovery, and service they provide, depend on the skills of the individual, the contribution of the loner and the cussedly independent. Independence, scholarship, commitment: those are the qualities universities seek in their faculty members. As long as the university exists to further knowledge and its humane application, those will remain the requirements.

Tenure allows freedom; it protects the heretical suggestion and the unthinkable hypothesis; it safeguards against the tyranny of orthodoxy, whether of internal forces like political correctness or external political pressure; it guarantees a hearing for the idea that is unpopular, unfashionable, or perhaps just ahead of its time. I do not argue that it is the *only* way to provide this protection; but I do argue that it is a demonstrably effective way.

Now that I have made the case, let me qualify it.

If universities are to continue to justify tenure, the process of achieving it must be very demanding. It already is in our best universities. It requires a terminal, professional, or doctoral degree. There may be 50–200 applicants for each advertised appointment. The successful candidate serves a six- or seven-year probationary period, broken into a three- and a four-year contract, separated by an interim review. He or she is paid a generally modest salary and then faces a comprehensive, rigorous review of his or her teaching, research, and service. This review is searching, demanding, extensive, and more or less public. Student critiques, faculty evaluations, expert outside opinions, teaching performance, published work, campus contributions — all these are reviewed and assessed. And the success rate is not high, ranging from about 20 percent to 60 percent. The winnowing that takes place in faculty appointment and tenure decisions is deliberate, effective, demanding, and severe. I believe it should be.

After tenure is awarded, the university should require periodic, say five-year, reviews, with a formal self-assessment and personal professional plan for the next five years, contributed by the professor. This would not jeopardize tenure once awarded, but it would provide accountability and would be beneficial to the future professional development of the individual. Personal interests and commitments change over the years; fields of study develop and mature; departmental and university needs evolve. Regular post-tenure reviews would bring these institutional changes into harmony with individual goals. Further promotion from associate professor to professor, merit salary increases, and teaching assignments should all be based on these reviews. The reviews should involve internal colleagues, members of other departments in related areas, and perhaps members of the standing external review committee of the department. Periodic post-tenure review of this kind for all faculty members would be time-consuming. It would, however, be time well spent.

An alternative solution would be to require reviews for any faculty member who does not receive a salary increase, who fails to publish over a certain period, or who receives successive negative teaching evaluations. Since the University of Hawaii adopted this practice, 17 percent of those faculty members scheduled for such review have resigned or retired, another 20 percent of those faculty members who underwent such review have resigned or retired, while another 20 percent received remedial plans. Grant or contract activity increased 12–15 percent in the same period, though it is not clear that this is the result of post-tenure review. Why then do I not accept this as an alternative approach? Because it allows review only of the "failures"; the "successes" can also benefit greatly from constructive review and advice.

Another aspect of tenure deserves some discussion: there is no necessary connection between a guaranteed appointment and a guaranteed salary. The present typical — perhaps universal — arrangement is for the salary of a faculty member to be "guaranteed" at the previous annual level, plus some modest increase. This expectation is generally unrelated to any clear and specific performance criteria.

It is time to unbundle tenure and compensation. I believe two changes are needed. The first is the development of personal and departmental performance benchmarks defined by agreement and including not only teaching effectiveness and productivity but also research and professional service. A recent court case emphasizes that in the eyes of at least one respected university (Northwestern), tenure involves a guarantee of an appointment, but not a salary.[16] But the overall purpose of these salary reviews should be not to punish but to improve performance and assist professional development.

The second change I believe would be useful is that individual compensation and the departmental "pool" should be subdivided into a base salary, say that of entry-level associate professor or professor, and an incentive component, based on institutional and departmental goals and priorities. The fringe benefits — sabbatic leaves, research and teaching assistantships, lab space, travel support, study leave, and so on — should also be used as incentives rather than taken for granted as entitlements.

One of the ironies of the present tenure system is that, though it was designed to encourage faculty members to challenge prevailing wisdom and conventional assumptions, it has become increasingly disciplinary-based, rewarding what is sometimes "production line" scholarship in conventional fields, rather than promoting creative, crosscutting research that challenges existing concepts and norms. One antidote to this is the regular participation of review committee members from outside the particular discipline involved.

Tenure should be one of several career options available to a faculty member. In a 1995 study of faculty attitudes conducted by the Higher Education Institute of the University of California, Los Angeles, more than a third of the 34,000 professors interviewed agreed "strongly" or "somewhat" that "tenure is an outmoded concept."[17] Asked in the same survey whether "tenure attracts the best to academe," only 54.3 percent agreed that it did. What other, nontenure options might be offered? Term contracts of perhaps three or five years; improved salary and/or perhaps benefits or scholarly support for those accepting nontenured, shorter-term, rolling appointments; substantial salaries and perhaps benefits for part-time faculty, and so on. But would such options be likely to attract the best candidates? There is some evidence that they already do, as the present number of poorly paid, part-time faculty attest, though I regard the salaries paid to many of them as irresponsibly low. At Rutgers, for example, the average assistant professor makes $46,015 a year, plus benefits, to teach six courses. The average pay for a part-time adjunct professor is $3,000 per course — or $18,000 for six courses — and no medical benefits.[18] In 1997, the newly created Florida Gulf Coast University had 4,000 applications for 120 positions it advertised — none of them tenured. Faculty members there will be offered three- or five-year contracts.[19]

But if such arrangements are attractive, why not extend the Florida Gulf Coast experiment and abolish tenure everywhere? Because this alternative has yet to prove as effective in providing a long-term supportive teaching, research, and service environment as does the traditional tenure system. That is why I favor a mixed appointment system.

Brent Staples comments, "Tenure does not guarantee vibrant and resourceful teaching. But the 'invisible faculty' system that is replacing it precludes the stability that makes the best teaching at least possible. Colleges need to find the midpoint between faculties that grow stale and stay in place no matter what and faculties of migrants dashing to and from their cars."[20] That seems to me to be a sensible approach to the problem.

Finally, I would require a Socratic Oath, the professorial equivalent of the

Hippocratic Oath that every young physician is required to swear before embarking on the practice of medicine. Patients committing their future to the hands of a surgeon have the assurance that the doctor has bound himself to a stringent and demanding level of practice, defined in the Hippocratic Oath. This is the physicians' ethical pledge to the patient. Why should students, committing four years, thousands of dollars, and their future livelihood to a university professor, expect any less commitment?

It might be argued that this is unnecessary; that it is implicit in the professor's role. Implicit it is; but explicit it is not, and so abuses exist unchecked. In other professions — law and medicine, for example — professional "guilds" such as the American Bar Association, state boards, the American Medical Association, and professional medical college boards monitor and regulate the conduct of their members. The ironic feature of the academic profession, as Frank Kermode has pointed out, is that scholarly disciplinary guilds and associations, which exercise virtually no control over their individual members' conduct, nevertheless command greater allegiance from their members than does the academic "profession" in which their members are employed. Furthermore, some of these professional guilds — from landscape architecture to accounting — monitor and accredit the institutions that employ their members.

So I'd have university presidents invite members of the faculty to develop such a draft oath. It must begin there to be accepted there. I'd discuss it from college to college; share it with others; engage the scholarly and professional societies in its development; consult students, alumni, trustees, and others in its refinement; revise it in extensive consultation; but ultimately have the faculty and board of trustees adopt it, require it, and enforce it. No professor should teach without endorsing an equivalent pledge.

Here's a first draft, presented in the hope of stimulating a wider discussion of the scope and content of such an oath.

A Socratic Oath for Faculty of Research Universities

I hereby devote myself to the advancement and extension of knowledge, recognizing that I have an obligation to my students, to my discipline, to my professional colleagues, to my university, and to the public.

I embark on teaching as a moral vocation. I recognize research and scholarship as a public trust and accept professional service as a societal obligation. In pursuing my responsibilities, I will devote to both teaching and research the same sustained, imaginative, and rigorous attention. I will pursue new knowledge and creative activities in a scrupulous manner that befits the high-

est professional standards in my field. And I will play my full part in service to the larger community. In undertaking these tasks I recognize that teaching, research, and public service are the fundamental responsibilities of every faculty member of the university; that they are responsibilities that must be continuously balanced; and that while they are responsibilities of comparable importance, teaching lies at the heart of the mission of the university.

Toward this end, I will accept the trust that the transmission of knowledge implies so that accuracy, fairness, balance, and integrity are exemplified in the way my subject is presented and arguments are handled. I will present my subject, whatever it may be, with rigor, but also in a liberal spirit, "illustrating the general within the particular," with a breadth of outlook and a humane concern for its foundations, context, relationships, and implications.

I will respect the integrity of the relationship between professor and student, in both personal and intellectual terms, so that hucksterism or improper advocacy are as unthinkable as abuse or harassment. I will be scrupulous in preparation for class, discussion, laboratory, or other exercises and supervise the same scrupulous preparation of any student teaching assistants who might assist me. I will be objective, rigorous, and fair in student evaluation, and I will be available for student conferences, office hours, laboratory sessions, and other formal contacts outside the lecture room.

Finally, I will participate in the life of the university community, cooperating with my colleagues in educational endeavors and participating in campus-wide activities. And, as I develop in my own career, I will encourage, help, and mentor my colleagues, especially those newly appointed, to become effective teachers and successful scholars.

This vow, which I freely take, I will keep, recognizing that the privilege of academic freedom that is entrusted to me carries with it the obligation of professional responsibility to honor and serve my students, my discipline, my profession, my colleagues, my university, and the larger society.

I would require such an oath of all those who are appointed to the faculty, and I would make the administration of the oath a public ceremony, a formal inaugural event at a university-wide convocation, held at the opening of the academic year. As in medicine, so in the university at large: all those who are already practitioners — the rest of the faculty — would also recommit themselves to this pledge.

If this oath is thoughtfully developed, and if faculty members are willing to pledge themselves to this high standard, tenure will take its rightful place.

To adopt the oath will lift the sights of the faculty and elevate teaching standards. It will rekindle community.

The Best (Imperfect) Solution

I see no way to avoid price increases, but they can be held near (though not necessarily at) the level of inflation if university administrators establish clear priorities and have the willpower to pursue them. Growing competition is likely to encourage such willpower. Universities must radically change the way tuition is set, and they must be ready to face the consequences — including reduction of the campus workforce. Instead of planning the ideal budget for the coming year and then setting tuition high enough to cover expenses, almost all universities are now reversing that sequence. That process is counterintuitive. Many businesses would not make such a decision if sales were brisk. Well, "sales" at the best universities are very brisk — with seven or eight applicants for each freshman place, several dozen for each place in many graduate areas, and several hundred for each place in some professional schools — but they still have a responsibility to control prices.

Linked to this new budgeting approach should be a strategic planning process that involves all constituencies, on and off campus, in identifying the university's most important goals and priorities. Clear identification of goals and priorities makes it easier to make hard choices — provided that the university's leadership has the willpower to live by those goals and priorities.

If strict tuition control is a priority, for instance, and an adequate financial aid program is also a priority, then some expenses must be excised from the budget in order to meet both. If very competitive faculty salaries are also a priority, it becomes more likely that the *number* of faculty and/or staff will have to be reduced. And that, in turn, will mean fewer classes or larger classes or increased teaching loads.

Each university must decide its own priorities for the future and develop its own methods. What they all must accept, though, is that any good faith effort to control tuition will require real reductions not only in programs but also in staff, who typically account for about 60 percent of expenditures. If this process is undertaken promptly, with wide consultation, adequate notice, careful planning, and humane implementation before large deficits loom, it may be carried out without wrenching consequences.

There is some evidence that this approach is already reducing the rate of increase of college costs. The 1997 National Commission on the Cost of

Higher Education, appointed by the Congress, heard evidence from one of its members, Martin Anderson — one of higher education's sternest critics, and author of *Imposters in the Temple* — that the cost of attending public universities grew by 37 percent from 1987 to 1990, by 40 percent from 1990 to 1993, but by only 3 percent between 1993 and 1996.

"There is a lot wrong with higher education — I even wrote a book about it," concluded Anderson, "but the one thing that colleges can't be accused of is gouging the public."[21]

There are those on the campus who will immediately complain that firm-minded cost control is a recipe for disaster, that excellence will inevitably be compromised, that "academic quality" will rapidly be undermined. It does not take long for the impartial observer to conclude that the academic appetite is insatiable. The characteristic culture of the campus is to demand more: more technical support, more faculty positions, more clerical assistance, more academic programs, more scholarly journals, more facilities, more research centers, more teaching resources, more of everything, in fact. This persistent, and sometimes shrill, demand for more is not a reflection of the fact that academics display a greater sense of selfishness, greed, or acquisitiveness than do their fellows. It seems to me rather to reflect a sincere conviction that they can offer "more for more," as Gilbert Whittaker has described it. Because expertise within a fully comprehensive discipline is never complete, because the richness of the student experience can be improved by a greater selection of course offerings, because improvement in quality of research can be expected from better equipment, or better performance from new facilities, they see it as their scholarly and moral obligation to become advocates for more. But the growing disparity between family income and tuition levels cannot continue unchecked. If universities do not themselves put a brake on rapid cost escalation, others, less informed and less sympathetic to their mission, will do it for them, as the experience of the nation's hospitals and physicians amply demonstrates.

I believe such efforts can and must be made if our universities are to remain sound and respected, and biting the bullet by establishing tuition limits — before allocating budget expenses — is the place to start.

But even this approach is not a panacea, except, perhaps, in the short term. For if universities do not make technological breakthroughs in teaching, they will in time again face the same challenge of controlling costs that rise faster than general inflation. However lean they make themselves and however committed to efficiency, the leading universities will retain some "inefficiencies" inherent in their nature.

The Transitional Nature of Progress

Most research universities have not yet adopted serious strategic planning programs. Nevertheless, they have taken steps proving they recognize the need for changes that will affect costs.

These efforts are not heroic — just realistic. They acknowledge that government support of universities is unlikely to return to the generous levels that followed World War II. They accept that, in spite of this, university pricing has become more of a public question than ever before. And they reflect the death of the old argument that universities are fundamentally different from business; universities may not turn a profit, but they certainly have to honor the bill payers.

As people of goodwill, on and off campus, strive to keep universities both great and affordable, it is worth remembering that a million-dollar house may be a great value, even a bargain. To the practiced shopper the reasons for the price are obvious in its location, size, construction, amenities, and quality of materials and infrastructure. But — bargain though it may be — it may still be unaffordable to the average buyer.

This is the challenge universities face in these transitional times: in the quest to bring prices under control, they must be cautious not to weaken the quality of their product, which remains the best in the world. There remains the risk that the call to cut back may ultimately become a call to downgrade. It can all too easily become a call not for increased access but for reduced access; a call not for high aspirations but for mediocrity; a call that, in the name of equality and economy, imposes the equality of dreary uniformity and the economy of lost opportunity. Economies there must be, but excellence must not be compromised, and excellence rarely comes cheaply.

RESEARCH
A PUBLIC TRUST

Research universities conduct research. They are not alone in this; industry, government, the Pentagon, financial analysts, and marketing specialists all conduct research, too. But research universities are different. They also teach students. They are unique in another respect: university researchers — the faculty — please themselves, literally please themselves, about the research they do. They select the area that interests them. They define it. They choose some aspect of it and decide how they want to pursue it. They decide how to spend their time on it; how to cooperate in it; how to interpret, share, and communicate their work; and how to use their conclusions. No one tells them what to study (unlike industry). No agency requires them to work within a plan, in a particular way (unlike a federal research lab). No superior sets targets, deadlines, or secrecy requirements (unlike the Pentagon). No one suggests their research has to be profitable in the long term (unlike financial analysts) or even useful in a specific sense (unlike marketing specialists). All the university expects is that faculty members will be self-starters, inquiring scholars, creative practitioners, and that they will go on learning, creating, and producing throughout their professional lives. That is the expectation for every faculty member, for philosophers as well as physicists, for sociologists as well as surgeons and sculptors. In fact, when we think of research, we typically think of work in science and technological fields, but research and the spirit of inquiry it requires permeate the whole of the modern research university — the arts, the humanities, and the social sciences, no less than scientific, technological and professional fields.

This macro view of research does not mean that the activity itself is random. Far from it. The individual researcher, and increasingly in science the team of which he or she is a part, plans a research strategy with meticulous care and painstaking attention. If the results of research are unpredictable, the pursuit of research is systematic, methodical, even plodding. But for all that, there is still a measure of informed hunch, of thoughtful intuition, of inspired guess and aesthetic insight. There is also a stern test of accountability, both at the time of initial funding and at the time of publication of the results. Whatever the source of funding and whatever the place of publication, the merit of the proposed research and the validity of its conclusions are judged by peer review. This is one of the great strengths of American science.

Almost every aspect of our day-to-day existence is touched by some research activity on the campus. Some work — the development of new nutritional guidelines, let's say, or a new therapeutic regime, or a new diagnostic procedure — will have immediate significance for many. But other work may have more limited appeal and more restricted impact: the composition of a new piece of electronic music or the discovery of a new fossil species, for example.

The research university supports all of this, supplying time in which the work is undertaken; space, including the most sophisticated laboratories; support facilities, including huge libraries (typically of five or six million volumes), studios, museums, data banks, schools, theaters, and hospitals; equipment, including supercomputers, radio-telescopes, and oceangoing vessels; assistance, including technicians, secretaries, and graduate research assistants; and general supplies. And it does all this without, in most cases, elaborate application and approval procedures on individual projects (though it does, of course, require these for experiments involving human subjects and for major new instrumentation or facilities); without project deadlines; without any real institutional scrutiny of short-term individual progress. It bases its support, which accounts for a substantial fraction of its budget, on the conviction that individual research prospers in an atmosphere of maximum freedom of inquiry and minimal red tape. That involves an act of faith, based on a wealth of positive results — including, but hardly limited to, the discovery of the Salk polio vaccine, the widely used Pap test for cervical cancer, skin grafts for burn victims, artificial wrists and artificial knees, synthetic insulin and several common antibiotics, and the standard malaria-preventive pill. From the first digital computer to today's supercomputers, from advances in rocketry that literally got America's space program off the ground to design codes that keep concrete buildings and bridges from falling down, from the economics of regional development to insights about early childhood development that led to the establishment of Head Start for children — basic research at America's universities has produced positive results. Indeed, no other country relies on the universities for the conduct of basic research to the extent that America does. Much of that research is supported by the federal government, based on the bipartisan conviction that it serves the national interest. Federal support does involve detailed planning, budgeting, deadlines, and peer scrutiny, of course. But even here, it is chiefly the individual investigator who initiates new proposals.

Under the Microscope

Yet the underlying conviction that the public benefits most by supporting the private curiosity of individual scholars at research universities is now under scrutiny. Research, it is argued by some, takes too much time away from teaching; or it is too costly; or it is inconsequential. Others claim it is too consequential, that bioengineering poses health hazards, such as those supposed to arise from the use of bovine growth hormone to increase milk supply in dairy herds. Still others argue that it is too freewheeling, too unplanned, that only "strategic" science, for example, deserves support.

Whom should we believe? Has an arrangement from which we have gained so much social benefit during the past 120 years, and particularly the half century or so since the end of World War II, outlived its usefulness? Is the disciplined pursuit of private curiosity at the university a luxury society can no longer afford? Is there, in short, a better way?

To answer this question, I believe we must go beyond generalities and consider the particulars; that is, we must consider how some of the greatest scientific discoveries of our century developed. Consider, for example, some of the breakthroughs in biotechnology.

Behind the Front-Page News

Breakthroughs in biotechnology have become almost standard front-page news as researchers identify genes that produce lethal diseases; engineer hardier, more adaptable crops; and develop new products, new medical technologies, and new therapeutic drugs by manipulating and recombining genetic material. Herds of dairy cattle are being injected with a genetically engineered growth hormone so that they will produce more milk. Strawberries are being bred with a gene that enables them to resist frost damage. Tomatoes are being developed that ripen without rotting.[1]

Perhaps most striking are the implications of biotechnology for human health. The human genome has now been mapped, an achievement announced jointly by then-president Bill Clinton and Prime Minister Tony Blair on June 27, 2000. This and some of the most remarkable recent advances in medical diagnosis and therapy result from the discovery of the structure of DNA by a young American named James Watson and his senior British collaborator, Francis Crick. These and subsequent studies by other researchers deciphered the genetic code that living cells use to translate the sequence of bases in the molecular "rungs" of the helical strands of DNA into the mass production of proteins. "Incorrect" pairing of these bases tends to cause a cell to produce either a "wrong" protein or a "wrong" amount of protein, and this often results in a disease. A single mismatched base may be sufficient to cause a disease, such as sickle cell anemia. These mismatches or genetic errors are thought to be responsible for three thousand or more hereditary diseases, including cystic fibrosis, Duchenne muscular dystrophy, and Huntington disease, as well as influencing cancer, heart disease, diabetes, and other maladies. The forty-six chromosomes in the nucleus of a human cell represent about six feet of DNA strands, made up of three billion base pairs. Clearly, the possibilities for mismatched bases are considerable, and it is estimated that as many as half the human population will develop a hereditary disease, arising from the interaction of this genetic predisposition with environmental and lifestyle factors.

Subsequent studies have made it possible to use so-called restriction enzymes to snip long DNA sequences into smaller fragments which can then be isolated and identified. In this way, the distinctive gene sequences of individuals suffering from specific inherited diseases can be confirmed. More than fifty such disease genes have been identified, including those listed above, as well as genes for some types of Alzheimer's disease, breast cancer, and colon cancer. For example, the genes that cause one form of colon cancer (hereditary nonpolyposis Colouchal cancer, HNPCC) were identified, their sequence analyzed, and tests for them developed. It is thought that as many as one in two hundred Americans carry one or the other of the two mismatched genes, so genetic screening can identify those at risk, allowing more effective preventative or therapeutic treatment, long before symptoms appear. In some cases, including cystic fibrosis and Duchenne muscular dystrophy, experimental treatments have been developed to correct or replace the faulty genes that produce the diseases.

The results of this technology have already been spectacular in some diseases. A prenatal screening program for the gene responsible for a fatal neurological disorder — Tay-Sachs disease — led to a twentyfold reduction in the incidence of the disease in the Baltimore area, for example. Not all hereditary diseases thus identified are yet treatable — Alzheimer's disease, for example — but the completion of the Human Genome Project, which has mapped and described the complete sequence of human DNA, some one hundred thousand genes, offers hope that those individuals carrying genes for inherited diseases may benefit from early detection, preventative treatment, and possibly repair or replacement of the faulty gene.

So great is the promise of the Human Genome Project for developing new drugs and medical techniques that private investment now exceeds the $165 million that the federal government is spending on the project each year. And despite intense competition from other nations, the U.S. remains the world leader in biotechnology, with significant, positive impact on our balance of trade.

America's preeminence in biotechnology did not just happen, however. It grew out of basic research in genetics and molecular and cell biology, much of it conducted in universities in this country and in Europe a generation and more ago. What is noteworthy about this research is that its medical benefits — great though they are — were not the goal of most of the basic studies that subsequently made them possible. The basic studies in the 1960s and 1970s that led to the understanding of the genetic code and its hereditary mechanisms, for example, were mostly aimed at a series of unrelated issues, such as the mechanism by which bacteria resist viral invasion. It was only later that their transforming medical benefits were understood. That kind of serendipity has characterized the history of scientific discovery again and again. Only in rare cases have the beneficial applications of the most significant discoveries in basic science been foreseen.

The Discovery of DNA — At Cambridge

"We wish to suggest a structure of the salt deoxyribonucleic acid (DNA). This structure has novel features which are of considerable biological interest." So opened the now-famous paper, published in *Nature* on April 25, 1953, in which Francis Crick and James Watson, working in the Medical Research Council laboratories in Cambridge, England, described the double helix structure of the molecule of life — a structure that suggested a way that genetic material might be copied and passed from cell to cell and generation to generation, and eventually snipped apart, rearranged, and put back into living cells in order to achieve specific results.

"The discovery of the structure [of DNA] by Crick and Watson, with all its biological implications, has been one of the major scientific events of this century," wrote Sir Lawrence Bragg, whose X-ray method of studying crystal structure developed forty years before was at the heart of Crick and Watson's discovery. "The number of researches it has inspired is amazing; it has caused an explosion in biochemistry which has transformed science." (His words ring even more true today, when biotechnology is on its way to becoming a multibillion-dollar industry, than they did when he wrote them in 1968, when the practical applications of Crick and Watson's discovery were still in their infancy.)

But the story of Watson and Crick's search for the structure of DNA is instructive as much for the process involved as for the scientific significance of the result. They did not set out with the goal of establishing a new industry or a major aid to human health or agricultural productivity. Their work involved blind alleys, wrong turns, dead ends. It involved transatlantic competition, personal passion, and ambition among the principals, who, in addition to Crick and Watson, included Maurice Wilkins and Rosalind Franklin of Kings College, London, and Linus Pauling, who was pursuing his own line of research at CalTech. It involved intergenerational partnerships between professors and students. It involved the piecing together of information from a variety of disciplines — structural chemistry, crystallography, genetics, even quantum mechanics — and relating it to the work at hand. And it involved what might seem to some a substantial waste of time.

The morning after the discovery of the double helix, Watson recalled that he awoke feeling marvelously alive. "I slowly walked toward the Clare Bridge, staring up at the gothic pinnacles of the King's College Chapel that stood out sharply against the spring sky. I briefly stopped and looked over the perfect Georgian features of the recently cleaned Gibbs Building, thinking that much of our success was due to the long uneventful periods when we walked among the colleges or unobtrusively read the new books that came into Heffer's Bookstore."[2]

But if Crick and Watson's work at Cambridge provided the foundation of basic knowledge on which biotechnology rests, it was the work of a Stanford professor of biochemistry that led to the first work in the field of genetic engineering.

The Birth of Genetic Engineering — At Stanford

Paul Berg is a Nobel Prize–winning professor of biochemistry who might have learned more about his father's garment business than about the nature of genetic engineering had it not been for the clever prodding of a high school science club adviser at Abraham Lincoln High School in Brooklyn, N.Y., fifty years ago.[3]

"One rarely got a straight answer from her," said Berg, now considered "the father of genetic engineering" and director of the Beckman Center for Molecular and Genetic Medicine at Stanford. "If you asked a question, she would ask you a question back or give you a lead as to how you might find out what you wanted to know." This teaching approach helped foster in students a natural curiosity and confidence in digging for an answer on their own.

The question Berg pursued, after joining the faculty at Stanford, was "Why do some cells turn cancerous?" He quietly pursued it in the laboratory for years. Then one day he did something no one had ever done before. As the Royal Swedish Academy of Sciences said in naming him co-winner of the 1980 Nobel Prize in chemistry, he became "the first investigator to construct a recombinant DNA molecule, i.e., a molecule containing parts of DNA from different species."

In other words, Berg was the first to demonstrate how scientists could transplant or splice genes from one organism into another — in essence, kicking off genetic engineering. After his discovery, he also took the lead in addressing ethical concerns about the new technology, among other things by presiding over the 1975 Asilomar Conference which gathered 134 scientists from around the world to agree upon a set of regulations for genetic engineering experiments.

What resulted from Berg's foray into DNA recombination is nothing less than the field of biotechnology, one of the most promising new industries in the world. Economically, it is projected to become as large as the computer industry, Berg says. Medically, as we have seen, it holds out the hope of genetic cures for numerous diseases and has the potential to radically alter the practice of medicine as we know it. "Indeed, most — perhaps all — human disease results from the inappropriate gene structures that alter or prevent normal cellular functions," Berg says. "These discoveries and the promise of others to come have profound implications for the future of medicine, for they have placed us at the threshold of new methods of diagnosis, prevention and treatment of human disease."

Socially, there also are many implications that will stem from the new information being made available through genetic screening. Being able to know one's predisposition to major diseases will have consequences, for example, in the areas of health care, insurance, government regulations, and employment.

Looking back on the host of new developments that have followed from the experiment he conducted in his laboratory some twenty years ago, Berg says he never envisioned this result. But that is not unusual in university research. "One of the great things about science," he says, "is you make a little opening and a lot of smart people out there see how it can help them solve their problems, of many of which you aren't even aware. The applications create ripples and then the whole thing explodes."

"The applications create ripples and then the whole thing explodes." That's been the pattern of research over the years. And the knowledge produced by genetic engineering — already of such immense importance in medicine, agriculture, manufacturing, and even in the understanding of life itself — exists because the Medical Research Council employed and supported Professor Francis Crick, the National Foundation for Infantile Paralysis supported a fellowship for graduate student James Watson at Cambridge, and Stanford supported faculty member Paul Berg. Because of that support, the future prospects for the human race have literally been transformed.

From Abstruse Questions to Laser Therapy

The physicists who carried out the early work on lasers were intrigued by basic questions about the interaction of molecules and magnetic spins with microwave and millimeter-wave radiation, and they wondered whether atoms or molecules could be used to generate such radiation. That, it might be argued, was a rather narrow and rarified interest — "very academic," perhaps — but its results have been far-reaching. Writing about the development of the laser, Nicholaas Bloembergen notes where such curiosity has led:

> The widespread commercial applications of lasers include their use in fiber optic communication systems, surgery and medicine, printing barcode readers, recording and playback of compact disks, surveying and alignment instruments, and many techniques for processing materials. Laser processing runs the gamut from sculpting corneas by means of excimer laser pulses to the heat treatment, drilling, cutting and welding of heavy metal parts in the automotive and shipbuilding industries by CO_2 lasers with continuous-wave outputs exceeding 10 kilowatts.... Lasers have revolutionized spectroscopy, and they have given birth to the new field of nonlinear optics. They are used extensively in many scientific disciplines, including chemistry, biology, astrophysics, geophysics and environmental sciences.[4]

From Basic Research to NMR

Fundamental questions also spurred the development of nuclear magnetic resonance (NMR) techniques, which were originally used to investigate nuclear properties but soon became powerful tools for other disciplines including structural chemistry, biochemistry, and, not least, medical imaging. Magnetic resonance imaging has revolutionized medical diagnosis, but it developed, not out of research in medical radiology, but out of what many would regard as esoteric research in basic physical science. Physicist George Pake, former provost at Washington University and former vice president for corporate research at Xerox, has noted:

> Magnetic resonance imaging could arise only out of non-directed research, not focused upon ultimate applications, that give rise to what we know today as NMR. The key was the series of basic quests to understand the magnetic moments of nuclear spins; to understand how these nuclear magnets interact in liquids, crystals and molecules; and to elucidate the structure of molecules of chemical interest. Out of these basic quests came the knowledge that enabled a vision of an imaging technique. Without the basic research, magnetic resonance imaging was unimaginable.[5]

America's Commitment to University Research

Research universities have proved to be such productive environments for creative work that it is easy to forget that they have not always been a feature of higher education in America. The colonial colleges, including Harvard, William and Mary, Columbia, Princeton, and Yale, were founded primarily as selective teaching institutions. In the nineteenth century, as the country was adjusting to the demands of independent nationhood, universities became more inclusive in their membership and more expansive in their scope. But except for the land-grant institutions established by the Morrill Act of 1862, which took on some additional responsibility for agricultural research and outreach, they remained primarily teaching institutions for the first three-quarters of the century.

That changed rapidly with the founding of Johns Hopkins University in 1876. Drawing heavily on the model of the German universities, with their emphasis on research, Hopkins's first president, Daniel Coit Gilman, brought together a faculty of scholars selected primarily because of their capacity for independent inquiry, pursued in the vigorous forum of the university. I believe that in his insistence on both independent inquiry and community Gilman identified the secret of the research university: community, inquiry, and breadth.

The Johns Hopkins approach, with its emphasis on scholarship, remains the predominant one at the American research university today, having been validated by the achievements of countless individual faculty members and the students they have trained. Not only have the overwhelming majority of the world's Nobel laureates conducted their prize-winning research at American universities, for example, but a remarkable number of laureates have studied with a prior Nobel laureate at an earlier stage of their career.

The value of basic research carried out in our universities is reflected in the extent to which basic research has been encouraged and supported by the federal government, particularly in the years since World War II. Recognizing the contributions that university scientists had made to the Allied victory — work that began at the turn of the century with new insights into the laws of physics, included the development of radar and the first computer, and culminated with the Manhattan Project that produced the first atomic bomb — President Franklin D. Roosevelt asked Vannevar Bush, longtime MIT faculty member, former president of the Carnegie Institution, and then director of the Office of Scientific Research and Development (the wartime agency for the mobilization of science), to suggest ways in which the power of science could be harnessed for the national good in times of peace.

In his report, *Science — The Endless Frontier* (1945), Bush wrote that "scientific progress is one essential key to our security as a nation, to our better health, to more jobs, to a higher standard of living, and to our cultural progress. . . . Without scientific progress no amount of achievement in other directions can insure our health, prosperity, and security as a nation in the modern world." He argued that "the simplest and most effective way in which the government can strengthen industrial research is to support basic research and to develop scientific talent."[6] His assessment set the stage for the establishment of the National Science Foundation and for a major federal investment in fundamental research at American colleges and universities. Because the government has embraced the dual aims that Vannevar Bush identified for university-based research — the discovery of new knowledge and the development of new talent — it has been willing to pay not only for the direct costs of the work (such as graduate student research assistants, major facilities such as telescopes and oceanographic survey ships, and laboratory equipment) but also part of the indirect costs (such as the library and the maintenance and operating costs of research buildings).

Why a 120-Year-Old Idea Works

Of course, not every basic research project has led to a major breakthrough, even with a lead time of a generation or more. Basic research is, by its nature, both high-risk and high-reward. But the pattern of basic research, much of it conducted in universities, leading to broadly applicable discoveries and inventions and even to paradigm shifts that have had profound commercial implications, is one that has been repeated time and again. Research is not a guarantee of economic success; that requires the ability of firms to capture and commercialize the results. But it is an absolute requirement for economic success.

Yet the benefits of basic research have rarely been predictable. There is a story told of Michael Faraday, perhaps the greatest experimental scientist of all time. Faraday had demonstrated his latest discovery, electromagnetic induction on which the dynamo depends, to Prime Minister Benjamin Disraeli and was asked what use it was. "As much use," he is said to have replied, "as a newborn babe." (There is also another version of this story in which Faraday is alleged to have replied, "Some day, sir, you may be able to tax it.") Years later, another British prime minister, Margaret Thatcher, remarked that Faraday's invention had generated more wealth than the entire capital represented by the London Stock Exchange. There are, it has been said, no useless discoveries; there are only those whose usefulness has yet to be discovered.

No one pretends that all university research is of equal merit, or every publication of equal consequence. No one argues that every discovery will enhance the quality of life or that every scholarly book contributes significantly to the richness of our culture. Nor does anyone assert, so far as I know, that all faculty members, at every stage of their professional lives, are as productive as they might be, however productivity is defined. What is claimed is that, on balance, this huge investment is a prudent and profitable one, that the benefits far outweigh the costs, both in direct results and in indirect benefits — the educational value for students associated with the activity.

For this reason, university research is widely supported, not only by funding from universities themselves, but also by all the major agencies of the federal government, by all the states, by industry on a considerable scale, by foundations, hospitals, churches, benevolent associations, public bodies, artistic groups, charitable trusts, and individual benefactors, investors, and clients. This pattern of widely based external support has existed for forty years or more. It represents a collective vote of confidence from a wide group of satisfied supporters.

The extent of this external funding is substantial. For example, in 1998 an estimated $26.3 billion was spent for research and development in America's universities and colleges. About $15.6 billion came from the federal government, about $4.9 billion from the academic institutions themselves, $2.1 billion from state and local governments, $1.8 billion from industry, and $1.8 billion from other sources. Of that total, an estimated 67 percent of the funding was concentrated in basic research, 25 percent was applied research, and 8 percent was development. The universities continue to perform over 50 percent of all basic research in the United States. Federal support as a proportion of the total has fallen from 65 percent in the early 1980s to less than 60 percent in 1997, being concentrated in three agencies: the National Institutes of Health (57 percent), the National Science Foundation (15 percent), and the Department of Defense (10 percent). Some 217,500 academic doctoral scientists and engineers are employed in the academic sector.

The extent of research funding in the leading universities is shown by the following expenditures for 1997:

Amount Spent for Research in U.S. Universities (in millions)[7]

University of Michigan, all campuses	Public	483
Johns Hopkins University	Private	421
University of Wisconsin-Madison	Public	420
Massachusetts Institute of Technology	Private	411
University of Washington-Seattle	Public	410
Johns Hopkins University Applied Physics Lab	Private	408
Stanford University	Private	395
University of California-San Diego	Public	378
University of California-Los Angeles	Public	375
Texas A&M University, all campuses	Public	367

America's larger confidence in the power of science has been well expressed by former vice president Al Gore. Speaking to the American Association for the Advancement of Science in 1996, he commented that for much of this century "Americans have benefited from a virtuous circle — a virtuous circle of science and success. As the nation generated wealth, a portion of that wealth was invested in research, science and technology. Those investments helped answer what seemed answerable — and eventually spawned still greater wealth, which was then invested in still more research. On and on it went. In this virtuous circle — launched with bipartisan agreement — prosperity generated investment, investment generated answers, and answers generated future prosperity."[8]

Research and Public Benefit

But it is one thing to claim that all this research activity is generally useful; it is quite another thing to prove that it makes any impact. Does it all add up to produce any real economic benefit? Consider the impact of just one research university: MIT. A 1997 study by the Bank Boston Economics Department,[9] the first to measure the job impact of a single research university, is based on an intensive study of MIT. It concludes, "If the companies founded by MIT graduates and faculty formed an independent nation, the revenues produced by the companies would make that nation the 24th largest economy in the world. The 4,000 MIT-related companies employ 1.1 million people and have annual world sales of $232 billion. That is roughly equal to a gross domestic product of $116 billion, which is a little less than the GDP of South Africa and more than the GDP of Thailand.

"Eighty percent of the jobs in MIT-related firms are in manufacturing (compared to 16 percent nationally) and a high percentage of products are exported. . . . The MIT-related companies have more than 8,500 plants in 50 states."[10]

Apart from quantifying this impact, two other conclusions of the report are of interest. First, innovation is not confined to graduates of any one major or discipline. Though the large majority of company founders are engineering graduates, architecture graduates founded more companies (171) than those in aeronautics (151), materials science (91), or life sciences (88), while those in the humanities (44) founded more than those in nuclear engineering (37), and those in political science (35) more than those in earth science (31).[11] So much for the fate of those graduating in "irrelevant and unemployable" disciplines.

All this creative entrepreneurial activity develops, not because MIT exists to create new industries, products, or companies, but because of the day-to-day experience of students learning together at a research university. That's why a second aspect of the report proves particularly useful — the record of interviews with company founders and their comments on how their experience as students at MIT influenced their subsequent careers. One founder summed it up this way: "I knew I was not going to work for big companies when I was about to leave MIT. I would rather take the risk of failure than the risk of becoming nobody. There must be many alumni who felt the same way I did.

"MIT offers great mentors (professors) and more opportunities (professors' consulting/research activities) for students to test the water in establishing their own businesses. MIT exposes students to cutting edge technologies and new ideas. . . . It seems to be quite natural that MIT becomes a cradle of entrepreneurs."[12]

"It's a 'hands on' place; if there's a problem, students are encouraged to go down to the basement, build the appropriate equipment, and develop a solution," another company founder observed.[13]

Another commented that "students get to work on 'real stuff' right in the middle of something big" — topics being argued about and worked on at that moment in the industrial world. Professors don't hesitate to work on real-world industrial problems. Other founders mentioned the importance of ties forged at MIT with fellow students who later became customers or co-founders.[14]

The larger impact of MIT is also characteristic — though sometimes to a lesser extent — of all research universities. Investment in research produces direct but unpredictable economic benefit. One of the problems in justifying support for basic research in terms of its economic importance is that its precise future usefulness is unpredictable. No one would have supposed, for example, that research on the operating mechanism of heart valves conducted at Berkeley would lead to the commercial development of the ink-jet printer a decade later. And few would have predicted that research at MIT on data compression would lead thirty years later to the development of the CD player.

But though unpredictable in detailed application, basic research in science has proved repeatedly to provide long-term human benefits. Take the GPS (Global Positioning System), for example, which is increasingly used to pinpoint any location on earth to within a hundred feet. GPS depends on a system of twenty-four Navstar satellites, each about the size of a large automobile, in orbit eleven thousand miles above the earth, each emitting coded signals and each containing four high-precision atomic clocks, accurate to a billionth of a second. Each satellite orbits the earth every twelve hours, and their spacing within the system insures that every point on the earth's surface is always "covered" by at least four satellites, from whose signals a small, hand-held receiver calculates latitude, longitude, altitude, and time by comparing the signal and the time transmitted by the satellite with its own time, and uses the difference between them to calculate its distance. With the aid of several such readings, the position of the receiver is calculated. Although first developed as a military device, GPS was made available to the public in 1996, and already its use has exploded to become a multibillion dollar industry. GPS receivers are being used for everything from rescue missions to measuring automobile traffic flow; from trucking and transportation to aircraft navigation and airport landing and controls systems; from mapping and surveying to earthquake monitoring. The receivers themselves can now be purchased by anyone for less than two hundred dollars.

The source of this huge new technology was a search not for an accurate positioning system but for an accurate clock, sufficiently precise to test Einstein's theory of relativity. The atomic clocks, now refined to an accuracy of within one second in one hundred thousand years, were developed on basic studies of the magnetic resonance of atoms — scarcely the stuff that could have been seen to lead to a new defense technology and later to a global system of precise navigation, available to any user for a few hundred dollars.[15]

What is true of the GPS is true of almost every other area of technology, from the study and control of ozone depletion to human gene testing and remediation. In almost every case, technology has been developed upon a foundation of basic science, carried out to resolve quite different questions and explore quite different phenomena.

The question of economic returns from investment in research, especially in science, is not an easy one, but various studies suggest that the rates are very high. Science, in the words of the 1993 White House policy document *Science in the National Interest,* is "an endless and sustainable resource with extraordinary dividends." The 1995 *Economic Report to the President* describes the "dramatic improvements in agricultural productivity, . . . successful new drugs, new treatments and new medical equipment" that have resulted from federal support of research. Joseph E. Stiglitz, of the President's Council of Economic Advisers, has suggested that, while the average rate of return on capital investment in the United States ranges from 10 to 14 percent, the private rate of return on research is some 2.5 to 25 percent, while the rate of return on research to society, rather than to the private investigator, may average as high as 50 to 60 percent. This is the rate of return to the nation as a whole.[16]

The Association of University Technology Managers (AUTM) has been collecting data on licensing activities by academic institutions in the U.S. and Canada for almost a decade. Its FY 1999 survey showed that academic discoveries were developed into health care products, software programs, agricultural products, and other new products — some 417 new products in all. Licenses on these discoveries generated $40.9 billion in economic activity and supported 270,900 jobs. At least 344 new companies based on an academic discovery were formed in FY 1999, some 82 percent of them in the state of the academic institution that licensed the discovery.[17]

But crude financial estimates may understate the human benefit and social impact that this return represents: the steady growth of knowledge and with it our growing ability to conquer disease, alleviate hunger, achieve technological progress in every area, and address the needs and ills of our society. And such estimates may not reflect the wider benefits of the personal commitment from which this larger public good is derived, as our universities, open to all who have the abilities to benefit from them, nurture in their graduates the knowledge and skills that enable them to play productive roles as citizens and to excel as individuals. No percentage return expresses the real riches that a society enjoys from such investments.

New Factors in University Research

Traditionally the federal government has awarded research funding to the nation's universities through merit-based competition, where research proposals are carefully reviewed by both the funding agencies and outside experts in relevant fields. This system, while not infallible, has ensured that by and large the most promising research, carried out by the most capable investigators, receives support.

Unfortunately, factors other than merit now play a significant role in the awarding of grant funds. Members of Congress have come to see federal research awards as a way to gain favor in their home districts, in much the same way they have viewed federal highway and water projects that they could bring back home. Rather than inviting competing proposals, they simply funnel funds to favored institutions. Scientific pork barrel projects are as appealing to voters, one supposes, as other kinds of pork.

Although in the recent past some members of Congress have attacked the use of congressional earmarking as a prime example of government waste, it is now back with a vengeance. Between fiscal 1990 and fiscal 2000, the total value of congressionally earmarked academic research projects increased from $270 million to $1.044 billion. That was a 31 percent increase over the 1999 record total of $797 million.[18]

These funds are awarded without direct competition, usually as a result of congressional patronage. Many of the awards are made to relatively weak institutions in states with powerful senators and representatives. In very few cases do the federal agencies from whose budgets these funds originate request or even support the projects.

The FY 2000 appropriations include a variety of projects. By far the largest ($36 million) went to Loma Linda University, a Seventh-Day Adventist school east of Los Angeles, where a portrait of local congressman Jerry Lewis, chairman of the Defense Appropriations Subcommittee in the House of Representatives, hangs in the lobby of a research building. In West Virginia, represented by Senator Robert C. Byrd, $7 million was earmarked for the Robert C. Byrd National Technology Transfer Center at Wheeling Jesuit University, and a further $2 million for the Erma Ora Byrd Center for Educational Technologies, named for the senator's wife.

The temptation to use federal research awards to further political aims is particularly unfortunate, given that there will continue to be more good research ideas than there are funds to carry them out. Those currently working at the nation's research universities find themselves having to write more and more proposals in order to cover the cost of their research, and also to gear up and slow down their efforts, to dismiss staff and then rehire others, in response to variable funding levels. The momentum and the continuity of research efforts can suffer significantly as a result.

But the federal government is not the sole supporter of university research. To point out the need for continuing federal support for basic research distributed on the basis of merit is not to diminish the importance of finding other sources of research funds. Cooperation between universities and industry, often supported and encouraged by the federal government, has opened new research opportunities for both universities and industries in recent years. Early fears that industry support would somehow taint the research have proven to be largely unfounded, thanks to careful negotiation of ground rules about such issues as patent and licensing procedures, publication of results, use of graduate student assistants, and the character of the research itself.

University-industry cooperation is likely to increase with the growth of technology-based industries. In these fields the old linear pattern of basic research–applied research–development is obsolete. What were once distinct and separate activities now tend to be closely associated, with marketing interacting with research, and design jumping conventional boundaries and playing a catalytic role in manufacturing. These changes put a huge premium on the availability of a skilled workforce of adaptable, creative, imaginative, and talented people, and recruitment of these workers will be intense and international. Ideas, capital, technology, communications, resources, and even people are now global. For these new global corporations, as much as for universities, university-industry alliances offer remarkable new opportunities for productive partnerships.

Research: The Larger View

To justify research solely on the basis of future commercial value or social benefit or other quantifiable gains is to miss the larger point. We humans are a curious species, driven to explore our past, our present, our relationships, our surroundings, our feelings, our fears. If we are to exist at all, we *have* to know. That is the underlying motive of all research. Research is organized human curiosity. It is the systematic searching and inquiry about everything around us and within us. If science is the "interrogation of nature," then research is the endless interrogation of existence, the constant analysis of experience.

We cannot be sure, without the test of time, which research will be of lasting benefit or enduring significance. Perhaps half of it will be confirmed in some fields, but generally we need time to know which half. Perhaps two-thirds of the work in some fields will have no lasting significance, but we can never identify in advance — and often not at the time of its publication — which third to embrace. We need variety of viewpoint, breadth of insight, multiple working hypotheses. Natural selection operates within ideas as well as within species. The floor of the cutting room of human understanding is littered with discarded hypotheses and outdated knowledge. There is — as in evolution — no alternative method known to us by which new understanding arises.

Although as a nation we may argue about the appropriate level of support for such work, given the many other pressing social needs we face, we must also acknowledge that research is an essential dimension of our humanity. It's not just scientists and scholars who take this view. The late Congressman George Brown, former chairman of the House Science, Space, and Technology Committee, put it this way. "The promise of societal benefit through technology development is often illusory, but the potential of science to empower the human intellect is not. My personal view — subjective in the extreme — is that the ultimate enrichment of the human spirit comes from our ability to explain our realm of experience and knowledge. Scientists must seek to share the privilege of their enrichment with others, not by promising more, faster, stronger machines, but by sharing what they know and how they feel."[19]

Because as humans we *need* to know, we are driven to explore; we cannot tolerate the constraints of ignorance, and no knowledge, however abstruse, is without benefit or usefulness. Our species is distinguished, not chiefly by its anatomy, but by its perception, by its ability to acquire and use knowledge. All knowledge is of value to life. Life depends on understanding as well as on information. We need insight as well as data. That is what creativity, scholarship, and research also provide: insight, experience, perspective, understanding, and sometimes, in moments of illumination, a new view of ourselves, glimpses of the beauty of a larger order, a broader understanding, a sense of linkage to things beyond ourselves and to reality beyond our immediate surroundings.

That is the reason, of course, that research universities' involvement in research has had a salutary effect, not only on the progress of science and scholarship, but also on the education that students at research universities receive. Faculty members known worldwide for the strength of their research — people like Paul Berg and others profiled in this book — not only contribute to the increase of knowledge, but also attract to their universities students with the ability and potential to carry out original research themselves and to carry the fruits of such research into society. Exceptional researchers are often the very best teachers, offering courses on the cutting edge of their respective fields, which are simply unavailable at institutions that place a lower priority on research. Perhaps even more important, involved, productive, successful researchers convey to students an approach to knowledge, a way of thinking about problems, and an excitement about the process of discovery that are nothing less than the survival skills of the future — skills that all members of society need to avoid obsolescence and deal productively with change.

On October 9, 1996, I learned from an early morning radio program that two Cornell faculty members, Bob Richardson and David Lee, and their former graduate student, Douglas Osheroff, had just received the Nobel Prize in Physics. I waited until 8:15 A.M. to call and congratulate them; by then, Bob Richardson was in Washington, leading a review of current developments in materials science and condensed matter, and David Lee was teaching his customary 8:00 A.M. class for freshmen and sophomores, Physics 213: Electricity and Magnetism. (He told me afterward that he felt a little guilty at deviating from the curriculum to answer questions about the work that won him the prize!) Professors Richardson and Lee exemplify the commitment of individual researchers, not only to their own research, but also to the application of that research to national issues and opportunities and inspired teaching of the next generation. Those tasks still lie at the heart of the university's mission.

I had an interesting glimpse of the long-term impact of Bob Richardson's teaching when I met Robert M. Kolbas, professor and head of the Department of Electrical and Computer Engineering at North Carolina State University. Professor Kolbas told me that he was a student in Physics 315, an undergraduate class taught by Richardson in 1973. Because it was an "off-semester class," enrollment was small, about twelve students, as Kolbas recalled. That, to many, would be an ideal class. Not to Bob Richardson. Instead of lecturing to the class of twelve as a whole, he divided the class into four groups of three, meeting with each twice a week, and running the class as a small tutorial. "Without realizing it," Bob Kolbas remarked, "we had a future Nobel laureate for our personal instruction, at our beck and call, twice a week. . . . That class really got me going. That's why I went on to graduate school. It really stands out in my memory. Whenever I go back to Ithaca, I always look up Bob Richardson in his basement lab or stop by his office on the fifth floor of Clark Hall."

Experiences like Professor Kolbas's refute the charge that a commitment to research reflects a lack of commitment to teaching. Bob Richardson could easily and justifiably have taught his class of twelve students as a group: contact time, two hours per week. He chose instead to teach them in small tutorials: required contact time, eight hours a week. Those self-appointed pundits who condemn the "inefficiency" of universities would, no doubt, deplore such a decision. I can visualize the complaints: "duplication of effort," "inadequate student enrollment," and all the rest. Only a dedicated teacher — or a grateful student, I suppose — would understand the value, as well as the price, of such devotion.

It is because of this intimate relationship between discovery and learning that I am always puzzled at the rigid distinctions that some make between research and teaching. The excitement of discovery energizes both; at our best universities, it permeates the life of the campus. For the successful faculty member, each is a face of scholarship, and scholarship itself is indivisible.

The Value of "Useless" Research

While science, medicine, and engineering account for the vast majority of research expenditures, they represent only a part of the larger research and scholarly enterprise of the universities. The academic appetite for knowledge is voracious: new musical compositions, studies of inner city poverty, new methods of educating high school dropouts, contemporary literary criticism, city and regional planning, new works of drama and poetry, the study of industrial competitiveness, improved systems of criminal justice, patterns of ethnic conflict, population growth and family planning in China, the languages of Indonesia, trade unions in Detroit, the atmosphere of Jupiter, or human evolution in the African Rift Valley: these and a thousand more research topics reflect its omnivorous character.

Some of these studies — industrial competitiveness, population growth, and criminal justice systems, for example — might prove to be useful. But what of the rest? What of literary criticism, or Egyptian archeology, or the history of the Ottoman Empire? Should the university support these activities? And what of literature, the arts, music, drama, and all the rest? What of those irritating literary fads and incomprehensible new works of art that provoke such indignation? Can they be said to be useful? Do they contribute to the larger public good? Only in this sense: they help us to know ourselves, to understand what it means to be human; they help us wrestle with the paradox of existence and the ambiguity of experience. They illuminate and they provoke; they inform and they bewilder.

Surely life itself is like that. We are surrounded by the unknown — perhaps by the unknowable — but we do not give up. "Decay is inherent," the dying Buddha is reported to have said: "Strive on with diligence." And we do. We must. We are human. Annie Dillard may be right that we are moral creatures in an amoral world, where the universe that suckled us is a monster. But how does she know? To others, we are the glory and wonder of creation. How do I know? And yet how do I live without grappling with these questions?

In the end, human life is more than the existence that depends on biological processes and economic survival, on scientific facts and numerical data. It is more personal and less quantifiable, more ambiguous and less explicable.

We need facts and data and equations and processes for our survival and well-being. But we need as well the things that belong to our peace. These things are as old as the yearnings of the psalmist and as fresh as the challenges of this morning. These are the things of the heart as well as the mind: our longing for love, our search for significance, our innate sense of duty, our commitment to justice, our groping for meaning, our quest for linkages and relationships.

Perhaps one day we shall be able to understand these deep longings. Perhaps one day we shall be able to understand the neurophysiology of love and the information processing that underlies our sense of justice. I hope and expect that we shall, for that "enchanted room" that we have called the brain has much to teach us. But to understand the mechanism is not to explain away the reality of need. Our understanding of the anatomy and physiology of the digestive tract and the biochemistry of nutrition "explains" the process of digestion, but it does not explain away our need of food or refute the reality of hunger. Nor is a Cézanne painting of Mont St. Victoire made redundant by the latest photograph or topographic or geological map of the area. Indeed, in one sense, every scrap of knowledge, every glimpse of reality, every insight contributes perspective to all the rest.

It was Lewis Thomas, physician and scientist, who once described music as the effort we make to explain to ourselves how our brains work. Knowledge is indivisible. It is indivisible because our experience is indivisible, because we are whole persons before we are neurologists or poets. John Maynard Keynes, in his economics surely one of the most practical of men, once wrote of those who prefer the good to the useful: "We shall honour," he said, "those who teach us how to pluck the hour and the day virtuously and well, the delightful people who are capable of taking direct enjoyment in things."[20] I like to think that, at their best, the arts and the humanities demonstrate and illuminate just such virtue and delight.

Does that make them useful? Surely it does, in that most beneficial sense of all: providing glimpses of ourselves; celebrating the mystery of life; making existence meaningful; making life worth living. What could possibly be more useful than that?

The Culture of Creativity: The University as Incubator

No one directed Watson, Crick, and Berg to do the work that blossomed into biotechnology. No one foresaw, or perhaps could have foreseen, the results. They happened because there are universities in this country and elsewhere that regard research as both an intellectual calling and a public trust. Pathbreaking research is far more than a matter of technique. It depends for its success both on individual creativity and on conditions that allow it to flourish. Good research is conducted in many settings, but universities seem to have characteristics that have proved to be especially conducive to fostering that kind of work:

The presence of the world's most outstanding scholars within an interacting community provides an implicit benchmark to which other members of the community are challenged to aspire. There is in all research and scholarship, as in much else, a world of difference between the best and the worthy second best. The thin stream of superior talent in most fields flows into research universities, and the benchmark of excellence is reinforced by the presence of that talent.

Freedom for the best scholars in their fields to pursue their own ideas adds unmatched vitality and originality to a university community. University research is unmanaged and undirected because attempts at management are likely to be counterproductive in the long term. It is individuals, not committees — whether congressional or industrial or academic — who ultimately develop creative new ideas and insights. "Managed research" is an oxymoron, like "postal service," or "airline cuisine." It is individuals, often at odds with conventional wisdom, often in disregard of accepted approaches, who make the most creative discoveries. Freedom for the irritating oddball has often been the basis for new understanding and fresh application. The university is hospitable to difference. The faculty member is often one who thinks otherwise.

Universities foster receptivity to new information, openness to new ideas, a welcoming climate for new people and alternative viewpoints, and an eagerness for new understanding. This openness springs from a deep conviction that knowledge can be developed and increased only to the extent that it is free to build on the work of others and is, in turn, subject to their review and criticism. No American university of which I know accepts support for secret or classified research; none I know permits restricted publication of results, beyond a delay of a month or two to provide priority of information to the sponsor. This openness goes back to the universities' earliest days, and though it has sometimes been severely tested by critics both on and off the campus, it remains a matter of conviction. Some years ago, when the federal government sought to limit the access of some foreign students to supercomputer facilities, the universities mounted a spirited and successful defense of the need for openness. The reason was not lack of loyalty, but rather the belief that the spirit of inquiry on which research depends cannot prosper behind locked doors. It is only by sharing, both in personal contact and in formal publication, that knowledge can be challenged, tested, and fully utilized. And since the public provides the ultimate support of university research and inquiry, it is proper that the public should have full access to its results.

Universities offer a huge range of resources and facilities. Universities provide access to facilities of unmatched breadth and quality that embrace every aspect of human knowledge. A Bell Labs or GE Labs has superb resources of technical journals and scientific instrumentation. A university has all that, plus comparable facilities in many other fields, from medicine to art history. Even in the age of electronic analysis and retrieval, this concentration and breadth of resources are unique. The Harvard library subscribes to some 91,000 current periodicals. That's 4.5 for every student, 44 for every faculty member. Most other research universities subscribe to at least 50,000 such journals. That coverage is costly, but it is essential in a world of sweeping intellectual change in which knowledge in one area can have such significance for another.

A remarkable blend of collegiality and individuality unites members of the institution in a common mission and enables them to embrace common interests, even as they pursue their individual goals. This collegiality is less extensive than it could or should be, but it is nevertheless real, and it is a distinctive feature of universities. So, too, is a feisty independence and individuality, and the combination of these qualities is more than the sum of the abilities of individual members.

Cross-pollination among disciplines comes from being part of a university community, as well as a member of a single professional field. No other institution comes close to the university in its breadth of scholarly interest. The association with specialists from other fields, both related and unrelated, can often provide vital insight and suggest creative applications. Even the competition and tension between them can be positive at times. This is increased when the community is international in its membership. Nor is this cross-pollination limited to closely related fields. Charles Darwin and Alfred Russel Wallace were each independently led to develop their theory of evolution by natural selection by reading a book not on biology but on human population by an English clergyman, Thomas Malthus. Serendipity is a major factor in discovery, and though it can take place anywhere, the university provides a particularly fertile cultural medium.

Intergenerational and international partnerships involving faculty members and students, both graduate and undergraduate, often provide unusual insights on a particular question and encourage rigorous scrutiny of ideas and effective explanation of results. To an undergraduate, authority exists to be questioned; little is sacred. To a graduate student, no premise goes unexamined. Iconoclasm reigns. Such an approach to education benefits not only researchers — present and future — but all who, as adults, will assume the responsibilities of citizenship. Similarly, the presence of iconoclastic students places demands on faculty researchers not only for an explanation of their assumptions but also for continuing explanation of their conclusions; these are constant incentives to further understanding.

In practice, these linkages work superbly for graduate and professional students, but they are less frequent and less beneficial than they should be for undergraduates. For undergraduates, the professor all too often is one who lectures and then vanishes to another realm called research. In spite of good intentions, in spite of the lip service paid to the interaction of research and teaching, in many institutions professors and undergraduates enjoy proximity but no relationship, as one commentator observed recently. They are as neighbors in a giant apartment building, who do not speak. Their mutual silence and self-isolation are not the result of disagreement or quarrel, for they have never met, never recognized one another beyond a cursory nod and dismissive "Hi." They have been too preoccupied, too busy, having interests, colleagues, and friends elsewhere. They are simply uninvolved with their neighbors; their true focus is elsewhere; their real community is with others. That is a tragedy, no less for the researchers than for undergraduates, for each has so much to offer the other. Universities need to develop added incentives that encourage the linkage between the two, breaking down the unintended walls that too often separate the worlds of faculty research and undergraduate experience.

Research as a Public Trust

I have argued in this chapter that the university provides a uniquely favorable setting for student inquiry and a demonstrably successful incubator for research and discovery. Its uniqueness lies in its variety of interest, its wealth of professional talent, its diversity of viewpoint, and its success reflects its unconstrained freedom of inquiry and its partnership between the generations. Yet it is a frail plant that requires careful cultivation, and whose nurture involves the recognition of paradox.

- Research demands investigative freedom and independence, but it represents a public obligation and trust.
- Research arises from private curiosity, but it depends on public support.
- Research involves personal discovery, but it provides public knowledge.

- Research requires individual insight, but it yields societal benefits.
- Research results in basic knowledge, but it produces practical applications.

This balance between the independence and responsibility of the individual investigator and the support and interest of the general public depends on an unwritten social contract that has served our nation well. For more than half a century, bipartisan congressional support has recognized the benefits of that compact and the "virtuous cycle" of public investment in research and the discovery, application, generation of wealth, and renewed investment it has supported. In this cycle, research is the seed corn for the harvest of benefit. It is a cycle we must continue to support, for the well-being and security of the nation depend upon it.

SERVICE AS A SOCIETAL OBLIGATION

FROM FARMS TO CORPORATE AMERICA TO INNER CITIES

Public service, carried out chiefly through teaching, was the motive for the creation of the earliest universities; teaching was the means by which the faith of the church and its service to the community were transmitted to the next generation. Today, teaching remains the core of the university's public service. It is by far the simplest and most effective method of technology transfer, supplying the economy with a continuing stream of new graduates, whose skills and knowledge have been developed in an atmosphere blending formal instruction with personal discovery and certified through the awarding of degrees. But, at the beginning of the twenty-first century, the university's public service also extends far beyond teaching and certification in ways that affect people in almost every walk of life. Indeed, the university of the twenty-first century is an institution heavily involved in all areas of public life, engaged in addressing every societal need.

Town-Gown Partnerships

The early universities — financed chiefly by fees for instruction, which the students paid retroactively only if they approved of the quality of teaching — were fiercely independent of both local and sometimes national communities. But as economic and social pressures have shown the mutual benefits of cooperation, a new alliance between universities and their communities has developed. In many areas, universities have become partners in addressing community concerns. For example:

- Boston University superintends the Chelsea public schools.
- Harvard sponsors a health maintenance organization for the residents of Cambridge, Massachusetts.
- The University of Illinois at Chicago sponsors a Great Cities Program that harnesses the skills of the faculty in health care, technology transfer, business, and urban affairs to the needs of the community.
- The University of Iowa has produced a statewide economic development plan, charting the future for agricultural programs and products.
- The University of Southern California provides counseling, tutoring, and college preparatory classes for children in South Central Los Angeles.
- Yale has invested $50 million in local improvement projects, and more than half its students are involved as community volunteers.

Many of these projects involve the use of student volunteers, on the theory that such arrangements not only benefit the community but offer valuable experience to the students. At Cornell, for example, a Public Service Center coordinates a student-staffed Homework Helpline, which offers homework assistance to high school students in fifteen school districts through an 800 telephone number. The Public Service Center also coordinates student work with elderly shut-in citizens, prison inmates, the homeless, and at-risk youth. Some projects develop student leadership in local chapters of national groups such as Habitat for Humanity, American Red Cross, and American Cancer Society. Others are strictly local in character, such as "Into the Streets," an annual effort that brings out about four hundred Cornell students to clean up local sites and assist in neighborhood projects, such as the design and construction of a children's playground and the development of a science center. Other students train as volunteer firefighters and EMS crew members, teach outreach minicourses in local schools, and participate in countless other activities.

These Cornell activities are linked with similar programs through Campus Compact, an alliance of over 560 university and college presidents committed to the promotion of the values and skills of citizenship through public and community service. Member campuses engage faculty, staff, and students to promote a renewed vision of higher education — one that supports not only the civic development of students but "the campus as citizen" as well. With member campuses in forty-four states and twenty-one network offices, the partnership includes twenty State Compacts, in partnership with the Education Commission of the States. Over 830,000 students contribute some twenty-two million hours of community service through the Campus Compact each year.

Other projects take place far off campus. Students from the Cornell School of Hotel Administration have sponsored a nationwide program in which restaurants and hotels cooperate in distributing surplus food to feed the homeless. Other students have helped develop community gardens in the Bronx, while medical students staff drug treatment clinics in Harlem and others serve in medical clinics in refugee camps in Asia and Africa.

In addition to programs such as these, in which most of the service is provided by students, there are several areas of public service in which university faculty and staff are particularly active. Let me describe three of these, each of them in an area of acute national concern: improving the quality of public schools, aiding technology transfer, and fostering new business ideas through the support of research parks and incubator centers.

Helping to Improve Public Education

One of the most widely acknowledged areas of public concern is the quality of the schools, and one of the most frequently heard suggestions is that universities become more involved in the effort to improve it. The question, however, is how to structure university involvement so that it complements the universities' responsibilities for teaching and research and does not drain resources away from those essential tasks.

Perhaps the best place to start is to overhaul and improve the teacher-training programs offered at the universities' schools of education. There also is room for additional research on effective teaching, the cognitive process, the causes of school failure and success, effective educational management, and other topics of direct interest and utility to parents, schoolteachers and administrators, and those in public policy roles. The availability of a pool of talented future teachers and faculty members trained in education also offers the potential for internships beyond the traditional student-teacher opportunities and for the limited development of experimental or model schools. Many universities are already deeply involved in these efforts, though they seldom make headlines.

But even at research universities that do not have schools of education, there are opportunities to reach out to the schools in ways that utilize the resources already available on the campus in new and productive ways: offering specialized continuing education programs for teachers, particularly during the summer, in the sciences, the humanities, and other fields, as well as in business methods and leadership skills; conducting tutoring and mentoring programs staffed by college student volunteers; donating surplus or outdated research equipment; and providing guest lectures and special programs.

Consider, for example, one particularly successful program: every summer, about forty high school teachers attend a four-week-long residential course on the Cornell campus for instruction and practical experience in molecular biology. Organized by the university and funded by a number of federal, foundation, and industry sources, such as the National Science Foundation, the Howard Hughes Medical Institute, and Apple Computer, the program has as its goal to update teaching skills; provide challenging experimental courses and the equipment needed to present them; and help teachers foster professional contacts.

More specifically, the program involves a set of laboratory exercises in biology, carefully developed for use in high schools, plus the materials and equipment needed to conduct them. An equipment-lending library allows teachers to use more elaborate equipment for demonstrations in their own classrooms. And a computer network keeps participants in touch with one another and their Cornell mentors, as do return visits to the campus.

In another Cornell program, "Expanding Your Horizons," female graduate students, faculty members, research associates, and other women working in mathematical, technical, and scientific fields host a day-long program of workshops and hands-on experiments designed to excite middle-school girls about careers in these fields. In another program, Cornell students under the guidance of English professor Scott McMillin have worked in the Bronx to improve literacy by helping middle-school youngsters become better readers. And in cooperation with two other local colleges, Cornell has been involved for several years in a program to help middle and high school youngsters who might not otherwise have considered college learn more about higher education and acquire the necessary academic skills.

These are some of the ways in which research universities address many of the problems facing the schools while creating new opportunities for their students to have a role in their solution. Of course, these efforts alone will not solve the school problem, but because such programs exist at every major university, the long-term impact on the school system is likely to be significant.

Technology Transfer

A major reason for the success of the U.S. computer industry has been the development of a host of small firms in Silicon Valley in California and along Route 128 in Massachusetts. These firms, whose enterprise has led the success of whole industries, grew directly out of basic research at Stanford and MIT, and the proximity of the Silicon Valley and Route 128 to those campuses reflects the ongoing benefits of the science-business links that lead to technology transfer. Faculty members have acted as consultants; new graduates have provided the workforce; and research projects have contributed much of the intellectual capital for these firms. The companies benefit, and so does the nation, with new products, new jobs, and new market strength.

Similarly, biotechnology, which has emerged as a major industry in the last decade and in which the United States is clearly the world leader, was established chiefly as the commercial application of basic discoveries in molecular biology and genetics made in the nation's leading universities. These discoveries, in turn, are partly the result of the federal investment in basic research, chosen because of its inherent scientific interest and promise rather than its direct commercial value, and partly because the scientists involved have moved freely between the academic and corporate worlds. Some scientists have created their own companies, others serve as consultants, and still others as board members of these embryonic corporations. Some, like Genentech, are Wall Street favorites, while others are virtually unknown.

One such company, Phyton, Inc., is seeking new ways to develop and commercialize valuable plant-derived compounds, including pharmaceuticals. Its initial work has been focused on Taxol, an antitumor compound originally extracted from the bark of a threatened tree species.

Phyton, Inc., is one of several new ventures that have been assisted by their membership in the Cornell Center for Advanced Technology in Biotechnology, a center funded by the State of New York and a consortium of industries, ranging from small firms to corporate giants like Bristol-Myers Squibb, Pfizer, and Procter and Gamble. The center supports biotechnology research in areas such as medicine, environmental conservation, agriculture, and food processing, and encourages commercial applications in all these areas. It views biotechnology, not just as a narrow technique involving recombinant DNA and cell fusion, but as the comprehensive use of living organisms and biological processes to modify products, improve organisms, and develop biological systems for specific uses. The potential range of benefits from the research of such a center is immense: drought-, pest-, and disease-resistant plants, more effective medications, improved livestock, and bioremediation of polluted sites, among others.

All the scientific research of the Biotechnology Center, including that on which Phyton, Inc., is based, is published in the professional literature and so is widely available. It is the techniques that are patented.

The potential for conflict of interest surely exists within Cornell's Center for Advanced Technology in Biotechnology, within the Human Genome Project, and in many other partnerships that have been established between research universities and the companies with direct interest in putting research findings in these areas to commercial use. While the record to date has been good, and the incentive of the marketplace is seen by most as the best means to exploit the benefits of basic research for the good of the country as a whole, the potential for conflict remains and becomes a growing concern as the university derives more and more financial benefit from its own discoveries. Columbia, for example, was reported to anticipate royalties of some $144 million in the year 2000. The year before it earned nearly $100 million of its $1.5 billion budget from patents and royalties. The University of California received patent earnings of $89 million in the year 1999–2000, and Stanford $35 million.[1] That Columbia and other universities reinvest this income in other academic ventures reduces the problem but does not eliminate it.

Two particular issues emerge. The first concerns the integrity of the universities' own activities, especially in research, and the temptation both to follow the dollar in research priorities and to turn what should be independent research labs into secretive development facilities, answerable more to short-term corporate interests than to the longer scientific horizons and the best interests of the university.

The second issue involves the threat that overdependence on such patent revenue may erode — or appear to erode — the impartiality and independent judgment of the university. Once that impartiality is weakened, the university's effectiveness in public service is at an end.

These are serious issues for the university that must be addressed both openly and directly. What is required is a comprehensive protocol and an effective monitoring system, involving the participation, not only of the faculty and administration, but also public members of the board of trustees. I have drafted an outline protocol in the Appendix. Only with the scrutiny that such a system provides can the public be assured that the university can provide apolitical, balanced, and impartial advice on the most pressing bioethical and other issues of the day.

Research Parks and Incubator Centers

It is the success of projects like Cornell's Center for Advanced Technology that has led many universities to establish research parks and incubator centers on their campuses. In these parks, space is rented to small, developing companies — often headed by recent graduates — and the university provides facilities, as well as scientific and business advice and support. Let me give some examples of the way this works.

Corporate liaisons now frequently involve direct participation in joint research projects. The Cornell Electronic Packaging Alliance undertakes precompetitive research in areas that represent the foundation of the dataprocessing industry, whose gross annual revenues already exceed and are growing faster than those of the automobile industry. Electronic packaging involves mounting microchips into arrays in carriers, computer cards, and circuit boards. The Semiconductor Research Corporation and the Electronic Packaging Alliance involve a consortium of leading U.S. semiconductor companies ranging from suppliers of raw materials to systems manufacturers. Under this arrangement, industrial scientists work in the lab alongside Cornell faculty members and graduate students, to the benefit of all.

The Cornell Nanofabrication Facility provides a somewhat different example in which a national facility is supported by federal funds (via competitive funding from the National Science Foundation) to provide research facilities and services to both university and industrial users. The facility provides access, in one service-oriented laboratory, to all the equipment needed to design, manufacture, and test micro- and nanocentimeter devices (chips). (A nanocentimeter is one billionth part of a centimeter.) The revolution in electronics and computing has been based largely on the miniaturization of these devices, and users from industry and universities work closely together in that process, studying both the basic science and the technical fabrication needed to support it. At any one time, some 250 students will be working on associated research topics, and more than sixty graduate degrees are awarded every year. A joint corporate-university policy board, most of whose members are not affiliated with Cornell, administers the center.

Success in the international marketplace in the coming years will depend chiefly on the successful and swift application of new science and technology to manufacturing processes and products. And that, in turn, will depend increasingly on close and effective partnership between the government, industry, and the universities.

The Greatest Success Story

The Morrill Act of 1862 set the stage for the most distinctive and most success-ful example of public service by American universities. We have already seen the influence of this act in the development of a new curriculum for universi-ties. But its influence *beyond* the campus was even more dramatic, as it brought the new universities into active partnership in the agricultural life and work of the nation. It is a success story that begs to be told — and extended.

Justin S. Morrill, a prosperous merchant from Vermont who served in the Congress from 1854 until 1898, was concerned that the United States, then an overwhelmingly agricultural nation, lacked the capacity to educate those in agriculture and manufacturing on whom the nation's prosperity depended. Aided by Ezra Cornell, then the chair of the Committee on Agriculture in the New York State Senate, and Andrew Dickson White, chair of the Senate Com-mittee on Education, he introduced in 1857 a bill to make available grants of federally owned land to states that would create public colleges. The object of these new colleges, now found in every state, was "to teach such branches of learning as are related to agriculture and the mechanic arts . . . in order to promote the liberal and practical education of the industrial classes in the several pursuits and professions in life."

The Morrill Act was followed by the enactment of the Hatch Act in 1887, which allocated federal funding for agricultural research stations, and the Smith-Lever Act (1914), which made the federal government a partner with state and local governments in outreach extension programs for "giving in-struction and practical demonstrations in agriculture and home economics to persons not attending or resident in colleges."

The motive for the Morrill Act was to supply the nation's need for well-educated engineers and farmers. But the motive behind the Hatch and Smith-Lever Acts was both to provide off-campus instruction in existing practices, and to develop, extend, and apply new knowledge, not only in the traditional classroom, but in the factory and the field.

Even before the passage of the Hatch Act, Cornell was hosting "Farmers' Institutes" on campus — the forerunners of "Farm and Home Week" — and its faculty members were publishing bulletins for the state's farmers on such topics as fungicides and insecticides. In 1894, the New York State legislature approved $8,000 for experimental work of direct interest to the state's farm-ers, and by 1898 annual state grants for extension work had reached $35,000. Under the leadership of Liberty Hyde Bailey, extension evolved into a coherent program that included, along with the bulletins, a correspondence course for farmers, a reading course for farmers' wives, and a series of nature study leaflets developed by Anna Botsford Comstock for use in the state's rural schools.

The results of such extension efforts have been dramatic. In our own lifetime, the percentage of the adult workforce employed in agriculture has fallen from 45 percent to only 2 percent. Food, once scarce, is now exported to the rest of the world, and huge government subsidies are aimed at discouraging increased agricultural production. How has this success come about?

Cooperative Extension at Work in Agriculture

The land-grant universities, some seventy in number, provide a nationwide program of extension services, supported by a mixture of federal, state, and local (county) funds. In New York, for example, the extension service is represented by at least one extension agent in every county of the state. These agents are closely linked with professors on the campus and in the agricultural research stations attached to the campus, so there is a continuing interaction between the work of the lab and the problems of the farmer. New problems are identified and tackled as they occur. The county extension agent, there on the scene, provides a trusted link between the land and the lab. The new crop variety, the new treatment, the novel technique, developed in the lab, is freely available for trials in the field. Workshops, demonstrations, classes, expert advice — all these are a regular part of life on the land.

The cooperative extension system is a pattern of almost irreducible simplicity, but it is one that works. It works, not just in a rural setting, but also in urban settings. And it works, not just for agriculture, but for all the topics that now come under the heading of "human ecology": food, nutrition, child development, drug abuse, consumer economics, social services, housing, and a dozen others. In fact, it works so well that in New York State, there are more than eight million individual contacts with these educational programs each year. In many cases, the extension educators are the lifeline for those in the inner city; the single-parent family, the neglected child, the elderly tenant can testify firsthand as to how effective a program cooperative extension is.

There are three qualifications to this success story. First, the financial support for inner-city projects has never been adequate, has never come close to the level provided for agriculture, for example. Second, people problems are far less easily solved than plant problems or livestock problems. Simple "scientific solutions" hold little promise for resolving the tensions and complexities of modern cities. Third, there is little or no direct governmental responsibility for most of the problems of the inner city or for those of economic competitiveness. Unlike agriculture, where a single government agency has chief responsibility, inner-city issues, for example, may involve half a dozen federal agencies, a dozen city offices, and hundreds of volunteer agencies, each understandably conscious of its own role and its own turf.

A Proposal to Expand a Good Thing

The genius of the cooperative extension program, nonetheless, has been its success in linking the knowledge and expertise of the campus to the pressing issues of society and vice versa. It would be naive to pretend that the universities and their extension/outreach programs can solve all these pressing and complex social problems. But they can make four vital contributions toward their solution.

They can experiment with a variety of potential solutions, using the latest knowledge and methods to develop creative approaches, and testing the effectiveness of one approach against another. Many of the problems I have outlined have, at present, no solutions. Identifying solutions that work is the essential first step. We rely on hunches and depend on traditional remedies for problems that grow steadily worse. We need bold experiment, novel solutions, and apolitical, impartial, rigorous evaluation of results. Extension services have a degree of flexibility that federal and state agencies lack in developing these new strategies.

They can develop effective solutions and run them as demonstration models. Nothing so persuades a community to take action as to see a working pilot program that effectively addresses the community's own most urgent problems. Effective child care, job training, and other model programs already exist and have already been shown to be a sound social investment. These model programs will not resolve or remove all the underlying problems, but incremental improvement and amelioration at the margins are still useful contributions.

They can educate and encourage individuals, families, and community groups to cooperate effectively. So many societal issues lie unattended because of a lack of common will to address them. Educational outreach is the key to building community resolve, and resolve is the key to effective action.

Extension programs can provide linkages — impossible to achieve through conventional agencies — between problems and programs. Let me give one simple example. An engineering extension program to provide technical and business advice to small manufacturers could be linked to a job-training program to provide entry-level workers with appropriate skills. That, in turn, might be linked to a child care program to encourage single teenage mothers to enroll in job training. This type of linkage scarcely exists at present.

Cooperative extension's remarkable success in agriculture has been demonstrated repeatedly over the last ninety years, and it continues to be as effective as ever. This raises a question: Can the cooperative extension model be used more widely as a model for other areas? I believe it can, though its effectiveness is likely to be both uneven and less than that in agriculture, and its success will depend directly upon the level of state and local involvement.

Consider the case of small manufacturing businesses. Small businesses account for the majority of new jobs created in this country. They also account for the majority of jobs that are lost. The reason is that small businesses are particularly vulnerable in the first few years of their existence. Perhaps it is time to direct some of the federal surplus to explore the value of a national industrial extension-type program, aimed at assisting small start-up manufacturing and other firms. The Morrill Act was to have fostered teaching the "mechanic arts," but support for the extension of training and advice in this area beyond the campus has not been forthcoming. Perhaps now we have a remarkably favorable time to experiment with a new government-industry-university partnership, similar in substance to the way in which the Hatch and Smith-Lever Acts extended the benefits of the Morrill Act.

We have prototypes of such a system in the modest industrial extension programs developed at a handful of universities with assistance from the state and federal governments. But if the nation is to reap the maximum benefit from these efforts, something equivalent to a network of extension agents will be required to link the needs of industry to the knowledge available in major research universities.

Such a new industrial extension system would be unlikely to resemble the traditional network of agricultural extension agents — those "enormously productive busybodies" as Harold Enarson, president emeritus of Ohio State University, has called them, who have carried the results of research "to the farthest reaches of muddy farm roads." More likely, an industrial extension service would be built on a computer network, since manufacturing involves scores of industries, producing thousands of products in processes that often present problems of great technical complexity and scientific subtlety. Such an outreach network would link the specialized skills of individual faculty members in many research universities to the particular technological needs of individual companies. The network might also respond to industrial needs in fields as diverse as management and public health.

The foundation for such a network already exists in the Internet. The benefits of such a network would lie partly in gaining immediate industrial access to some of the world's foremost scientific and technical experts and to sophisticated research facilities and equipment, and partly in the opportunity to work with and recruit advanced students who will be the next generation of industrial scientists and engineers. It would also provide a window into new research and technology and a chance to tackle major studies where the critical mass of scientists required exceeds the capacity of a single firm to provide it.

The results of this effort in manufacturing technology could improve the nation's competitive edge in many fields. The success of the extension program in agriculture has been built on a simple formula: knowledge gained, knowledge integrated, knowledge shared, knowledge multiplied, knowledge applied, knowledge trusted. It is time to apply the same formula to our manufacturing industry. Even in an era of reduced government funding, a government-industry-university pilot program of this kind represents a remarkable opportunity.

What about our most pressing social problems? Can we harness knowledge more effectively in the quest for their solution? There are already some encouraging results from existing cooperative extension programs in our cities, ranging from the Food and Nutrition Education Program for young mothers and low-income families to community economic development.

Let me give a few examples of low-profile but high-impact programs that are, I think, typical of the contributions a university extension program can make. I choose Cornell because that is the university program I know best.

Most job growth occurs from the expansion of existing companies, rather than the creation of new ones. So Cornell's Business Retention and Expansion Program provides help for New York State communities by forming task forces that focus economic development on the needs of local businesses. These task forces supply companies with follow-up business strategies, as well as access to business support programs, technical assistance, and training.

Agricultural productivity is heavily dependent on the control of pests, but continuing use of chemical pesticides has produced both environmental hazards and insecticide-resistant pests. A statewide program of integrated pest management (IPM) achieves high crop productivity, lower production costs, reduced chemical applications, and decreased environmental impact by designing optimum combinations of biological and chemical insecticides and herbicides. This program, which is now used by more than 2,700 food producers in the state, involving twenty-five different crops, has reduced production costs by at least $14 million, reduced use of chemical pesticides, and led to the development of more than twenty-five new products.

About 15 percent of New York's population — including more than 20 percent of its children — live in poverty and are vulnerable to the inadequate nutrition, chronic diseases, and poor pregnancy outcomes often associated with it. Through a Food and Nutrition Education Program, the Cornell Cooperative Extension teaches families how to stretch their food budgets and improve their dietary habits. Each year, more than eight thousand adults and eleven thousand young people participate in these programs.

The seafood industry in New York is made up primarily of small businesses, which add over $1 billion a year to the economy and employ some twenty-five thousand people. Cornell Extension educators provides a program of research, technology, alternative products, and marketing, which reaches at least twelve hundred seafood businesses.

Water supply is becoming a major problem in many areas of the country, where the need to preserve "clean" water catchment areas for major metropolitan areas conflicts with the pressures for alternative land use, especially agriculture. Cornell Cooperative Extension is the key partner in the New York City Watershed Agricultural Program, a voluntary partnership that seeks to protect the water supply of the city's eight million people, while preserving the economic viability of farms in the watershed by handling such problems as waste management. This program, the first of its kind in the nation, has so far enabled the city to avoid the cost — estimated at $6–$8 billion — of installing a massive water filtration system.

Reducing waste is a growing challenge in most industries. Some 24 percent of the municipal solid waste in the United States comes from construction and demolition activities. Building one average single-family home, for example, generates from two to four tons of waste. By developing a training program for builders, Cornell Extension educators have helped them reduce such waste by 60–90 percent.

Youth development and life skill programs — teaching leadership, critical thinking, and decision making — now help some three hundred thousand youth in the state each year to become productive, contributing citizens. In a period of broken families, drug and alcohol abuse, teen pregnancy, and crime, these programs, mounted with the help of twenty thousand volunteer leaders, represent a powerful influence for good in many communities.

Effective local government is the key to effective communities. In recent years, Cornell's Community and Rural Development Institute has worked with various associations to bring well-known experts, respected political leaders, and experienced public officials together with newly elected officials, some seven hundred of whom recently participated in more than fifty such postelection gatherings.

New York's dairy industry lagged behind those of western states in the mid-1980s. An extension program of dairy herd management and business and marketing strategies led to both cost savings and increased output. The five thousand farmers participating in the program account for more than 50 percent of the state's milk production.

Outreach is enhanced by an electronic network connecting the sixty-three county- and city-based centers to each other and to the campus, as well as to other universities, businesses, professionals, and databases. Some two thousand publications are in stock, twenty-seven university departments participate, and some 830 professional staff are involved, supported by over sixty-five thousand volunteers. Over eight million people participated in the programs offered.[2] This represents grassroots service at its best, harnessed and used under the guidance and direction of local community leaders. And every one of the other forty-nine states could recount a comparable story.

Let's consider a few issues that have been addressed in these and other pilot schemes and that might be addressed at a wider level. Increasingly, community leaders need expert but impartial advice on a host of technical issues, from economic stability and job creation to environmental impact and tourism. Extension educators have had marked success in organizing workshops, consultant services, networks, youth apprenticeships, and other arrangements, developed in new alliances between local governments, businesses, and the university, by which community members can cooperate in common efforts toward common goals.

Environmental problems, ranging from waste disposal to water quality and industrial pollution, now present major challenges to many communities, where solutions involve costly developments and decisions. Sophisticated technical decisions lie behind these issues, and county agents have shown great skill in linking these community issues to technical expertise.

Public health issues are among our most pressing. More individuals die during the first year of life than during any other year before age sixty-five, for example. Adequate nutrition, pregnancy monitoring, lifestyle changes, and education could prevent a major part of this wastage, and these are all areas where the cooperative extension system has a long and successful record. The overwhelming problems involved in drug abuse and the spread of AIDS might also be usefully addressed by comparable programs, as might the grievous effects of family instability and joblessness.

But could this be done? Could it be coordinated effectively? I believe it could be done, but it would require the creation of a new Smith-Lever-type act, one that would do for the metropolitan and urban areas what the original act did for the rural areas eighty-five years ago.

Anticipating Concerns

Praise for the achievements of cooperative extension programs is widespread and strong, but it is not unanimous. Some recent critics have argued that existing agricultural programs favor capitalist models of large-scale, specialized farming, others that they have devoted inadequate attention to sustainable agriculture and the limitation of fertilizers and pesticides, and still others that they have neglected the contribution of "farm wives" and the larger interests of rural communities. While opinions will differ on any program as extensive as extension, there are compelling answers to all these concerns, not least that cooperative extension programs are just that — cooperative — dependent on local initiative and grassroots community support and partnerships. Without the engagement of families and communities, the programs would not exist. The directions programs have taken and the support they have provided have always been in response to local needs and in partnership with local communities.

It may be argued that this proposal establishes yet another government bureaucracy. But one great feature of the cooperative extension system is that there is no such bureaucracy. It is demand-driven, not centrally directed. It responds to local priorities and depends on local county funding, typically around 35–40 percent of the total, with some 25–35 percent coming from the state, 15–25 percent from the federal government, and 5–20 percent from contracts and other sources. It is direct local initiative and effort, not remote federal administration, that guide and energize these programs. If a program offers promise, if it works, it wins local support. If it does not, it loses support, and funding with it.

It may be argued that this proposal is a paternalistic, even a "socialistic" big government solution to deep-seated problems best left, as in the past, to the volunteer and private sectors. A large part of the cooperative extension system is, in fact, based on volunteer staff, some sixty-five thousand of them in New York State alone. Existing government programs are costly, often ineffective, and offer little encouragement to their recipients, with no prospect of making substantial progress. How long must we wait? As for socialism, perhaps one observation may be made: Justin Morrill was a Republican, the founder, in fact, of the Republican Party in Vermont. If ever a program had a legitimate entrepreneurial pedigree, it is this one.

Can we afford the extension of our present program? That depends on how serious we believe our present problems to be. Consider the situation in one state, New York. About 25 percent of the children under fourteen live in poverty. More than one-third of ninth grade students do not graduate from high school. Over 60 percent of all children have mothers in the workforce, most in full-time jobs. Teenage pregnancies account for 92.6 out of every 1,000 births, about 9 percent of the total.

Against that background, consider these limited results. In one county, 72 percent of pregnant teenagers participating in an extension program either returned to school or completed a high school equivalency program. Statewide, young people who participate in 4-H clubs do better in school, are more motivated to help others, and achieve more than children who are not 4-H participants — even those who participate in other group programs and clubs.

So far as financial costs are concerned, the federal Smith-Lever funding in 1997 was $14.8 million. Add to that the $27.8 million spent on the programs by the state, and the $27.8 appropriated by the counties, for a total of $70.4 million. If by increasing this investment we can make even marginal reductions in the costs of enormously costly law enforcement and welfare programs, the gains will be significant, not just in dollars spent, but in lives that are saved and families that are transformed.

The real purpose of federal budget reduction is not to provide a balanced budget as an end in itself, as though a balanced budget were a guarantee of nirvana. A balanced budget is a means and not an end: the end is a robust economy that produces national prosperity.

The federal budget amounts to $1.6 trillion, and half of that formidable total consists of entitlements of one kind or another. Of the rest, defense accounts for 18 percent, and interest on the national debt another 15 percent. The civilian discretionary budget amounts only to 17 percent of the total. It is vital that this particular portion of the federal budget be creatively and effectively spent. That is the context in which the costs of a program of this kind must be judged.

Concluding Thoughts

To this discussion of the university's wider role should be added the following cautions:

The knowledge and skills that universities can supply will not guarantee a solution to society's most pressing problems. Knowledge is necessary, but it is not sufficient to solve them. The problems of the schools, for example, have as much to do with economic issues, entrenched power structures, local educational political agendas, and union contracts as with the primary educational issues. Many tasks now imposed on the schools, from alcohol awareness to AIDS education, are at best ancillary to their primary task of academic preparation. These tasks would once have been performed by families, organized religion, or youth groups such as Scouts and Campfire not formally affiliated with the schools. While universities can offer significant help in social issues, they are unlikely to be able to provide comprehensive solutions.

Public service by the university, important though it is, must be based on precise expectations of and clear assignments to faculty members and staff involved, and it must receive adequate funding, incentives, and rewards. One of the greatest frustrations, even with some of the most needed outreach programs, is that they are done on the cheap, with short-term funds, bare-bones support, and inadequate resources cobbled together from half a dozen sources. Foundations, anxious to establish model programs, will often provide start-up funds for two or three years, but will then withdraw support, leaving the university scrambling to continue to meet the needs of communities they have just begun to assist.

For most universities, in the absence of gifts or uncommitted endowment funds, there is only one alternative source of funding if they are to continue these research and outreach programs, and that is student tuition. I regard that as an illegitimate charge, so Cornell, like many sister universities, has been forced to discontinue some highly successful public outreach programs in the schools, inner cities, and elsewhere that have clearly served the public interest.

Public outreach must not detract from the university's central mission: the effective teaching of its students. Teaching remains the most important and the most effective form of public service. If that is neglected, no amount of outreach will atone for it. Outreach should be undertaken only if its character and content enhance the university's teaching mission and if its financial support does not detract from it. Most of the time, these two requirements will be met: where they are not, the university should be willing to decline to become involved in public outreach, however worthy the cause.

Where they are met, everyone will gain. For the professors, teaching will be enriched by illustrations from the larger society. Students will be exposed to participation in outreach projects that will expand their understanding. And the ethos of the campus will be enlivened, with the notion of service pervading the inreach toward its own members as much as the outreach beyond its walls. For this is one great benefit of public service: the servant gains as much as the one who is served.

And, finally, the university should assist and advise in such outreach programs, but it must not dictate or direct. "Assistance" should be just that: the university must not presume to become the arbiter of local priorities or policy issues. Those decisions involve local concerns and competing needs, and the autonomy of the host community or government is crucial. This becomes especially sensitive in discussions on the major redirection, refinancing, or termination of a program. Foresight, forethought, and clear lines of responsibility will avoid many disappointments here. But whatever the details, local autonomy must be respected.

Outreach and public service will succeed only to the extent that the emphasis and motives are not paternalistic but rather fraternal, based on the assumption that the search for solutions will be a joint one, whose benefits are mutual, in which experience is shared and in which each partner and each institution gains through a common commitment.

Nowhere is this more important than in projects involving other cultures and communities. I like the story of the Virginia colony in the 1770s that as a concession and a gesture to the local Native American people invited them to send six of their young braves to Williamsburg College. The reply from the Native American community went as follows:

We thank you heartily. But you, who are wise, must know that different nations have different conceptions of things, and you will therefore not take it amiss, if our ideas of education happen not to be the same as yours. We have had some experience with it. Several of our young people were formerly brought up at your colleges; they were instructed in all your sciences; but, when they came back to us, they were bad runners, ignorant of every means of living in the woods, unable to bear either cold or hunger, knew neither how to build a cabin, take a deer, or kill an enemy, spoke our language imperfectly, were therefore neither fit for hunters, warriors, nor counsellors, they were totally good for nothing.

We are, however, not the less obliged by your kind offer, tho' we decline accepting it; and to show our grateful sense of it, if the gentlemen of Virginia will send us a dozen of their sons, we will take care of their education; instruct them in all we know and make men of them.

The need here is for mutuality of respect as much as of contribution. The culture of the campus may be as different from that of the inner cities as it is from peasant cultures in developing countries. Each participant in an outreach program must make a contribution, and each can learn from the other participants. Programs to provide water for rural villages in India, for example, or to provide start-up capital for rural women's cooperatives in Africa, can yield models for this country. International students training reading coaches in the inner cities of the United States can draw on that experience in developing models for their own countries. Successful extension efforts are joint ventures: jointly selected, jointly undertaken, jointly developed, jointly evaluated, and jointly extended.

Mutuality, in short, has to be the basis on which universities reach out to others, and the emphasis must be on service and sharing, not on off-the-shelf prescription. That way, we shall all be the beneficiaries.

{ 11 }
INFORMATION TECHNOLOGY

Entertainment, communication, shopping, banking, travel, marketing, design, manufacturing, health care, and news: all these and more are being transformed by Information Technology (IT) and the Internet. This ongoing revolution, gathering momentum before our eyes, promises to reshape almost every aspect of our lives. Yet, paradoxically, the research universities, which created and developed much of the new communications technology, have — unlike business and industry — been slow to apply it to their mainstream activities. Certainly, the use of computers has improved research and professional practice in every field, and has revolutionized information storage and access for faculty and students alike, while it has facilitated university business operations and management. The business of learning, however, remains largely untouched by this revolutionary technology. Most instruction is still a cottage industry, little influenced as yet by the benefits and support of modern technology. It is as though industry had computerized its business and management activities, but left its manufacturing operations and sales distribution essentially unchanged and unimproved.

Developments and partnerships now under way hold considerable promise of application to more conventional learning methods, both on and off the university campus. Possibilities now emerge for wholly new kinds of educational alliances and learning strategies to deliver information on any topic, to any person, in any place, at any time, and universities need to explore the mutual gains of such new partnerships.

Because universities are in the "information and communication business," this increasingly sophisticated information technology will have a major impact on their work, though precisely how it will affect the future of the traditional campus and its members is still unclear. What is clear, however, is that the effects will be substantial.

Increased Access

Distributed learning is likely to give many more students access to the university and college courses. Nor is it only individuals who will be enrolled; corporations, government agencies, and institutions are all likely to become institutional members of this larger alliance. Changing technology and new skills will require not only a more skilled workforce (the Department of Commerce projects that 60 percent of the workers in the twenty-first century will need computing skills that only 22 percent now have) but a workforce with constantly updated and upgraded skills. (It has been suggested that degrees should have an expiration date!) This will require less emphasis on linear, sequential programs and formal degree schemes and more on ad hoc, short-term access to knowledge in modules, workshops, and interactive electronic programs. Time, distance, and institutional resources will no longer be barriers to this access as learning partnerships become the norm.

Improved Quality

Distributed learning will improve the quality of traditional educational programs as new technological developments in multimedia communication and reduced costs increase interactive capacity. I see six ways in which improvement is likely:

Improved learning and retention. Studies of comparative pass rates for students taught in on-line and traditional settings suggest the superiority of the former. At California State University, Fullerton, for example, the use of a "mediated software" on-line program in remedial algebra increased the pass rate from less than 50 percent to more than 70 percent. This does not mean, of course, that the results of every course at every level will be similar, though all are likely to benefit from increased emphasis on educational outcome as opposed to input.

At Cornell's Medical College, for instance, the fourth-year pharmacology elective is taught entirely via computer, after an initial meeting between teacher and students. It is pedagogically efficient and very popular. Substantial parts of the second-year pathology course also rely on computer-assisted teaching. Surprisingly enough, while this pattern of teaching improves the quality of learning, it does not necessarily reduce costs. The demands on faculty members' time are far greater in this case than in traditional teaching. On the other hand, while instruction in surgery or painting or music or acting or creative writing may benefit from some computerized instruction and inter-active demonstrations, students are still likely to require intense, personal attention from a live teacher.

Although these interactive programs are generally offered on the campus, they also allow students to pursue them at any convenient time and place — late at night or on the weekend, in residence hall or in an off-campus apartment, for example — thereby providing far more flexibility and choice in developing a course schedule.

Such interactive programs as these are also likely to improve course quality and transform the role of the campus instructor, who may no longer "teach" the course, but may become more of a coach and mentor. The introductory course might be designed and "taught" "off-campus" by the most celebrated individual scholars in the field, enriching the student experience and allowing the local instructor to devote less time to lecturing to the class and more time to teaching and counseling individual members (see below). This will not necessarily reduce costs to any great degree, at least if earlier experience of computerization is any guide. But a significant improvement in quality would represent real value added.

Expanded scope of curriculum. Information technology will allow enrichment of the curriculum. "Visiting" lecturers; improved ongoing evaluation; "visits" to museums, factories, historic sites, and other localities in every part of the world; interactive access to symposia and legislative hearings; discussions with practitioners, leaders, and mentors in every area; CD-ROM access to performances, archives, libraries, collections, and data banks; multimedia visualization; group studies; simulations of medical diagnosis and treatment; scientific experiments; business decisions; and environmental constraints — all these will be readily available.

Increased personalization and flexibility. The old degree structure and instructional style assumed that one size would fit all, that a single learning pattern would serve all. New technology will allow the instructor to personalize the courses so as to recognize the differing educational needs, capacity, and interests of the students. Monitoring will be continuous, with the emphasis on capacities and skills, as well as the retention of information. Many students will enter a lifelong learning contract with the institution, providing updated information and continuing access to faculty members, campus programs, and events.

More effective teaching role. The instructor will cease to be a lecturer dispensing the standardized information to a passive class and will become a mentor, coach, and learning adviser to each student. Far from reducing the role of the instructor, new technology will expand it, adding value, advice, and enrichment to each encounter, whether in person or electronically. In some cases, there will be a continuing instructor-student electronic relationship, long after the completion of the formal course.

Greater group interaction. The student will become a member of an extended class, international in its membership, cosmopolitan in its interests. Student participation and group interaction have been shown to increase under this system. The walls of the traditional classroom will collapse, as it ceases to be a confined space, an isolated island, and becomes a node on a worldwide network, in real-time contact with other scholars, practitioners, resources, and remote sites.

Expanded access to vital information. The requirement for continuing professional recertification and the growing demand for access to databases (from poison treatment to new synthetic materials) will place growing demands on, and provide new opportunities for, service by the university. Will this reduce costs? Perhaps, although developing courses and databases is costly. What it will certainly do is increase access and improve service for industry, for health care providers, for government officials, and for the public at large, for whom the benefit will be substantial.

Growing Partnerships

Information technology will create new institutional partnerships, not only with students, but also with corporations such as publishers and software manufacturers. Information will become a shared commodity, selected, packaged, and employed for particular users and tastes. The design of programs will be two-way, with users as well as providers initiating new projects characterized by their timeliness, responsiveness, flexibility, and competitiveness. Subcontracting for specific courses and services is likely to increase.

Costs and Effectiveness

The provision of information technology will not automatically reduce costs of traditional instruction, though it will enrich it. It can reduce costs only if each instructor is willing to share software and course materials. This will be seen by some traditionalists as inviting a bland uniformity of content, but it is not necessarily more threatening than the adoption of common textbooks, or even the study, under different professors, of a common text. The value of a class study of *Hamlet,* for example, is not reduced by the sharing of a common text. The value comes partly from the richness of the text itself and partly from the contextual richness added by the instructor.

But the greatest cost reductions will come from another source: competition. The unique role enjoyed by traditional colleges and universities as purveyors of knowledge will be challenged by for-profit competitors. Some see this as a looming threat to the survival of the university.[1] I see it as a bracing cold shower, a stimulus that will benefit both the public and the universities (much as they will deplore it!).

There is one other aspect of costs that will prove increasingly challenging: the ownership rights and royalties of electronic courses and the extent to which faculty members are free to invest substantial time in teaching beyond their own institutions. Already there are major differences between comparable institutions in these arrangements. Nor is it only royalties that will be contentious. If universities choose to enter the field of on-line learning, whether as a nonprofit or a for-profit venture, they will require talented producers, designers, and directors, whom they must recruit head-on with the entertainment industry. Issues of relative compensation and reward are likely to be highly controversial.

Teaching and Technology

How rapidly will technology change the traditional pattern of college going? That is still far from clear, but what is clear is that the choice of "cyberschools" is growing rapidly. Peterson's College Guide listed ninety-three in 1993. A 1997 count listed 762, with over 1 million students enrolled in cybercourses, in contrast to about 13 million in traditional colleges. But 55 percent of traditional four-year colleges are reported to have off-site courses available,[2] a figure that is estimated to increase to 84 percent by 2002, when an estimated 2.2 million students (15 percent of the total student higher education population) will be enrolled in distance-learning courses.

Any person now has access, not only to any study, but often to the foremost scholars and best lecturers, at any time, at any place. While present enrollment in these courses is dominated by older, working students, that will probably change, and these courses may well represent tough competition for some colleges. In fact, two hundred colleges closed in the last ten years, twice as many as in the previous decade.

The research universities are unlikely to encounter problems of survival from cyberschools — "Cyber League, not Ivy League," as two observers remarked — but they themselves are joining the trend.[3] Duke's Fuqua School of Management, for example, offers a nineteen-month remote M.B.A. degree, which enrolled forty-five executives in forty-five nations in its first class. It requires eleven weeks' residence "on campus," made up of attendance at two-week sessions every three months at centers on four continents. Other work is done in a virtual classroom. Duke charges a premium tuition for this program ($82,500 in comparison with $50,000 for the traditional course). Thirty-five other business schools have developed similar on-line M.B.A. programs, including Illinois, Michigan, Purdue, and Tuck (Dartmouth).

The scale of these operations is dwarfed by that of several mega-universities already in existence, which use remote teaching techniques such as televised courses and the Internet to reach a huge audience with quality instruction, often at a fraction of the unit cost of conventional research universities. Turkey's Anadolu University, for example, has 578,000 students and a unit cost of one-tenth that of the average for other universities in that country. China's TV University has 530,000 students; Indonesia's Terbuka University, 353,000. Eleven countries have such mega-universities, each with more than 100,000 students. Such programs do not have to be of low quality: Britain's Open University, which has 157,000 students and a unit cost of 50 percent that of other universities in the United Kingdom, and which pioneered massive distance learning, ranked tenth out of seventy-seven universities in a national survey of teaching quality.[4]

The new communications technology will create a new model for education. This model will not replace the traditional pattern of campus-based learning, but it will extend its reach and compete with it for both students and support. Let me compare the two:

- The traditional model of education has as its goal knowledge and a degree. The new model has as its goals competencies and skills.
- The traditional model is site-based, requiring physical classrooms and labs. The new model is unconstrained, requiring only an interactive terminal to give a virtual classroom.
- The traditional curriculum is standardized, with choice constrained. The new curriculum is individualized, with unlimited choice.
- The traditional model is based on faculty presentation. The new model is based on student discovery.

- The traditional model is based on a fixed calendar. The new model allows a flexible schedule.
- The traditional model is faculty-centered. The new model is student-centered.
- The traditional model is cost-intensive. The new model is cost-effective.
- The traditional model involves buying the "whole package." The new model involves personal choice of particular courses or programs from many competing institutions.
- The traditional model involves one-time presentation with limited interaction. The new model allows repetition of presentation and is highly interactive.[5]

There are two quite distinct views of the future of the traditional research university, given this growing competition. One view, widely held by thoughtful observers both inside and outside the academy, believes that future to be dim. Eli Noam, for example, professor of finance and economics and director of the Columbia Institute for Teli-Information in the Graduate School of Business at Columbia University, asks whether the impact of electronics on the university will be like that of printing on the medieval cathedral, ending its central role in information transfer. "Have we reached the end of the line of a model that goes back to Nineveh, more than 2,500 years ago?" he asks.[6]

Milton Friedman, Nobel laureate economist at the University of Chicago, thinks the private, for-profit companies will be successful in challenging the universities, because the universities "are run by faculty, and the faculty is interested in its own welfare."[7]

The other view, more widely held within the academy, regards such predictions as unfounded at best and alarmist at worst. "That's not the way we do it *here*. That's an impoverished, go-by-the-cookbook, stripped down kind of learning, scarcely worthy to be called education. What's offered here on our own campus is much broader, much better. After all, Jeremiahs were probably predicting the same thing with each new development: when printing was invented, with the birth of the correspondence course, with the advent of TV, with the creation of the Open University and all the rest. But look what's happened. The traditional university is as strong as ever." So the comments go.

Somewhere between the two extreme views lies reality. The new technology will change traditional patterns of learning, and there is neither exemption nor immunity for the research universities.[8] Nor is there any shelter for them from the chill winds of competition, coming from "new purveyors" of knowledge, both for profit and without it.

The questions that confront universities involve more than the degree to which they will compete in the rapidly growing distance-learning market. The recording and multiple use of lectures and courses now delivered once and then "lost" forever will create issues of intellectual property rights. There is also likely to be an unbundling of the content, presentation, production, packaging, marketing, and distribution of distance-learning courses, with "stars" providing core presentations, backed up by skilled production teams and professional distribution. All this will change both the traditional role of the faculty and the traditional relationships between faculty members and students, with purchased presentations interpreted and mediated on a highly individual basis by local specialist instructors and advisers.

The monopoly of an established campus location, public support, scholarly resources, and a powerful faculty with the right to grant degrees (self-accredited, but still widely recognized) is about to be challenged by the new information technology, growing competition, mounting financial pressures, and public demands for a more effective, less rigid, more responsive, and less expensive system. Passive learning with lectures on particular topics given at set times at the convenience of the faculty will be replaced by the creative response to individual needs and the design and oversight of personalized learning experiences. For many universities and their faculties, that will be a demanding and sometimes painful transition.

Most faculty members, most universities, and most professional practitioners are not yet prepared for the transformation that IT and associated distance learning will bring. Although all universities are already testing new ways to apply technology to teaching, the social interactions and intellectual cross-pollination of the campus, which are essential components of any meaningful undergraduate education, are not easily replicated in cyberspace. But other forms of learning are helped by the use of IT, and in the long term technology will both improve and extend the quality of learning and reduce costs.

For over nine hundred years, the effectiveness of the university has been dependent on a social compact under which society supports the university financially and grants it a remarkable degree of autonomy, while the university uses its resources and its freedom to serve the larger public interest. The custodian of that social compact is the board of trustees, which exercises both a fiduciary and an oversight role on behalf of the public.

The most cherished values of the university — integrity, impartiality, excellence, community, openness, civility, freedom, responsibility, all exercised within an autonomous community of learning — are not merely items of intellectual convenience but also a practical means to a practical end: they are the essential requirements for the effective pursuit of knowledge. Developed and refined over centuries, sometimes contested from within and sometimes tested from without, these values have proved the essential means for effective learning and discovery and their humane application to society's needs. Without respect for these values, there can be no university worthy of the name. In fact, in those countries where these values have been neglected or suppressed, universities have become places of political turmoil, pedestrian training, or dogmatic propaganda.

Effective Governance: Board, President, Faculty

In general, public universities in the United States are governed by boards of public members selected either by constitutional, gubernatorial, or legislative appointment or, more rarely, by statewide election. In these public universities, the board has wide powers within a budget approved by the state legislature. In the private universities, the board is typically self-appointed. In both public and private universities, the board is the final governing body for all decisions, though in practice many responsibilities are delegated to others.

The members of governing boards represent the public interest in a broad sense and are responsible for the appointment of the president, the approval of the institution's mission and goals, the oversight of its programs, its financial health, and the good order of the campus. It is the board that each year gives the president the authority to grant degrees, subject to the recommendation of the faculty. It is the board that approves all new construction, new programs, and new ventures. The board approves tenure appointments and has a distinctive fiduciary relationship to the institution, acting literally as trustees for its health and well-being.

This public governance, exercised by lay boards of trustees or regents, remains generally stronger and more responsible in private than in public universities, where political pressures, regional interests, ideological issues, and obsessive notions of accountability have sometimes divided boards, while sunshine laws — scrupulously applied — have limited their ability to interview and recruit outstanding and outspoken presidential leaders. It is perhaps no accident that the average tenure of presidents of public universities is significantly shorter than that of their counterparts in private institutions. But, by and large, most boards — public and private — function well, and strong and responsible boards have kept America's universities strong and effective.

The president is the link between the board and the campus and as such has a degree of influence — for good or ill — unknown in other countries. The president is responsible for all major administrative appointments, for developing the budget, new programs, and facilities, and for the overall effectiveness of the institution. But the role of the president is now seen by many external observers as less influential, and by potential aspirants as less desirable, than it once was, so that the average incumbency has declined to less than five years in public institutions and less than seven in all institutions.

Both the board and the president delegate substantial responsibility to the faculty. The ancient universities developed their autonomy around self-governing bodies of scholars, and vigorous faculty governance continues at the heart of the university. The faculty, in one sense, are the university. They determine who should be admitted, what should be taught, and who should graduate, for example, and that trust supposes responsible consideration and informed, impartial judgment.

At its best, faculty governance and responsibility remain strong. Over time, however, faculty loyalty has tended to drift from the university toward external professional guilds, funding agencies, corporate sponsors, and pri-

vate patrons, so that institutional engagement of faculty members has declined. Furthermore, shared governance has sometimes been used to promote
special interests or obstruct proposed reforms. The solution to this problem
is not, as some critics have advocated, a reduction in faculty authority. The
solution is for all three governing entities — trustees, president, faculty — to
clarify their roles, develop trust, and exercise leadership.

Governance in Practice

The pattern of governance I have just described is simple, reasonable, and
clear-cut. In practice, however, it is generally rather less tidy. The untidiness
arises when the aims of the three major players — board, president, faculty
— diverge. Let me give one or two examples.

One of the most divisive issues during my tenure at Cornell was whether
the university should hold stocks of companies doing business in South
Africa during the apartheid regime. All agreed that the regime was evil. The
debate, lively and prolonged, concerned whether one university could exercise a more responsible influence by retaining stocks of companies that followed an ethical code of business practice (the Sullivan principles) — thus
bringing jobs and products to all South Africans and influence and support
to those companies — or by divesting those stocks and so showing its opposition to apartheid. The board held several lengthy and noisy public hearings
and appointed a broadly representative committee to review the matter. A
formal faculty vote favored divestment, as did the noisiest student sentiment.
Frequent demonstrations, the creation of a large shantytown on the main
Cornell quadrangle, and repeated sit-ins occurred during this period. A rock
was thrown through a window of my home, and a pie was thrown in my face
during a discussion with a large student group. Feelings ran very high.

Two things were clear. First, the issue was difficult and complex; reasonable people could differ, and they did. Second, whatever the intensity of the
feelings, it was the responsibility of the board — specifically charged with the
oversight of the university's investment portfolio — to make a decision. And
it did. Though deeply divided, it followed the recommendation of its review
committee and voted in a tense public meeting to retain its investment in
companies judged to be responsible participants in South African business.
That case, though divisive and prolonged, was resolved because of clear designation of responsibility and authority.

Another, less contentious, example arose within campus governance.

There had long been public concern — which I shared — that teaching skills and effectiveness received considerably less consideration in promotion and tenure decisions than did research. The recommendations for faculty promotions originated in the faculty and, subject to review and approval by the president, were approved by the board. The undue emphasis on research in these decisions — unacknowledged, but real — did not serve the interests of either students or the university, but the balance was unlikely to be restored by directives from the president or declarations by the board. The culture could be changed only from within the faculty, and it had to be done by respecting and maintaining the concern for research. Cornell has an elected spokesperson for the faculty — the dean of the faculty, in this case Walter Lynn, a widely respected professor with whom I worked closely. He appointed a committee of senior faculty members to review the issue, and as a result, all nominations for tenure must now include a review of teaching performance at least as rigorous as that devoted to research. Here was the faculty monitoring itself, in a thoroughly professional and responsible way.

Occasionally, the formalities of board responsibility run into conflict with the legitimate concerns of the faculty or the role and responsibility of the president. Early in my presidency, a talented young associate professor in the School of Industrial and Labor Relations was recommended for promotion to the rank of professor. By any measure, he was, and is, a major asset to the Cornell faculty. Although the board awards tenure, its review of promotions is normally pro forma. But in this case a board member — himself a senior trade union official — strongly opposed the promotion on the grounds of the faculty member's alleged lack of sufficient concern for "labor's interests." This was, and is, to me an inappropriate judgment for the board to make, and for the first and only time in my eighteen years as president, I insisted that the vote was also a vote of confidence in me. The professor was appointed to tenure by a unanimous vote. Other personnel actions over which the board has no formal authority can still sometimes be controversial: the dismissal of a winning coach, or the censure of a popular professor, for example. But just as the authority of the board must be upheld in the face of faculty and student opposition, so must the authority of the president and the faculty be upheld in the face of board opposition.

Other cases are less clear-cut. The president of a respected private research university recently resigned, for example, after prolonged faculty opposition to his plan — fully supported and approved by the board — to increase the size of the undergraduate student body and to modify the long-established curriculum. The lines of authority here are less clear, so that personal leadership and diplomacy become of even more importance in reaching a resolution.

In public universities the ancient faculty prerogative to decide whom to admit has recently run into conflict with the public policy of ending affirmative action. Over the substantial opposition of the faculty and the campus chancellors, the board of the University of California system changed its admission system a few years ago to discontinue affirmative action policies.

Particularly challenging jurisdictional problems are emerging with regard to the university's role in distance and other off-site learning. Here the faculty members' personal interest in intellectual property and professional obligation to the university, the board's interest in institutional policy and financial prudence, and the president's interest in educational opportunity and outreach may run into conflict.

Differences of this kind are neither unexpected nor necessarily regrettable. They are probably inevitable in a vigorous academic community. The key to their resolution, in almost every case, is presidential leadership, exercised on a basis of mutual trust, understanding, and respect developed over time with both the board and the faculty.

Effective Governance: The Board

Effective governance involves deliberate respect on the part of each participant for the role of others. Such governance, responsibly exercised, is as vital to the well-being of the university as is the distinction of the faculty or the effectiveness of the president's leadership.

Governing boards must delegate some appropriate and well-defined authority to other responsible groups and bodies (the president, the faculty, and so on) with the understanding that decisions made by others under such delegated authority may sometimes be subject to board review and reconsideration, and that the board may not delegate its ultimate authority for the mission, integrity, and financial viability of the institution.

Board members must recognize that as citizen representatives they not only exercise institutional oversight and provide accountability but — like the president and faculty — also have the responsibility to defend the autonomy of the institution and promote and nurture its well-being.[1] Their loyalty to the larger public interest can be served only by their concern for the institution as a whole, rather than for any constituency or special interest, whether internal or external. That gives the board a particular responsibility for ensuring due process, orderly procedures, and appropriate levels of decision making and appeal.

The role of the board is governance, and there is a world of difference between governance and management. Governance involves the responsibility for approving the mission and goals of the institution; for approving its policies and procedures; for the appointment, review, and support of its president; and for informed oversight of its programs, activities, and resources. Management, in contrast, involves the responsibility for the effective operation of the institution and the achievement of its goals, within the policies and procedures approved by the board; the effective use of its resources; the creative support of the highest standards for teaching, research, and service. The responsibility of the board is to govern, not to manage. "Noses in, fingers out" remains sound and tested advice to board members.

The most important single responsibility of the board is the selection, appointment, periodic review, and continuing support of the president. Candor, fairness, understanding, and trust are essential ingredients in this critical relationship. The president, while performing at a satisfactory level, is entitled to the sustained support, candid advice, and personal encouragement that the board is uniquely able to provide. That removes neither the need to question and to challenge, nor the obligation to understand the views of other interested parties, but the president has both a unique claim on and a substantial need for the understanding and support of the board.

The most effective boards are those that have developed a board code of conduct and that practice regular self-assessment of their own performance as a board. In the case of public universities, for example, improved effectiveness might involve weighing the benefits of public meeting law requirements against the "tyrannies of transparency"; improving selection of public trustees, perhaps by the appointment of an independent screening board to provide impartial assessment; and reconsidering board size (often now only eight members in many public universities) in relation to function, with the possibility of adding additional independent members.

Effective Governance: The Faculty

In research universities the authority delegated by the board to the faculty is substantial, and the more effectively it is exercised — in the department, the school or college, and the university as a whole — the more effective the institution.

There exists at present in most universities a one-sided obligation in which the university is expected to provide tenure, compensation, professional support, technical services, facilities, equipment, and the protection of academic freedom to the professoriate, while the reciprocal obligations of the faculty member are nowhere specified.[2] A Socratic Oath — a professional code of conduct such as I have proposed in Chapter 8 — would redress this imbalance, and there is a need for cooperative development and implementation of such a code by the president and the faculty.

Campus governance is by its nature collective. Decisions reached by committees may be imperfect or even wrong. There are two ways of minimizing this situation. First, all decisions should be made at the lowest appropriate level of responsibility — the department, say, rather than the college — so improving participation and understanding, and encouraging added responsiveness and accountability. Second, subject to the framework of the campus code, an aggrieved individual should generally have the right to appeal a particular decision to a level one step above his or her immediate supervisor. Both these procedures need to be pursued responsibly; the goal should be to reach timely, informed, and appropriate decisions.

Not all "stakeholders" have an equal claim to participate in campus governance. For example, those with little experience and knowledge (students, for example) do not have equal claim to guide curriculum development with those with substantial experience and knowledge (the faculty, for example). Similarly, only the chairman of the board and the president can speak for the entire institution. The best systems of campus governance reflect these various levels of responsibility, avoiding burdensome proliferation of committees in favor of a tested system, with clear guidelines concerning the respective authority of each of the participants and with clear definition of particular areas involving variously the right of information, consultation, consent, or approval. Much of the present cumbersome ineffectiveness of campus governance reflects confusion about the right of the faculty to be informed, their right to be consulted, and their right to approve.

The elaborate structure of campus governance will experience growing strain in the face of the increasing need for making difficult and sometimes unpopular decisions, responding promptly to rapid changes, and satisfying the burgeoning demands of government oversight and requirement. Unless campus governance is seen to be both effective and responsible, governing boards and the public may well become less tolerant of both the autonomy and the shared governance of our universities.

Effective Governance: The President

Our discussion so far has been concerned with governance. But effective governance requires both shared goals and forthright leadership, and that is the responsibility of the president. The essential link between the governing board and the constituencies of the institution it represents is the president or chancellor. Without strong and effective presidential leadership, no system of campus governance can be effective. It is the responsibility of the president, not only to explain the role and concerns of the board to the campus community, but also to interpret for the board the distinctive role and concerns of the faculty and other members of the campus community.

But the president is far more than an intermediary between the faculty and the board. The president must lead. It is to the president that both the board and the campus look for leadership and direction. It is the president who is the crucial catalyst in effective campus governance.

Academic leadership will be viewed by some as an oxymoron, yet there was a time when both the uniqueness and the importance of presidential leadership were unquestioned. When Yale was searching in the nineteenth century for a new president, one of its board members characterized the search for the individual — assumed, in those days, to be inevitably a man — as follows:

> He had to be a good leader, a magnificent speaker, a great writer, a good public relations man, a man of iron health and stamina, married to a paragon of virtue. His wife, in fact, had to be a mixture of Queen Victoria, Florence Nightingale and the best dressed woman of the year. We saw our choice as having to be a man of the world, but an individual with great spiritual qualities; an experienced administrator, but able to delegate; a Yale man, and a great scholar; a social philosopher, who though he had the solutions to the world's problems, had still not lost the common touch. After lengthy deliberation, we concluded that there was only one such person. But then a dark thought crossed our minds. We had to ask — is God a Yale man?

In those days Americans looked for a degree of perfection in their college presidents that the British hope to find only in their butlers. Today the job of the president is more likely to involve maintaining the fragile equilibrium of the campus than rising to the noble challenges of leadership. Kingman Brewster of Yale once declared that the typical college president roars like a lion away from home, but murmurs like a mouse on the campus. To Clark Kerr, the task of the president was to provide football for the alumni, parking for the faculty, and sex for the students. Small wonder, then, that the average incumbency of a college president is seven years, and falling.

But in spite of financial pressures and political concerns, in spite of public disenchantment and campus discontent, the academic presidency is one of the most influential, most important, and most powerful of all positions, and there is now both a critical need and an unusual opportunity for effective leadership.[3]

The college presidency is one of the most influential of all positions because the future leaders of the world sit in our classrooms. The academic presidency also is one of the most important of all positions because it is chiefly on the campus that knowledge — the foundation of the future — is created. The university presidency is one of the most powerful of all positions because of its persuasive influence and its long-term and wide-ranging leverage.

How, then, can a college president become an effective leader? The task of the college president, reduced to its essentials, is to define and articulate the mission of the institution, develop meaningful goals, and then recruit the talent, build the consensus, create the climate, and provide the resources to achieve them. All else is peripheral.

The most important task, and also the most difficult one, is to define the institutional mission and develop its goals. Everything else follows from that; everything else will depend upon it. The mission and goals must be ambitious, distinctive, and relevant to the needs and interests of campus constituents. Too many mission statements are shallow and self-serving, full of academic buzzwords and scholarly hyperboles, but empty of substance and bereft of significant purpose. The tone and substance of the mission statement will be reflected in the aspirations and achievements of trustees, faculty, students, and alumni, as well as the expectations of the public.

The president should devote his or her best skills to dream the institution into something new, to challenge it to greatness, to elevate its hopes and extend its reach, to energize it to new levels of success and galvanize it to higher levels of achievement in every area of its institutional life.

And it is here that most presidents fail. "Make no little plans," Daniel Burnham once urged. "They have no magic to stir men's blood." But it is not setting small goals, it is setting no goals that leads to presidential failure. Aimless day-to-day management, busy inertia, preoccupied drift, and high-minded indecision mark too many presidencies, because incumbents set no goals. The first and greatest task of a president is to articulate the vision, champion the goals, and enunciate the objectives. "There can be no great creation without a dream. Giant towers rest on a foundation of visionary purpose," Morris Bishop once declared. He was right.

Creating this visionary purpose is not the work of a day or a week. Nor can it be a solo effort. It requires imagination, perception, cultivation, creativity, and boldness. It also requires help, criticism, and time. By building on the traditions of the institution, harnessing its strength, recognizing emerging needs, seizing new opportunities, developing new niches, building new constituencies, the president shapes the vision and the mission, which are then tested, refined, and sharpened in active debate with all the stakeholders, both on and off the campus.

The vision drives the goals, as the president establishes the expectations and articulates the values on which the day-to-day life of the institution will depend. Those goals, developed item by item, unit by unit, set the agenda, the blueprint for action, the mandate for change. This, too, like the development of the mission, is a joint effort. Trustees, officers, faculty, staff, students, alumni, the public, advisers, and consultants all have a role and a proportionate voice, but it is the president who outlines the process, frames the discussion, and establishes the tone of the debate. It is the president who carries it through to conclusion, not as a finished report, but as a living program, actively influencing decisions, motivating effort, and channeling resources.

It is the president's task not only to ensure the development of the vision, mission, and goals, but also to carry the flag for them once they are developed, to encourage understanding, promote discussion, and develop support.

Three more things must be accomplished for success, and each is a presidential responsibility: creating the climate, recruiting the team, and providing the resources to achieve the goals.

Creating the campus climate is among the most challenging and most subtle of all presidential roles. It is also one of the most vital. It means generating trust, encouraging initiative, building partnerships, promoting teamwork, rewarding achievement, celebrating success. It means not only tolerating but encouraging a willingness to break out of the box, to question orthodoxy, to experiment with new approaches, dismantling bureaucratic barriers, eliminating administrative layers, nurturing an expectation of success and an atmosphere of openness, exemplifying enthusiasm for the task in hand and commitment to the well-being of the institution and all its members.

The president creates the atmosphere. He or she is everywhere, walking the campus, meeting with students at breakfast, faculty at brown bag lunches, alumni at reunions, everyone at campus events, entertaining at home. The president understands the hopes and concerns of the campus, energizes its efforts, challenges its complacency, raises its aspirations. No encounter is too brief, no event too small, no action too limited to have an influence — positive or negative — on the atmosphere of the campus.

And, if this task is demanding because the president is never "off duty," it is also exhilarating and satisfying. The effective president will embody a level of energy and enterprise, of optimism and openness that is infectious. It is this spirit, and the teamwork it promotes, that achieve success.

But the campus atmosphere requires and reflects a foundation of values. The fact that values are not emblazoned over every campus doorway or discussed in every lecture does not make them any less real or less significant. No effective president has ever been value-neutral. The traditional virtues of the academy — reason, integrity, fairness, respect, civility, community, discipline, and industry — are values that the successful president will embrace and embody. They will be reflected by the president in every speech, every relationship, every meeting, every priority, every decision, every policy. The president is the personal embodiment of the institution's values. The successful president accepts that high obligation.

The successful president also recruits the leaders who will carry the institution forward. These must all be championship players, at the top of their form; they must be what Jack Welch, chairman of General Electric, calls A players, single-minded in their commitment, unswerving in their loyalty to the university, and unambiguous in their willingness to serve its members. Search committees, headhunters, faculty advice, and student input will all play a part in the selection of these campus leaders, but the president must establish the structure, define the tasks, and have the ultimate voice in making these appointments. Their incumbents will share the president's dreams and will be committed to achieving his or her goals.

These people are the "A team," and the president will be the manager, coach, and cheerleader for the team. But he or she is *not* the owner and not the quarterback. The president will achieve results through others, designing the strategy, coaching, shaping, encouraging, and inspiring the team to success, trusting their various skills, and celebrating their victories. If I overstate the athletic model, it is to emphasize the difference between this winning style of leadership and the dreary, budget-bound, "management style" of so many campus leaders. Achieving results requires high morale, joint effort, shared objectives; it also requires frequent contact, regular meetings and close working relationships with all these team members. There is a particular energy that comes from this contact; energy, enthusiasm, and confidence are highly infectious qualities.

The president is also responsible for providing the resources to support the life and work of the campus. It is a natural law of academic life that every program could be far more effective, every institutional ranking elevated by ten places, every facility greatly improved, and every program wonderfully enriched by having another million or so dollars. No curriculum is ever properly covered, no program ever adequately supported, no need ever fully met.

Many presidents — never recognizing that the academic appetite is insatiable, as it should be — become slaves to a mendicant treadmill, camping out on unwelcoming legislators' doorsteps, endlessly wandering inhospitable Capitol corridors, crisscrossing the globe in weary pursuit of prosperous but uncaring alumni, exhausting themselves in the search for financial support. Let me be clear: the president *must* raise funds, *must* provide resources, *must* cultivate the legislature, *must* somehow scratch together the extra funding needed for important stretch goals and ambitious new developments. But in doing these things, he or she must be concerned as well about the things that matter most. I believe fund-raising is immensely important — I've just edited a book on the subject — and I believe an inattentive and ineffective fund-raiser is most unlikely to be an effective president. But fund-raising must not become all-absorbing. It is generally easier for the president to find first-rate help in fund-raising than in those things that matter even more: the mission and goals, the climate, the programs, and most of all the people who make up the larger campus family. Fund-raising can so divert a president's attention that those other things are dangerously neglected; the successful president will be committed to both fund-raising and friend raising, but they will not displace these other vital tasks.[4]

But why do so many fail so soon, departing, by desire or direction, frustrated, exhausted, and disillusioned? And why do so many who continue to occupy the position regard the presidency with such ambivalence? Why do so many constantly represent themselves as the burdened victims of administrative burnout, trustee neglect, faculty mistrust, and campus opposition? There are, I suppose, as many reasons as there are presidents, but the following areas of presidential neglect seem to be all too frequent causes of frustration and failure.

Personal exhaustion takes a terrible toll. Lack of sleep, no time for exercise, shortened vacations, and repeated involvement in crises are the warning signs on the road to personal exhaustion. Only a disciplined routine, a managed calendar, appropriate delegation, a willingness to say "no," effective personal support staff, and the unswerving personal conviction of the ultimate value of the university's work can prevent personal exhaustion. Overburdened university presidents do not *suffer* burnout; they *create* it, inflicting it upon themselves by their lack of responsible work habits. The campus is unlikely to prosper if its leader is so worn down by the burdens of office that he or she conveys a sense of joyless routine and weary resignation.

Muddled priorities, and no priorities, contribute to presidential failure. Every task is not of equal importance; every invitation not equally pressing; every meeting not equally urgent; every objective not equally vital; every decision not equally significant. Choices have to be made, and the priorities I have listed above should top the president's list.

Too many college presidents neglect their families and those naturally closest, the very ones who can best support and encourage them in their role. Family members are always next on the list for attention but easily displaced, always close but easily overlooked and taken for granted. The president is impoverished and the family deprived by this neglect.

Personal isolation is an occupational hazard of the busy college president. Meeting hundreds of people, the president is friends with none. Addressing scores of listeners, he or she remains a stranger to them. And if family estrangement undermines personal support, personal isolation can undermine institutional effectiveness. It leads to lack of insight and understanding, lack of trust, lack of cooperation and teamwork, lack of joy. Too many presidents become prisoners of the office.

Because most college presidents are drawn from the faculty ranks, intellectual starvation is a particularly threatening disease. Busy with this, preoccupied by that, distracted by a dozen pressing issues, presidents develop an inner emptiness and personal hollowness; they are starved of the intellectual and spiritual nourishment that is the sustenance of the campus. Hollow men and moral nomads — Robert Bolt's phrase — are found as frequently in the president's chair, perhaps, as in any other. But there is something particularly poignant in this inner poverty in the midst of the intellectual riches the campus provides.

And the antidote? Serious reading, continuing teaching, participation in lectures and symposia of substance, maintenance of a meaningful research interest, nurture of the inner life: these are the means of intellectual grace, the essential basis of the scholarly community. The effective president's schedule will have a place for each of them, though not, inevitably, to the degree once enjoyed as a member of the faculty. The president should teach, in however limited a role; should be a serious reader; should participate in the intellectual life of the campus; should remain an informed scholar in his or her own field. The pressures of the day will converge to squeeze out these activities. They must be resisted. Time must be found.

One final thing: the president must lead. Everything I have written so far is a prelude to leadership. But it is not a substitute for it. For all its supposed limitations, the authority of the office is substantial; the president must exercise that authority. Effective leadership is blunted all too often by endless debate, excessive consultation, and unwise accommodation. Effective leadership requires the president to be both a listener to others and a teacher, clarifying, simplifying, and specifying the nature of governance, the division of responsibility, and the process of decision making. Effective presidential leadership means not only framing the agenda but also driving it to a conclusion. It means being accountable but also being bold. It means building support but retaining a degree of independence, if sometimes support is not forthcoming. Perhaps there was never a time when the opportunities for presidential leadership were so extraordinary or the consequences of presidential failure were so great.

THE NEW
UNIVERSITY

"Predictions are very difficult to make," Mark Twain is reputed to have reflected, "especially when they deal with the future." Dan Quisensberry of the Kansas City Royals was more specific. "I have seen the future and it is just like the present — only longer," he is said to have observed. He was wrong. The future always has been different, and it becomes less and less like the present or the past.

Every generation, I suppose, believes that it is living in a period of unprecedented change, in which the pace of transformation dwarfs anything experienced before. And every age, I presume, has seen technological development as a major influence in its social transformation. From the Paleolithic savanna of Ethiopia and Kenya to the banks of the Egyptian Nile, from the hills of ancient Rome to the industrial heartland of Victorian England and the production line of Detroit, wave upon wave of technological invention has crashed upon its creators and swept up the societies of which they were a part in ways they scarcely anticipated. But those changes, great as they were, were heavily dependent on natural resources and were limited both in their scope and in the range of their impact by national boundaries, wealth, and communications.

No longer. A nation's present well-being and its future destiny are no longer constrained only by its "givens" (its geography, its population, its natural resources). Knowledge has become the prime mover; science and technology represent the new driving force. Economic prosperity, energy supplies, manufacturing capacity, personal health, public safety, military security, and environmental quality — all these and more will depend on knowledge.

Although knowledge will be the fundamental resource of the twenty-first century, it is not a natural resource in the conventional sense. Most natural resources — mineral deposits, petroleum, coal, and industrial materials, for example — are nonrenewable. When they are used, they are gone, even though recycling can sometimes extend their usefulness. But unlike these conventional natural resources, knowledge is undepleted by its utilization. Far from diminishing knowledge, sharing increases its usefulness and multiplies its benefits. Unlike other natural resources, whose exploitation requires enormous capital investment and whose delivery depends on pipelines and vast transportation networks, knowledge is virtually unlimited in its accessibility, inexhaustible in its availability, and unconstrained by time, transport, and tariffs. Unlike other assets, whose utilization and investment are constrained by the law of diminishing returns, knowledge is autocatalytic, enlarging in the hands of its users; expanding in the range of its usefulness, even as it is applied; growing in scope, even as it is shared; increasing in refinement, even as it is questioned, challenged, and contested.

It would be naive, of course, to promise that knowledge will provide a panacea for the human race. New energy sources do not promise social justice, any more than miracle medicines and abundant agricultural products necessarily lead to personal fulfillment. Knowledge, and the science and technology it encompasses, does not guarantee the good life for all humankind, but increasingly it provides the conditions that make it possible. In the midst of poverty, knowledge creates new options; in the face of disillusionment, it opens up new possibilities.

But if knowledge will play an ever more decisive role in the society of the twenty-first century, it will be created, shared, and applied in ways startlingly different from those of the traditional university. The traditional laboratory will be supplemented by the virtual "collaboratory." The traditional library will be increasingly supplemented by massive data banks and networks. The college-age, full-time, residential student will become a small minority within a worldwide pool of lifelong learners, who will acquire particular skills and competencies as needed for changing careers and changing job demands, and who will shop for knowledge from many "brokers" and "providers," some of them for-profit companies. The "knowledge business" is already exploding in size, becoming global in scope, highly differentiated, and intensely competitive. If universities are to be successful providers in this huge new global market, they will have to adopt sweeping changes in governance, leadership, and structure.

The "learning industry" is about to face the same wrenching "restructuring" that health care, manufacturing, and other industries, as well as welfare and other public services, have already undergone. Mergers, acquisitions, and strategic alliances are likely to become unwelcome additions to the academic vocabulary. So are the terms "downsizing" and "outsourcing." Those pressures on the university will be intensified by growing demands to restrain the growth of tuition and other costs, which still continue to rise at rates well above the general level of inflation. Whether public or private, universities are now seeing growing resistance to the remorseless rise in tuition and other costs. The cost reductions described in Chapter 8, although they will help reduce cost levels, will not eliminate the larger problem of continuing rapid cost increases. Only structural changes can do that, and those changes will require painful choices and difficult decisions. Universities will be faced with the need to reduce costs by purchasing or contracting out some of their services and "components," for example, just as industry has already done. Several universities already do this in a modest way, contracting out their investment management, catering services, cleaning services, and computer services, for example. But bigger changes are likely to follow, with contracting for some educational services (elementary language or mathematics instruction, perhaps) and widespread adoption of computer-assisted instructional programs produced elsewhere.

Disposal ("spinoff") of other activities may well follow, as some universities have already sold or disposed of things as different as real estate, hospitals, works of art, and natural history museum collections, for example. Each such change is likely to be controversial, painful, and reluctant, but such changes may well be the price that has to be paid for continuing institutional strength.

The other prospect is that the multiple functions now performed by the university will be unbundled and redistributed, a possibility made more pressing by both financial constraints and for-profit competition and more feasible because of the benefits of IT. Precedents for this already exist. There are university hospitals, for example, that have separated from their parent institutions, though they still retain a close partnership with them, and though all the patient care is provided by university faculty and staff. Similarly, the outreach, or the applied research and development functions of the university, for example, might be separated and refinanced on a use basis, perhaps as independent financial enterprises. The development and possible extension of Internet II will create new opportunities for this unbundling.

The impact of such changes will be large: revenue sources, faculty roles, the character and range of partnerships will all be affected. So, too, will the nature and responsibility of the university itself, for it will become a hub in a series of enterprises, in some of which it may be one of many partners. In other functions, it may not be the hub but a junior partner in an activity in which the hub is a corporation, museum, publisher, library, professional consortium, federal laboratory, or community college. And in all such cases, what were once fiercely independent, competitive, freestanding enterprises, often of modest size, will be amplified and reinforced by a virtual partnership that gives them new synergy. The whole concept of a community of learning, both on and off the campus, will be expanded and transformed by the new virtual community. Face-to-face interaction will remain at a premium, both precious and uniquely important, but group interaction during the formative stages of research and scholarship — as opposed to the present pattern of critiquing finished, published work — will be a powerful catalyst.

These new alliances will enlarge the pool of research universities. The traditional strengths of the older, established institutions — faculty quality, size, breadth, facilities, instrumentation, library holdings — all become less formidable barriers for other institutions wishing to enter the research stakes when access to all of them — including real time experiment and instrumentation — becomes available over the Internet. The young Stanford Ph.D., recruited to a small, isolated liberal arts college in Nebraska, will remain an active member of a Stanford-based research team, rather than starting from scratch, with meager resources and inadequate facilities. The crowded community college in Alabama will have access to the full sweep of interactive electronics courses at MIT. Huge upheavals lie ahead before issues of credentialing, awarding degrees, accrediting programs, compensating institutions, rewarding faculty, and protecting intellectual property can be resolved. The race here will go not only to the swift but also to the nimble. And the research universities will need to shed their traditional torpor if they are to establish the standards and provide the substance of this new world of learning.

Nor will the individual faculty member be untouched by these sweeping changes. Just as the functions of the university will be unbundled, so too will those of the professor. He or she will be a member of several — perhaps many — virtual communities, each providing distinctive memberships, specialized skills, and multiple sources of support and also, probably, of compensation. The allegiance of the faculty member, already strained, will become even more divided by these extensive new alliances. Old patterns of organization and accountability will experience severe dislocation, as will long-established career paths and appointment criteria.

Knowledge itself will be modified and research and development transformed by the new capacities provided by IT. Nothing will be left untouched. The liberal arts will be revived and transfigured, liberated from their agelong reliance on text alone. The silos of the departments will topple as new approaches to bewildering issues are pursued with new vigor by scholars in mind-boggling combinations of once insular and isolated disciplines.

The reaction of the typical university president to this exhilarating degree of change — and all the confusion and uncertainty that will attend it — may well be to channel it and even to control it. He or she may want to bottle this fierce new wine into the dry wineskins of existing norms and established programs, to avoid the intellectual turmoil and administrative confusion that must accompany the birth of any major novelty. But it must not be constrained; it must be embraced. We should seek less to harness this fiery steed of IT than to release it, to give it its head, to allow it free rein and see where it can take us. That will take patience, nerve, flexibility, trust — and money. And all may become in short supply as the great experiment progresses, lurching from creative successes and impressive results to less evident progress, together with the inevitable dead ends, blind alleys, and false starts. It will be untidy, unpredictable, unceasing, this burgeoning intellectual revolution. But it will also be unimaginable in its potential capacity and in its influence for good. The technology exists to create unthinkable marvels; we lack only the rallying ideas and the boldness of vision to embark on the task and define its grand strategy. Here is where the universities must take the lead.

That is why another major change also seems inevitable. Universities tend to share a model of internal governance that is medieval and ecclesiastical in its origins, nomenclature, and offices (deans, rectors, provosts, chancellors, congregations, etc.) and cumbersome and conservative in its operations. It does provide a measure of collegiality that is prized, but it is inflexible and ponderous in an age that requires institutions to be nimble and adaptive. The successful university of the future will be one in which the cherished prerogatives of faculty governance are supplemented by more creative engagement by the governing board and more decisive presidential leadership (see Chapter 12).

All this may suggest that the universities, confronting the changing world at the beginning of the new millennium, are not after all unlike the dinosaurs contemplating the looming asteroid at the end of the Cretaceous period. But that would be too hasty a comparison. I do not believe the universities face extinction, but I do believe that the price of their effectiveness — if not their survival — will be their readiness to embrace changes, some of them quite sweeping, none of which they will welcome, and several of which they will regard as corrosive and even destructive. The future of universities, and the effectiveness of their future contribution, is likely to depend on how skillfully and creatively they are able to combine the virtues of their past governance and style of learning with the demands of a less benign future and a less deferential learning public. It is these tensions and ambiguities that we shall now explore.

The New American University of the Twenty-First Century

Although the traditional university will undergo substantial changes, driven by new learning technology, harsh financial constraints, changing public demand, and growing intellectual opportunity, it must keep learning, and especially student learning, at the heart of its mission. I include in "learning" not only mediated learning — teaching, that is — but also personal scholarship and organized research. And I include in student learning, not just undergraduate instruction, but also the education of graduate, professional, and postdoctoral students; continuing education and other formal outreach programs; and the great range of activities, from student volunteer service efforts to faculty research, consulting, and extension, by which knowledge is created, shared, tested, and applied.

At the heart of the university's mission, at the core of the concept of learning, will be the university's role in transforming "facts" into useful information, information into meaningful knowledge, and knowledge into useful judgment. The residential campus remains the best catalyst I know for achieving that wonderful alchemy. It is a quiet process, this transformation. It is rarely achieved, I think, by IT, however smart the software, but it is happening daily on the campus. That is why the campus community is of such surpassing importance. We need not only more people knowing more facts; we need also more people with judgment, discernment, and insight, able to distinguish not only truth from falsehood but the significant from the trivial and the best from the worthy. Perhaps it is too much to hope that the campus can any longer claim to transform knowledge into wisdom, but this much is clear: without knowledge that is ordered, tested, refined, related, and applied, wisdom will have but modest scope and little power in the larger issues of life.

If our future well-being depends in some measure on the effectiveness of our research universities, what expectations should we have for these institutions? What should the best universities of the twenty-first century look like? Without pretending that anyone can provide a precise blueprint for the research university of the future, several characteristics seem essential; the new American university will prosper to the extent that it can maintain a dynamic equilibrium between several inherent tensions.

The successful university will maintain institutional autonomy, lively faculty independence, and vigorous academic freedom, but will enjoy strong, impartial, public governance and decisive, engaged presidential leadership. The American university has prospered in part because it has enjoyed an effective and responsive pattern of shared governance. This has typically involved a threefold pattern of public oversight and trusteeship; shared, collegial internal governance by the faculty; and strong presidential leadership. Though the particulars have varied with time and place, this threefold pattern has proved both durable and effective. Its effectiveness has depended in the past on a large measure of external public confidence and internal institutional loyalty, mutual trust, professional commitment, and impartial judgment, but these qualities, together with the pattern of shared governance they have supported, now show signs of strain.

As a result of these pressures, institutions once admired as models of prudent judgment and strong participatory government are now seen by some as archetypes of bureaucratic bumbling and learned inefficiency, where effective management and decisive leadership are held hostage to a host of competing interests and divided loyalties, and where prompt, responsible action and responsive decisions are delayed by prolonged debate or diluted by ideological wrangling. The development of responsible, effective, and balanced governance, leadership, and management is one of the most urgent priorities for the American university as it enters the new millennium.

The division and distribution of authority and responsibility between the board, the president, and the faculty depend as much on the character of those involved and the context of the times as on tradition and statute. The new university is likely to see more formal designation of particular responsibility among these three participants, and it will prosper to the extent that it enjoys a judicious balance between healthy public trusteeship, responsible and collegial faculty governance, and creative, intelligent, and strong presidential leadership (see Chapter 12).

The successful university will be increasingly privately supported but increasingly publicly accountable and socially committed. Today's leading research universities include both privately endowed and state-supported, public institutions, though the financial differences between the two have declined in recent years as state appropriations have been reduced. One president of a public university has commented wryly that, within his own tenure, his university has changed from state-supported to state-assisted to state-located! As this trend continues, all major universities — public as well as private — are likely to become more dependent on private support. Two campuses of the

University of California, as well as the University of Michigan, for example, have already embarked on billion-dollar fund-raising campaigns.

Generally speaking, the private universities have been smaller in size, more selective in admissions, and more limited in range of academic programs than their public counterparts. But they have enjoyed more freedom — being unaffected, for example, by the requirement imposed on state universities to conduct virtually all their business in public. They have also enjoyed more effective governance than most public institutions, where trustees or regents are politically appointed or elected. Against this, private universities have generally been far less engaged in community outreach and extension activities than have their public counterparts, largely because of the lack of funding for such efforts.

It seems likely that as all universities become more dependent on private support, the new American university will see reforms in the governance of public institutions and greater emphasis by the private institutions on community outreach and service, with the land-grant extension model reinvented and reapplied on a new scale and in a new context.[1] While both public and private universities are likely to retain their distinctive identity, both are likely to face a new level of public accountability, based not only on costs but also on effectiveness (see below.)

The successful university will be campus rooted but internationally oriented. In spite of the growing benefits of information technology, the new American university will still depend on an established campus base as the essential platform for both its specialized facilities and its scholarly community. Though its role may change, the traditional concept of a university as a place is unlikely to be made redundant by a virtual institution, however powerful and inclusive distance learning may become. But the "real" university, though it may be located in a particular place, cannot be confined to a single place. Campus based in its location, it will be international in its orientation and cosmopolitan in its character; its graduates will pursue their careers within an increasingly global economy and an increasingly diverse workforce. Both its curriculum and its membership will reflect this diversity; the underrepresented and the underserved will still be recruited; directed community service, internships and study abroad will become the norm; both the student and faculty bodies will become conspicuously international in their membership; and living productively in a diverse community will increasingly come to be regarded as a "job skill." International students already form a significant proportion of the university's student body (typically 10–15 percent of its undergraduates and up to 50 percent of its graduate students), and foreign-born faculty members are already found within most of its departments. Boards of trustees of private universities already generally include several international members. New research partnerships, teaching exchanges, scholarly consortia, and institutional associations all serve to reinforce these growing international linkages. This emphasis on global knowledge is scarcely new; it recapitulates and reflects a characteristic as old as the university itself. While most colleges and universities will still draw their students from their local regions, the great research-intensive universities will become ever more international in their membership and outlook.

Perhaps, in fact, the new American university will no longer be an American university at all, but the American campus of an international university. At first glance, that may seem unlikely — even undesirable, perhaps — but the early signs of such new alliances are already discernible.

Columbia, the London School of Economics, the University of Michigan, the University of Chicago, the New York Public Library, the Victoria and Albert Museum, Cambridge University Press, the British Library, and Woods Hole Oceanographic Institute, among others, have already formed Fathom, an alliance for on-line education. Yale, Princeton, Stanford, and Oxford are partners in a similar venture. From such modest beginnings, it is not difficult to envisage an alliance with more comprehensive goals.

Giant corporate mergers are commonplace. Centuries-old hospitals have combined. Fiercely independent and long-established European and other nations are forming new unions. Perhaps farsighted university leadership will see similar opportunities. And if the obstacles to such an alliance are great, the potential opportunities are far greater.

The successful university will be academically independent but constructively partnered. The new American university will continue to enjoy the remarkable degree of institutional independence and academic freedom that has marked its recent existence and been an essential part of its success. That scholarly independence — exasperating as it has sometimes been to its detractors, and buttressed, as has sometimes been needed, by presidents, boards of trustees, and courts of justice — has served society well.

The new American university will continue to depend on that independence, but it will thrive to the extent that it also acknowledges its own dependence on others. For no institution, however wealthy, can "do it all." No university, however large, can be truly comprehensive in its programs. Nor should it seek to be. If the university is to meet the increasing range of societal needs, it will require new alliances within the academic community and new partnerships outside it, with communities, local, state, and national agencies, corporations, foundations, libraries, museums, publishers, hospitals, professional associations, scholarly societies, and other institutions. Because the traditional "university years" are but one part of a lifelong learning experience, universities will establish closer cooperation with other "providers" and "users" of knowledge, including not only other universities, professional associations, corporations, and local groups, but also commercial vendors of educational hardware and software. We are likely to see an increased blurring of distinctions between what have come to be called "brick universities," "click universities," and "brick and click universities," as these new partnerships develop and mature.

The successful university will be knowledge based but student centered, research driven but learning focused. The distinctive feature of the new American university will still be its commitment to learning in its widest sense. This involves, not simply the transmission of existing knowledge, but also the creativity that produces new achievements and research that leads to new discovery and new knowledge. World-class scholarship will require both greater selectivity and greater interaction among disciplines than is now the case. But this scholarship will be pursued in the context of a student-centered culture, with clear educational goals, explicit statements of curricular objectives, clearly defined professional skills, and new measures of educational outcome. The new university will require a new commitment to effective learning at every level — professional, graduate, and especially undergraduate — with emphasis on clearly defined standards, high competence, effective advising and mentoring, the cultivation of learning skills, personal growth, individual creativity, and meaningful assessment, all based on a variety of learning styles, teamwork, off-campus experience, lifelong learning, and the effective use of educational technology.

The "best" universities and colleges of the future will be those that demonstrate the most effective gains in learning and learning skills among their students. This new accountability will demand a better understanding of the learning process and a clearer statement of instructional purpose and effectiveness. The traditional pattern of a student accumulating information and a professor teaching "subjects" will be displaced by an emphasis on developing in students the initiative, skills, and discipline to pursue knowledge independently, to evaluate and weigh it effectively, and to apply it creatively and responsibly.

The successful university will be technologically sophisticated but community dependent. Already the quality of on-campus learning has been enriched by the use of IT, and the first fruits of its use in distance learning are now appearing. New uses in discovery and extended service, new approaches, new programs, new alliances, new groups of learners are emerging at dizzying speed, and we are only at the beginning of the exciting changes and opportunities that IT can provide. The challenge for the university is to match the vastness of the opportunities provided by the new technology with the boldness of vision to employ it in wholly new ways. Harnessing all the power of new information technology, both on the campus and in distance learning, the new American university will display a greater dependence on the power of the scholarly community in both teaching and research. The new electronic community will reinforce and complement the older resident community, each contributing the power of distributed intelligence in both inreach into the campus community and outreach beyond it. Intellectual cross-fertilization will become a more powerful learning tool and a more effective means of research and inquiry.

The successful university will be quality obsessed but procedurally efficient. Because scholarly discipline and analytical rigor are the keys to understanding, the new American university will continue to be obsessed with quality. It can have no other standard. But scholarly quality and academic excellence are not inconsistent with administrative efficiency and cost-effectiveness. Universities have too readily assumed that because quality is priceless, cost is no object, that no support level could ever be fully adequate for their needs. A new commitment to both excellence and cost-effectiveness will be required across the campus.

It is in this context that the unbundling of traditional campus functions is likely to emerge as a major issue. For most universities, this task will have to be undertaken within a context of continuing financial constraint. Cost-effectiveness is likely to be a major factor both in student choice in enrollment and in corporate — and institutional — choice in creating new partnerships and contracting out for educational and research services. The new university will require continuous improvement in the effectiveness of the learning process, not so much its cost-effectiveness as its effectiveness in improving quality and performance.

The successful university will be professionally attuned but humanely informed. The growth in importance of professional studies has been paralleled by a decline in the influence of the traditional liberal arts. This decline is influenced in part by the growing importance and increasing public role of the professions, by the growing popularity of professional studies among students, and by the declining influence and lack of internal cohesion within the traditional core disciplines of the liberal arts. The sciences have become powerful but increasingly unintelligible to nonscientists. The social sciences, entranced by microanalysis and quantification, have become increasingly irrele-

vant to social issues and public policy. The humanities, embracing fragmentation, otherness, and unreality, have neglected the great overarching issues of
human commonality in favor of increasingly internal discourse and sometimes advocacy, thinly disguised as scholarship.

Yet never has professional practice stood in greater need of enlightened
criticism and humane reflection. There is limited value and little benefit in
information undigested and unscrutinized by personal reflection, or in professional skills unguided by thoughtful insight and personal commitment. If
the university fails to educate free and responsible citizens, who will undertake the task? So the new university must reinvent the liberal arts, perhaps expanding the range of cultural statement by the creative integration of sound,
text, and image, and using the new communications technology to create
both a new form of expression and a new level of literacy, no longer limited to
text. This integration is as yet characterized more by trash than by pearls,
more by entertainment than by enlightenment. But it offers the possibility of
enriched cultural expression and a new cultural literacy to which the traditional liberal arts have yet to respond.

But suppose that the university—any university—strikes just the optimum balance in all these areas. What would it *look like*? Here are two models
representing distinct and extreme possibilities. The models reflect a choice
that the university is being forced to make regarding how to respond to globalization, IT, and the chance to serve a host of new clients and take on a formidable array of new functions.

The first model is based on accretion. Let's call this "Unmanageable U."
The expanded university would embrace more functions and educate more
students of all ages, levels, and locations; serve more clients in more tasks; en-
list more partners; employ more people—an army of new professionals in a
bewildering variety of new areas, garnering its support from a legion of
different sources. Global in its membership, its clientele, its governance, and
its programs, it would be open to the world, networking everything, everywhere, day and night, with the boundaries between teaching, research, and
service increasingly blurred. The residential community would be exploded,
replaced by scores of overlapping communities, both virtual and real, forming and dissolving around particular short-term tasks and longer-term functions. Freewheeling in its enterprise, it would be accountable to a host of
different paymasters; lucrative contracts, pro bono service, for-profit ventures, reimbursed studies, targeted corporate R and D, paid government surveys, franchised agreements, money-losing dreams, and profitable contract
services would mingle together, jostling each other across the sprawling bal-

ance sheet. The campus would become boundless, its reach limitless, its ambitions infinite, its thinking expansive, its focus diffused, its disciplinary barriers reduced, its tension increased. It would be a challenging, restless, undisciplined, freewheeling, sprawling, exciting place.

Model two is the divestiture university. Let's call it "Unimaginable U." This is the protect-the-core-at-all-costs model: replace, franchise, separate, give away, sell, reform, or close whatever detracts from the chosen central mission of the institution. The R and D would become a freestanding venture, a wholly owned subsidiary. Some academic activities—entertainment, business management, industrial design, health care, legal services, environmental analysis—would become service companies, perhaps with a judicious mix of pro bono service and profitable contract work. Most internal services—janitorial, security, maintenance, housing, food, health, and so on—would be outsourced. So, too, would some, or perhaps most, elementary educational services—language instruction, say—with the university itself becoming an off-site provider in other more profitable areas—continuing professional education, for example. Some peripheral services—hospitals, schools, museums, athletic facilities, presses, radio stations, and theaters—would be sold or given away, then leased back as needed. The mission would be clarified, the focus narrowed, the disciplines refined, the community purified. It would be a carefully planned, well-managed, financially accountable, predictable, responsible, inward-looking, and rather dull place.

Now, of course, both models are caricatures, but caricatures with enough authenticity to illustrate the inevitable choice with which globalization and IT confront the traditional university. In the past, universities have frequently made such decisions by indecision; direction has been determined by indeterminate drift; and long-term policy—such as it has been—has involved a varying mixture of territorialism, opportunism, competition, absentmindedness, and greed. There is clearly no right answer to the questions posed by these two options; nor is the matter ever settled once and for all. Both systems could be viable and useful. Different institutions may well pursue different courses; changing conditions will probably require changing choices, the results of which will have a profound influence not only on the universities themselves, but also on some aspects of our daily lives.

This choice between incorporation and disposition, and the eight characteristics described above, seem likely to shape, and perhaps define, the new American university. They will change the culture of the campus in much the same way that the changes of the late nineteenth century transformed the American college into the more comprehensive research-intensive university. The transformation will involve a combination of the best in the current model with the external connections and service ethic of the public land-grant university and with new global partnerships as strong as those of multinational corporations. But the university will be a place of learning only for an increasingly small proportion of the nation's students, both traditional and nontraditional. In that sense, it is neither a model for other institutions nor the pinnacle of the academic order. It is instead a distinctive and essential learning community.

Conclusion

It may well be argued that the view of the university of the future I have described is both limited and conservative. It is both, and I think it should be. It is limited because no one can foresee how countervailing tendencies will play out. But it is also conservative because universities, I believe, must not only adapt to contemporary forces but also sometimes resist them; they must both conform to the wishes of their various publics and patrons and also sometimes confront them.

Accountability, for example, is the newest buzzword for all institutions. It is an important — indeed, a vital — obligation, but it means very different things to different people. To one it means responding to students as "customers." But the university's students are not its customers; their relationship to the university is not that of a purchaser — let's say, someone paying to see a movie or subscribing to a cable TV service. The student relationship is more like that of a client coming to a professional for advice; that requires knowledge, discernment, and judgment. The worst service the university faculty member could offer to a student would be to withhold his or her judgment; to do so would be a denial of accountability, not an expression of it. Professional judgment may sometimes contradict that of the student; it may be unpopular and unpleasant, but still appropriate, reasonable, responsible, and — in the best sense — accountable.

Others see accountability as requiring accommodation to those who "foot the bill" — to the taxpayers or political legislatures, for example. But as David Saxon has remarked, if the university should not be an ivory tower isolated from the community, no more should it be a weathervane yielding to every political wind and popular demand.[2] It must, unlike almost every other contemporary institution, take the long view. It must stand for responsible deliberation and for deliberate responsibility. To ask it to respond to every passing political wind or breeze of fashion would be to make it truly unaccountable.

That is why I'm troubled by those, mainly outside but also occasionally inside the academy, who call for wholesale reinvention of the traditional university as a "more focused" agency for applied research or a more "businesslike" institution or a hub of a new system or major node in a distance-learning network. I do not deny that the university must — and will — change. But it must change deliberately and responsibly.

America's universities need to change, not because they are weak, but because they are strong. American universities are not "in trouble," not in decline. In spite of financial pressures, which are real, and public concerns, some of them justified, universities are doing well. They are world-class institutions; a dozen or so provide the benchmark for the rest of the world. The challenge is not to revive a flagging institution but to re-energize a vigorous institution and thus make it even better. The changes I propose are not remedies for the ailing but challenges for the healthy. To criticize present performance is not to condemn existing standards; it is, rather, as Adlai Stevenson once remarked, "to ask whether what is, might not be better."

University trustees, deans, provosts, and especially presidents must become the challengers of complacency, the voices of institutional conscience, the patient advocates for change, the champions of excellence, the midwives of new alliances and partnerships, the facilitators of teamwork, and the untiring exemplars of a new level of commitment.

Only those institutions that can provide significant value-added to the bare bones of information storage and transmission and research are likely to maintain their financial support. This will require a greater selectivity in research and service ventures and a growing responsibility for meaningful validation and certification. It will require a return to the ancient concept of learning as the education of the whole person and a commitment to the deliberate use of the university community as both the vehicle of individual learning and as a means of scholarly inquiry. It will require a reaffirmation of teaching as a moral vocation, of research as a public trust, and of service as a societal obligation. That combination can be achieved by a scholarly community; it is unlikely to be achieved in personal isolation and electronic estrangement.

But certain things will not change, and the most significant of these is the role of the traditional residential university as the place to create and nurture the leaders of each new generation. Like it or not, the campus of today is the larger society of tomorrow. The product of the campus is not simply learning; it is also the character of the nation and increasingly the character of many of the leaders of other nations. That does not mean that the traditional research university will be unchanged or educate a greater proportion of the population. On the contrary, more and more students will be nonresident, part-time, older, and "distance learners" in institutions quite unlike the research university. But there will still be a vital role for the residential university: the reformed university.

Today's government leaders are yesterday's undergraduates. Tomorrow's professional pacesetters are today's graduate students. The future leaders of the world stroll across our college quadrangles; future lawmakers, judges, and CEOs sit in university classrooms. The task in which universities are engaged — the pursuit of learning — is not the passive conveyance of information; it is the passing of the torch, the sharing of the flame.

If the universities trivialize that responsibility, if they reduce it to distributing the dead bones of disarticulated information or limit it to sharing the lifeless elements of technical competence, they will fail those who have entrusted them with responsibility, who have upheld their freedom, who have provided their resources, and who had supposed they were about a greater task.

In an age of limits and constraints, of cynicism and suspicion, the universities must reaffirm the soaring possibilities that enlightened education represents. In an era of broken families, dwindling religious congregations, and decaying communities, our nation desperately needs a new model of community — knowledgeable but compassionate, critical but concerned, skeptical but affirming — that will serve the clamoring needs of our fragmented society and respond to the nobler, unuttered aspirations of our deeper selves.

This is not to pretend that the universities have either wholesale solutions to humanity's ills or a monopoly on skills to address them. Universities are human creations, full of human imperfection, with as much sloth, envy, malice, and neglect as any other community and rather more than their share of pettiness, arrogance, and pride. But it is to assert that the universities, with all their imperfections, represent the crucible within which our future will be formed. Boiling, steaming, frothing at times, a new amalgam must somehow be created within them if we are to surmount our social problems and rediscover the civic virtues on which our society depends. And as leaders in every field of endeavor are educated within their walls, as knowledge is increased within their laboratories, new works created within their studios, and professional practice developed and refined within their facilities, so the universities provide each new generation of leaders, educated, influenced, and shaped within the culture of the campus. It is this emerging community — analytical and affirming, critical and creative, inclusive and inquiring, engaged and enabling — that will be the new university. And it is this new university that must be challenged and enabled to play an increasingly influential role in the creation of the future.

If university-industry-government partnerships are to prosper, they must operate within guidelines that respect the integrity and interests of all the institutional partners (university, government, corporations, foundations, and so on) and serve the legitimate needs of all the participants (faculty, corporate management, industrial scientists, students, and others). Self-evident as that may seem, it involves difficult questions and careful planning. How, for example, given a corporation's legitimate concern to protect and exploit a new technology to which it has contributed, does the university preserve its need to remain an open community? How does it ensure that financial support from a particular corporate sponsor — say, a pharmaceutical company — does not influence the outcome of clinical tests of their products? Or how can the university protect against the unreasonable targeting of graduate student thesis topics to narrow commercial ends?

The way to prevent such difficulties in these partnerships seems to me to lie in a general protocol, developed for each institution in consultation with external partners. It seems unlikely that a single such protocol could serve all institutions, still less all partnerships. What is needed, rather, is an institutional template protocol, within which each of its various partnerships may be negotiated. Let me suggest an outline within which such a protocol might be developed.

Any protocol will need to cover at least these major concerns:

- Participants: Who are they? By whom are they represented? How long is their commitment? What are the obligations/expectations of membership?
- Purposes: What is the purpose of the partnership? How are contributions to be shared between partners? Who provides capital

costs, equipment costs, benefit costs, salaries, and operating costs? Can funding be renegotiated midterm in the light of experience? Is funding renewable? If so, on what conditions?

- Governance: How is the partnership to be governed? What is the division of responsibility between governance and management? How is a governing body composed and appointed and how does it operate? What precise role does it play? How are activities reviewed/evaluated? How are results judged?

- Management: Whose responsibility is management? To whom does the manager/director report? What are the precise duties/powers of the director? What are the conditions/terms of his or her appointment?

- Appointments: How and by whom are appointments made/terminated? What are the expectations/obligations of team members? How are terms of appointment established and how, and by whom, is performance reviewed?

- Benefits: How are copyright and patent rights determined? How are royalties and other benefits established and divided between discoverer, sponsor, and parent company and institutions?

- Publication: What agreements govern publication? How is a spirit of openness protected? What, if any, prepublication review rights do partners have? How are proprietary rights safeguarded?

- Other issues: No two partnerships are alike. Each raises unique questions. These should be anticipated, reviewed, and — to the extent possible — resolved when the partnership is established. There should also be thoughtful provisions for amending the protocol when this proves necessary and for reviewing, renewing, or terminating the partnership. Probably no such protocol will be entirely satisfactory, and its success will depend as much on the spirit of the partners as on the letter of their written agreement. But partnerships of this kind can raise contentious issues, and the more these are anticipated, the more effective the results are likely to be.

NOTES

INTRODUCTION

1. John Masefield, speech at the installation of the new vice chancellor, Sheffield University, June 25, 1946, in *Simpson's Contemporary Quotations,* compiled by James Beasley Simpson (Boston: Houghton Mifflin, 1988), no. 2700.

2. Stanley Ikenberry, *American Council on Education Annual Report,* 1997.

3. Peter Drucker, quoted in Robert Lenzer and Stephen S. Johnson, "Seeing Things As They Really Are," *Forbes,* March 10, 1997, 127.

4. Alfred North Whitehead, *Modes of Thought* (New York: Free Press, 1968), 171.

CHAPTER 1. THE RISE OF THE AMERICAN UNIVERSITY

1. *New England's First Fruits: with divers other special matters concerning that country, 1643* (New York: Reprinted for J. Sabin, 1865), 23.

2. Frederick Rudolph, *The American University and College: A History* (New York: Knopf, 1962), 249.

3. Frederick Rudolph, *Curriculum: A History of the American Undergraduate Course of Study since 1636* (San Francisco: Jossey-Bass, 1977), 116.

4. Andrew Dickson White to Gerrit Smith, 1862, in Morris Bishop, *A History of Cornell* (Ithaca, N.Y.: Cornell University Press, 1962), 42.

5. Rudolph, *Curriculum,* 120.

6. Ibid., 117–19.

7. Bishop, *History of Cornell,* 190–91.

8. Rudolph, *Curriculum,* 10.

9. Ibid., 207.

10. Ibid., 131.

11. Nancy Cantor, "Affirmative Action: What Michigan Can Really Learn from California," *Detroit News,* May 17, 1999.

12. Frank H. T. Rhodes, "College by the Numbers," *New York Times,* December 24, 1999, 4. For an extensive analysis and comprehensive discussion of the results of affirmative action in selective colleges and universities, see William G. Bowen and Derek C. Bok, *The Shape of the River* (Princeton, Princeton University Press, 1998).

13. Howard Peckham, *Making of the University of Michigan,* edited and updated by Margaret L. Steneck and Nicholas H. Steneck (Ann Arbor: University of Michigan, 1994), 99.

14. See, for example, Hugh Davis Graham and Nancy Diamond, *The Rise of*

American Research Universities (Baltimore: Johns Hopkins University Press, 1997), 16.

15. There is a substantial literature on international differences in higher education. Graham and Diamond *(Rise of American Research Universities)* give a useful comparison. Other general reviews include Robert M. Rosenzweig, *The Research Universities and Their Patrons* (Berkeley: University of California Press, 1982); Burton R. Clark, *The Higher Education System: Academic Organization in Cross-National Perspective* (Berkeley: University of California Press, 1987); Burton R. Clark, *Places of Inquiry: Research and Advanced Education in Modern Universities* (Berkeley: University of California Press, 1995).

CHAPTER 2. THE AMERICAN RESEARCH UNIVERSITY TODAY

1. *Chronicle of Higher Education, Almanac Issue* 47, no. 1 (September 2000): 9.

2. Ibid., 25. See also U.S. Department of Education, National Center for Educational Statistics, Digest of Educational Statistics, 2000, NCES 2000–031, Washington, D.C., table 189, 2000. The figure for 18–24 year olds is 55 percent. The report shows 44.3 percent of 15–21 year olds and 43.5 percent of 18–21 year olds enrolled.

3. National Science Board, *Science and Engineering Indicators — 2000,* Arlington, Va., vol. 1, appendix table 4-18, 2000. In the United Kingdom, Norway, and Germany, many first-degree programs are three years long.

4. Older figures from Charles J. Andersen, Deborah J. Carter, and Andrew G. Malizio, with Boichi San, *1989–90 Year Book of Higher Education* (New York: American Council on Education, Macmillan, 1991).

5. National Science Board, *Science and Engineering Indicators — 2000,* Arlington, Va., pp. 4–6ff.

6. *Scientific and Engineering Research Facilities in Colleges and Universities,* NSF Publication 96–326 (Washington, D.C.: National Science Foundation, September 1996), 1. See also reference 2, appendix table 6-4.

7. Charles J. Clotfelter, *Buying the Best: Cost Escalation in Elite Higher Education* (Princeton, N.J.: Princeton University Press, 1996), 20.

8. Alan Wolfe, "The Promise and Flaws of Public Scholarship," *Chronicle of Higher Education,* January 10, 1997, B.4–5.

9. Jaroslav Pelikan, *Scholarship and Its Survival* (Princeton, N.J.: Carnegie Foundation for the Advancement of Teaching, 1983), 15.

10. See, for example, Martin Anderson, *Impostors in the Temple: American Intellectuals Are Destroying Our Universities and Cheating Our Students of Their Future* (New York: Simon & Schuster, 1992); Allan Bloom, *The Closing of the American Mind* (New York: Simon & Schuster, 1987); Page Smith, *Killing the Spirit: Higher Education in America* (New York: Penguin Books, 1990); Charles J. Sykes, *ProfScam: Professors and the Demise of Higher Education* (Washington, D.C.: Requery Gateway, 1988).

CHAPTER 3. TRANSFORMING PROFESSIONALISM

1. John Slaughter, speech delivered at Engineering Deans' Institute, Salt Lake City, Utah, March 29, 1982.

2. The oldest use of the term is in the description of the whole, or the entire number of a corporation or community regarded collectively. This usage persisted in legal contexts until the seventeenth century. The oldest recorded use of the English term "university" was in 1300, by which time it described a community devoted to the purpose of higher education. Though the earlier use stressed the notion of universality, early use of the term also implied a community or corporation.

3. See Walter Metzger, in *The Academic Profession: National Disciplinary and Institutional Settings,* ed. Burton R. Clark (Berkeley: University of California Press, September 1987), 19.

4. Julie Thompson Klein, quoted in Bruce Kimball, *The Condition of American Liberal Education: Pragmatism and a Changing Tradition* (New York: College Board, 1995), 147.

5. Alvin Kernan, ed., *What's Happened to the Humanities?* (Princeton, N.J.: Princeton University Press, 1997), 248, table 1.

6. Lewis Mumford, "The Fulfillment of Man," in *This Is My Philosophy,* ed. Whit Burnett (New York: Citadel Press, 1967), 15.

7. Frank Kermode, "Changing Epochs," in Kernan, *What's Happened to the Humanities?* 168.

8. Clark Kerr, *The Uses of the University,* 4th ed. (Cambridge: Harvard University Press, 1995), 15.

9. Bishop, *History of Cornell,* 190–91.

10. Peckham, *Making of the University of Michigan,* 25. See also George M. Marsden, *The Soul of the American University: From Protestant Establishment to Established Nonbelief* (New York: Oxford University Press, 1994).

11. Gerald Graff, *Beyond the Culture Wars: How Teaching the Conflicts Can Revitalize American Education* (New York: W. W. Norton, 1992), 181.

12. See, for example, John Henry Newman, *The Idea of a University,* ed. Frank M. Turner (New Haven: Yale University Press, 1996), 82.

CHAPTER 4. RESTORING COMMUNITY

1. Report of the Committee on Organization Presented to the Trustees of the Cornell University, October 21, 1866 (Albany, N.Y.: Van Benthuysen, 1867), 21.

2. J. Robert Oppenheimer, "Prospects in the Arts and Sciences" in *This Is My Philosophy,* Burnett, ed., 108.

3. Joe R. Feagin, "Soul Searching in Sociology: Is the Discipline in Crisis?" *Chronicle of Higher Education,* October 15, 1999, B4.

4. Jose Ortega, *Mission of the University* (New York: W. W. Norton, 1966), 39–40.

5. See, for example, Amitai Etzioni, *The Spirit of Community: The Reinvention of American Society* (New York: Simon & Schuster, 1994).

CHAPTER 5. TEACHING AS A MORAL VOCATION

1. Scott Elledge, *E. B. White: A Biography* (New York: W. W. Norton, 1984), 58–59.

2. "Teaching Assistants at University of California Vote to Unionize," *Chronicle of Higher Education*, July 2, 1999.

3. See, for example, Wilbert James McKeachie, *Teaching Tips: Strategies, Research, and Theories for College and University Teachers* (Washington, D.C.: Heath, 1994).

4. Craig Lambert, "Desperately Seeking Summa," *Harvard Magazine*, May–June 1993, 36–40. See also Ben Gose, "Efforts to Curb Grade Inflation Get an F from Many Critics," *Chronicle of Higher Education*, July 25, 1997, A41.

5. David Goldin, "In a Change of Policy, and Heart, Colleges Join Fight against Inflated Grades," *New York Times*, July 4, 1995, 8.

6. Irwin Kirsch et al., *Literacy in America: A First Look at the Results of the National Adult Literacy Survey* (Princeton, N.J.: Educational Testing Service, 1993), 26.

7. Freeman Dyson, *Disturbing the Universe* (New York: Harper & Row, 1979), 47.

8. "The Consequences of Failure," *Chronicle of Higher Education*, May 30, 1997, 39.

9. See, for example, *McBoyer Commission Report on Educating Undergraduates in the Research University: Reinventing Undergraduate Education: A Blueprint for America's Research Universities*, Carnegie Foundation for the Advancement of Teaching, Menlo Park, 1998.

CHAPTER 6. UNDERGRADUATE EDUCATION

1. Newman, *Idea of a University*, 105.

2. Anthony Flint, "Basics Urged for Academic," *Boston Globe*, August 1, 1993, 1.

3. Interview with David P. Gardner, president, the Hewlett Foundation, and past president, University of California, by Lisa Bennett, August 1993.

4. Interview with Vartan Gregorian, president, Brown University, by Lisa Bennett, August 1993.

5. Reports: (1) "Integrity in the College Curriculum: A Report to the Academic Community" (Washington, D.C.: Association of American Colleges, 1985); (2) "Contexts for Learning: The Major Sectors of American Higher Education" (Washington, D.C.: National Institute of Education, 1985); (3) William J. Bennett, "To Reclaim a Legacy: A Report on the Humanities in Higher Education" (Washington, D.C.: National Endowment for the Humanities, 1984).

6. Lynne V. Cheney, *Humanities in America* (Washington, D.C.: National Endowment for the Humanities, NEH-636, 1988), 5.

7. American Council on Education Survey, "Many Colleges Found Heeding Calls to Reform Undergraduate Studies," *Chronicle of Higher Education* 32, no. 2 (March 12, 1986): A1.

8. Sarah E. Turner and William Bowen, "The Flight from Arts and Sciences: Trends in Degrees Conferred," *Science,* October 26, 1990, 517–21.

9. Newman, *Idea of a University,* 126.

10. Literacy Council of Northern Virginia, Inc., www.nova_literacy.org, 2000.

11. Interview with William Brock, The Brock Group, Ltd., Washington, D.C., by Lisa Bennett, August 1993.

12. Interview with Edward O. Wilson, Pellegrino University Professor, Harvard University, by Lisa Bennett, July 1993.

13. *Higher Education for American Democracy: A Report of the President's Commission on Higher Education* (Washington, D.C.: U.S. Government Printing Office, 1947).

14. John Gardner, *No Easy Victories,* ed. Helen Rowan (New York: Harper and Row, 1968), 90.

CHAPTER 7. PROFESSIONAL AND GRADUATE EDUCATION

1. Not all the leading institutions on the list were research universities, although most were; many of those that were not, were located in states with very high overall pass rates. Ohio, South Carolina, South Dakota, Missouri, Minnesota, Utah, and Nebraska, for example, had "all-school" pass rates of 90 percent or more. Details from *Chronicle of Higher Education,* May 30, 1997, A.45. It should be noted, of course, that the leading institutions attract the most able students, with the highest academic aptitude. It is also the case that the "best graduates" typically join the "best law firms" who give special support in preparation for bar exams.

2. William G. Bowen and J. A. Sosa, *Prospects for Faculty in the Arts and Sciences* (Princeton, N.J.: Princeton University Press, 1989).

3. See, for example, R. C. Atkinson, "Supply and Demand for Scientists and Engineers: A National Crisis in the Making," *Science* 248 (1992): 432.

4. Phil Buchanan, "The Burden of Massive Debt on Graduate Students," *Chronicle of Higher Education,* June 13, 1997, B.6.

5. For an extensive review of these and other features, see the study by William G. Bowen and Neil L. Rudenstine, *In Pursuit of the Ph.D.* (Princeton, N.J.: Princeton University Press, 1992), 108.

6. See, for example, the Association of American Universities Report of the Committee on Graduate Education, Washington, D.C., 1998, and also, *Reshaping the Graduate Education of Scientists and Engineers* (Washington, D.C.: National Academy Press, 1995).

7. Kenneth E. Boulding, in William K. Frankena, ed., *The Philosophy and Future of Graduate Education* (Ann Arbor: University of Michigan Press, 1980), 144. See also the comments by John Passmore, 49.

8. Oliver C. Carmichael, *Graduate Education: A Critique and a Program* (New York: Harper and Bros., 1961), 196.

9. Boulding, in Frankena, *Philosophy and Future,* 144.

10. Passmore, in Frankena, *Philosophy and Future,* 58.

11. Ibid., 45.

12. Ibid., 52.

13. A telling example of the lack of any agreement arising from this inattention is provided by the published proceedings of an international conference on *The Philosophy and Future of Graduate Education,* organized at the University of Michigan in 1978. See Frankena, *Philosophy and Future.* In 13 papers, 10 formal comments, and 258 pages of text, no coherent philosophy of graduate education emerges, nor is there any common view of its future.

14. Thomas D. Snyder, *Digest of Education Statistics 1999,* NCES 2000–031 (Washington, D.C.: U.S. Department of Education, National Center for Education Statistics, 1999).

15. William G. Bowen and Neil L. Rudenstine, *In Pursuit of the Ph.D.* (Princeton, N.J.: Princeton University Press, 1992), 46 ff.

16. Ibid., 23.

17. William G. Bowen and Julie Ann Sosa, *Prospects for Faculty in the Arts and Sciences* (Princeton: Princeton University Press, 1989), chap. 6.

18. The conversion of "colleges" to "universities" continues apace; even though it may involve nothing more than a change in title, it is commonly seen as representing an elevation in status. In 1996, for example, 13 public four-year colleges in Georgia became "Regional and State Universities" with no changes in mission or in budget. A few years ago, all Britain's polytechnic institutions were renamed as universities in a nationwide change in nomenclature. "What's in a Name? Just Ask Colleges That Want to Be Called Universities," *Chronicle of Higher Education,* June 13, 1997, A.33–34.

19. Bowen and Rudenstine, *In Pursuit,* 68 ff.

20. Ibid., chap. 6, pp. 11–12, 142 ff.

21. Ibid., chap. 8.

22. Ibid., 131. In education, however, many Ph.D. students are working professionals, pursuing part-time or evening graduate studies.

23. Report of the Andrew W. Mellon Foundation, 1991, 8–12.

24. *Research — Doctorate Programs in the United States: Continuity and Change,* ed. Marvin L. Goldberger, Brendan A. Maher, and Pamela Ebert Flattau (Washington, D.C.: National Academy Press, 1995), 31, fig. 3–1. See also Association of American Universities, *Report and Recommendations of Committee on Graduate Education,* Washington, D.C., 1998.

25. National Science Board, *Science and Engineering Indicators — 2000,* NSB 00–1, 2–23, 2–32 (Washington, D.C.: U.S. Government Printing Office, 2000).

26. Ibid., 3–7, table 3–2.

27. "What's Happening in the Labor Market for Recent Science and Engineering Ph.D. Recipients?" Issue Brief, NSF 97–321, National Science Foundation, Division of Science Resources Studies, September 23, 1997.

28. Bowen and Rudenstine, *In Pursuit*, chap. 8.

CHAPTER 8. THE COST OF HIGHER EDUCATION

1. Fox Butterfield, "Crime Keeps on Falling, but Prisons Keep on Filling," *New York Times*, September 28, 1997, sec. 4, pp. 1, 4.

2. *Chronicle of Higher Education, Almanac Issue* 47, no. 1 (September 2000): 48.

3. "Anxiety Over Tuition: A Controversy in Context," *Chronicle of Higher Education*, May 30, 1997, A10–A19.

4. "Costs in Perspective," *NASULGC Newsline*, June 1997, 11.

5. Erik Larson, "Why Colleges Cost Too Much," *Time Magazine*, March 17, 1997, 46–55.

6. " 'oo Essays from the Edge," *U.S. Air Magazine*, January 1997, 50.

7. *U.S. News and World Report*, September 16, 1996, 91.

8. For a general discussion, see Arthur Hauptman, *The Tuition Dilemma* (Washington, D.C.: Brookings Institute, 1990), and Ronald G. Ehrenberg, *Tuition Rising: Why College Costs So Much* (Cambridge, Mass.: Harvard University Press, 2000). For a discussion of student financial aid, see Michael S. McPherson and Morton Owen Schapiro, *The Student Aid Game* (Princeton, N.J.: Princeton University Press, 1998).

9. Clotfelter, *Buying the Best*, 250.

10. Peta Appleborne, "Rising Cost of Education Imperils Nation, Report Says," *New York Times*, June 18, 1997, 38.

11. Stephen Martin, "House Passes Bill to Create Commission to Study College," *Chronicle of Higher Education*, May 23, 1997, A33.

12. Kim Strosnider, "For Profit University Challenges Traditional Colleges," *Chronicle of Higher Education*, June 6, 1997, A32.

13. *Chronicle of Higher Education, Almanac Issue*, August 27, 1999, 36.

14. Brent Staples, "The End of Tenure?" *New York Times*, June 29, 1997, sec. 4, 14.

15. See, for example, Denise K. Magner, "A Fierce Battle at the U. of Minnesota Comes to a Quiet Close," *Chronicle of Higher Education*, June 20, 1997, A14.

16. "Northwestern Professor Sues, Seeking Pay in Tenure Dispute," *New York Times*, November 24, 1997, A21.

17. Courtney Leatherman, "More Faculty Members Question the Value of Tenure," *Chronicle of Higher Education*, October 25, 1996, A12.

18. Bob Dart, "Part-Time Issue Elicits Response among Faculty," *Austin American Statesman*, August 23, 1997, A3.

19. Steven Girardi, "Faculty Yields Tenure for Creativity," *Tampa Tribune*, August 24, 1997, 4.

20. Staples, "End of Tenure?" 14. There is widespread literature on tenure. For a sense of the tone of recent discussions, see, for example, C. Peter Magrath, "Eliminating Tenure without Destroying Academic Freedom," *Chronicle of Higher Education*, February 28, 1997, A60, and Richard Chait, "Thawing the Cold War over Tenure: Why Academe Needs More Employment Options," *Chronicle of Higher Education*, February 7, 1997, B4 and B5, and the lively correspondence that followed these articles. Magrath, it might be noted, is president of the National Association of State Universities and Land Grant Colleges, and Chait is professor of higher education at Harvard Graduate School of Education.

21. William H. Honan, "The Ivory Tower under Siege," *New York Times*, Education Life Supplement, January 4, 1998, 44.

CHAPTER 9. RESEARCH

1. For these and further details, see "Human Gene Testing," *Beyond Discovery* (Washington, D.C.: National Academy of Sciences, 1996), 1–8.

2. James Watson, *The Double Helix: A Personal Account of the Discovery of the Structure of DNA* (New York: New American Library, 1969), 128.

3. Interview with Paul Berg, professor of biochemistry, Stanford University School of Medicine, by Lisa Bennett, June 1993.

4. Nicolaas Bloemberger, "The Birth of the Laser Era," *Physics Today*, October 1993, 29–30.

5. George Pake, "Nuclear Magnetic Resonance in Bulk Matter," *Physics Today*, October 1993, 50.

6. Vannevar Bush, *Science — The Endless Frontier* (Washington, D.C.: National Science Foundation, 1990), 2, 5, 21.

7. National Science Board, *Science and Engineering Indicators, 2000*, appendix table 6-4. See also tables 4-26 and 4-25 for Ph.D. data.

8. The White House, Office of the Press Secretary, February 12, 1996.

9. "MIT: The Impact of Innovation," a BankBoston Economics Department Special Report, March 1997.

10. Ibid., 1–2.

11. Ibid., A3, table A2.

12. Ibid., 9–10.

13. Ibid., 10.

14. Ibid., 10.

15. "The Global Position System," in *Beyond Discovery*, 1–2.

16. "Supporting Research and Development to Promote Economic Growth: The Federal Government's Role" (Washington, D.C.: Council of Economic Advis-

ers, October 1995), <http://clinton4.nara.gov/textonly/WH/EOP/CEA/econ/html/econ-top.html>.

17. "AUTM Licensing Survey FY 1999," ed. Lori Pressman (Northbrook, Il.: Association of University Technology Managers, November 2000), 8, <http://www.autm.net/surveys/99/survey99A.pdf>.

18. Jeffrey Brainard and Don Southwick, "Congress Gives Colleges a Billion-Dollar Bonanza," *Chronicle of Higher Education,* July 28, 2000, A29 and A44.

19. G. E. Brown Jr., "The Objectivity Crisis," *American Journal of Physics* 60 (September 1992): 779.

20. John Maynard Keynes, *Essays in Persuasion* (New York: Harcourt, 1932), 371–73. Quoted in William H. Calvin, *The River That Flows Uphill* (San Francisco: Sierra Club Books, 1986). The quotations from the Buddha and Annie Dillard are also included.

CHAPTER 10. SERVICE AS A SOCIETAL OBLIGATION

1. Karen W. Arenson, "Columbia Sets Pace in Profiting off Research," *New York Times,* August 2, 2000, B1 and B6.

2. "Cornell Cooperative Extension at Work," Cornell Cooperative Extension, Ithaca, N.Y., August 1999, 1.

CHAPTER 11. INFORMATION TECHNOLOGY

1. Kim Strosnider, "For Profit University Challenges Traditional Colleges," *Chronicle of Higher Education,* June 6, 1997, A32.

2. *Peterson's Guide to Distance Learning Programs* (Princeton, N.J.: Peterson, 1997).

3. Lisa Gubernick and Ashlea Ebeling, "I Got My Degree through E-Mail," *Forbes,* June 16, 1997, 85–86. For other examples, see Vicky Phillips, "Earn a Masters, Virtually," *Internet World* 7, no. 9 (1996). See also Patricia Senn Broivik, *Student Learning in the Information Age* (Phoenix, Ariz.: Oryx Press for American Council on Education, 1998).

4. "Schools Ponder New Global Landscape," *Science* 277 (July 18, 1997): 311.

5. I am grateful to David Lipsky for his help in developing some of these comparisons.

6. Eli M. Noam, "Electronics and the Dim Future of the University," *Science* 270 (1995): 247–49.

7. "Schools Ponder New Global Landscape," 311. See also Robert Lenzer and Stephen S. Johnson, "Seeing Things As They Really Are," *Forbes,* March 10, 1997, 127.

8. For a thoughtful discussion of the general issues involved in the use of IT within the traditional setting, see Gregory C. Farrington, "The New Technology

and the Future of Residential Undergraduate Education," in *Dancing with the Devil: Information Technology and the New Competition in Higher Education,* ed. Richard N. Katz (San Francisco: Educause and Jossey-Bass, 1998), 73–94; John Seely Brown and Paul Duquid, "Universities in the Digital Age," *Change,* July 1996, 11–19; and James J. Duderstadt, *A University for the Twenty-First Century* (Ann Arbor: University of Michigan Press, 2000).

CHAPTER 12. GOVERNANCE AND LEADERSHIP

1. *Statement on Institutional Governance,* Association of Governing Boards, Washington, D.C.

2. See, for example, Donald Kennedy, *Academic Duty* (Cambridge: Harvard University Press, 1997), and Henry Rosovsky, *The University: An Owner's Manual* (New York: Norton, 1990).

3. National Commission on the Academic Presidency, *Renewing the Academic Presidency* (Washington, D.C.: Association of Governing Boards, 1996).

4. Frank H. T. Rhodes, ed., *Successful Fund Raising for Higher Education: The Advancement of Learning* (Phoenix, Ariz.: Oryx Press, 1997).

CHAPTER 13. THE NEW UNIVERSITY

1. See, for example, Frank H. T. Rhodes, "The University at the Millennium" (La Jolla, Calif.: Glion Colloquium II at Del Mar, *Governance in Higher Education: The University in a State of Flux,* January 6, 2000); Frank H. T. Rhodes, "The Art of the Presidency" (Washington, D.C.: American Council on Education, Fall 1998), 12–18; Harold T. Shapiro, *Tradition and Change: Perspectives on Public Policy* (Ann Arbor: University of Michigan Press, 1987); Derek Bok, *Universities and the Future of America* (Durham: Duke University Press, 1990).

2. C. Kumar and N. Patel, eds., *Reinventing the Research University* (Los Angeles: University of California, 1995), 228. See also the comments of Cornelius J. Pings, ibid., 212–14.

INDEX

Frank Rhodes is professor of geological sciences and president emeritus at Cornell University, where he served for eighteen years. Before assuming the presidency at Cornell in 1977, Rhodes was vice president for academic affairs at the University of Michigan, having earlier served as dean of the College of Literature, Science, and the Arts. He was previously professor and head of the geology department and dean of the Faculty of Science at the University of Wales, Swansea, and has been a faculty member at the University of Illinois, where he was also director of the University of Illinois Field Station in Sheridan, Wyoming, and at the University of Durham.

Rhodes is a graduate of the University of Birmingham, England, from which he holds four degrees, a former Fulbright scholar and Fulbright distinguished fellow, a National Science Foundation senior visiting research fellow, and a visiting fellow of Clare Hall, Cambridge, and Trinity College, Oxford. He is a life member of Clare Hall, Cambridge, and an honorary fellow of Robinson College, Cambridge, and of the University of Wales, Swansea.

Rhodes holds honorary degrees from more than thirty institutions in the United States and abroad and is a fellow of the American Academy of Arts and Sciences and the American Philosophical Society. He is the recipient of the Bigsby Medal of the Geological Society, the Justin Morrill Award of the National Association of State Universities and Land Grant Colleges, the Higher Education Leadership Award of the Commission of Independent Colleges and Universities, and the Clark Kerr Medal of the University of California–Berkeley, Faculty Senate. He was the 1999 Jefferson Lecturer at Berkeley.

Rhodes was appointed by President Ronald Reagan as a member of the National Science Board, of which he is a former chair, and by President Bush as a member of the President's Educational Policy Advisory Committee. He has served as chair of the American Council on Education, the Association of American Universities, and the Carnegie Foundation for the Advancement of Teaching. He has also served as a trustee of the Andrew W. Mellon Foundation.

Rhodes has published widely in the fields of geology, paleontology, evolution, the history of science, and education. His books include *Language of the Earth, Geology*, and *The Evolution of Life*. He was chair of the 1987 National Commission on Minority Participation in Education and American Life that produced the report "One-Third of a Nation." The honorary co-chairs of the commission were presidents Gerald R. Ford and Jimmy Carter. He was the co-chair, with Donald E. Petersen, former chair of the Ford Motor Company, of the Business–Higher Education Commission, that produced the report "American Potential: The Human Dimension," and was co-chair, with Gary Tooker, chair of Motorola, of the

Council on Competitiveness 1995 report on research and development. He was also a member of the Association of Governing Boards 1996 Commission on Renewing the Academic Presidency.

Rhodes is a principal of the Washington Advisory Group, a member of the board of directors of the General Electric Company, and a member of the board of overseers of Koç University, Turkey. He is a member of the board of the Goldman Sachs Foundation and a member of the National Academy of Sciences Commission on the Future of the Research University. He is currently serving as president of the American Philosophical Society, and as chair of the Atlantic Foundation.